KEANU **REEVES**   MATT **KINDT**   RON **GARNEY**   BILL **CRABTREE**

BRZRKR ™

VOLUME ONE

Published by

BOOM!
S T U D I O S

Collection Designer
MARIE KRUPINA

Assistant Editor
RAMIRO PORTNOY

Series Designers
MICHELLE ANKLEY + SCOTT NEWMAN

Editors
ERIC HARBURN + MATT GAGNON

Special Thanks
ADAM YOELIN + STEPHEN CHRISTY + ROSS RICHIE

ROSS RICHIE Chairman & Founder
JOY HUFFMAN CFO
MATT GAGNON Editor-in-Chief
FILIP SABLIK President, Publishing & Marketing
STEPHEN CHRISTY President, Development
LANCE KREITER Vice President, Licensing & Merchandising
BRYCE CARLSON Vice President, Editorial & Creative Strategy
KATE HENNING Director, Operations
ELYSE STRANDBERG Manager, Finance
SIERRA HAHN Executive Editor
MICHELLE ANKLEY Manager, Production Design
DAFNA PLEBAN Senior Editor
SHANNON WATTERS Senior Editor
ERIC HARBURN Senior Editor
ELIZABETH BREI Editor

KATHLEEN WISNESKI Editor
SOPHIE PHILIPS-ROBERTS Associate Editor
JONATHAN MANNING Associate Editor
GAVIN GRONENTHAL Assistant Editor
GWEN WALLER Assistant Editor
ALLYSON GRONOWITZ Assistant Editor
RAMIRO PORTNOY Assistant Editor
KENZIE RZONCA Assistant Editor
REY NETSCHKE Editorial Assistant
MARIE KRUPINA Production Designer
GRACE PARK Production Designer
CHELSEA ROBERTS Production Designer
MADISON GOYETTE Production Designer
CRYSTAL WHITE Production Designer

SAMANTHA KNAPP Production Design Assistant
ESTHER KIM Marketing Lead
BREANNA SARPY Marketing Coordinator, Digital
GRECIA MARTINEZ Marketing Assistant
AMANDA LAWSON Marketing Assistant, Digital
JOSÉ MEZA Consumer Sales Lead
ASHLEY TROUB Consumer Sales Coordinator
MORGAN PERRY Retail Sales Lead
HARLEY SALBACKA Sales Coordinator
MEGAN CHRISTOPHER Operations Coordinator
RODRIGO HERNÁNDEZ Operations Coordinator
ZIPPORAH SMITH Operations Coordinator
JASON LEE Senior Accountant
SABRINA LESIN Accounting Assistant
LAUREN ALEXANDER Administrative Assistant

BRZRKR Volume One, September 2021. Published by BOOM! Studios, a division of Boom Entertainment, Inc. BRZRKR is ™ & © 2021 74850, Inc. Originally published in single magazine form as BRZRKR No. 1-4. ™ & © 2021 74850, Inc. All rights reserved. BOOM! Studios™ and the BOOM! Studios logo are trademarks of Boom Entertainment, Inc., registered in various countries and categories. All characters, events, and institutions depicted herein are fictional. Any similarity between any of the names, characters, persons, events, and/or institutions in this publication to actual names, characters, and persons, whether living or dead, events, and/or institutions is unintended and purely coincidental. BOOM! Studios does not read or accept unsolicited submissions of ideas, stories, or artwork.

BOOM! Studios, 5670 Wilshire Boulevard, Suite 400, Los Angeles, CA 90036-5679. Printed in Canada. First Printing.

ISBN: 978-1-68415-685-6, eISBN: 978-1-64668-229-4 [Softcover]
ISBN: 978-1-68415-716-7 [Hardcover]
ISBN: 978-1-68415-713-6 [Kickstarter Exclusive Softcover]
ISBN: 978-1-68415-719-8 [Kickstarter Exclusive Hardcover]
ISBN: 978-1-68415-722-8 [Blood Red Limited Edition Hardcover]
ISBN: 978-1-68415-725-9 [Bronze Age Limited Edition Hardcover]
ISBN: 978-1-68415-728-0 [Gunmetal Limited Edition Hardcover]
ISBN: 978-1-68415-731-0 [Platinum Immortal Limited Edition Hardcover]
ISBN: 978-1-68415-828-7 [Indigo Books & Music Exclusive Softcover]

Cover by
RAFAEL GRAMPÁ
Character Designs by
RAFAEL GRAMPÁ + RON GARNEY

Kickstarter Exclusive Cover by
TYLER KIRKHAM
with colors by **ARIF PRIANTO**

Blood Red Kickstarter Exclusive Variant Cover by
LEE GARBETT

Bronze Age Kickstarter Exclusive Variant Cover by
JONBOY MEYERS

Gunmetal Kickstarter Exclusive Variant Cover by
RON GARNEY

Platinum Immortal Kickstarter Exclusive Variant Cover by
INHYUK LEE

Indigo Books & Music Exclusive Variant Cover by
DAN MORA

Created by **KEANU REEVES**

BRZ

RKR

Written by
KEANU REEVES + MATT KINDT

Illustrated by
RON GARNEY

Colored by
BILL CRABTREE

Lettered by
CLEM ROBINS

CHAPTER
ONE

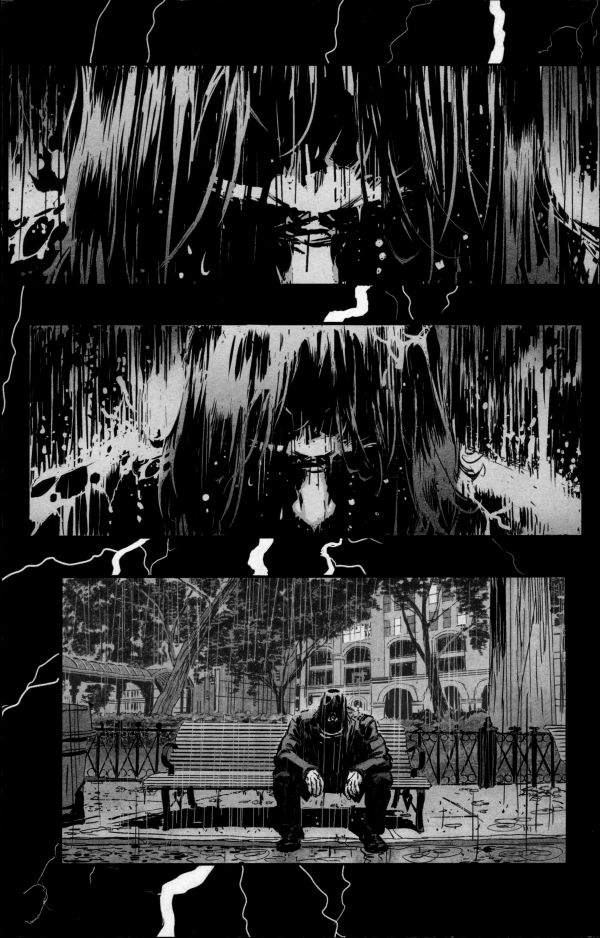

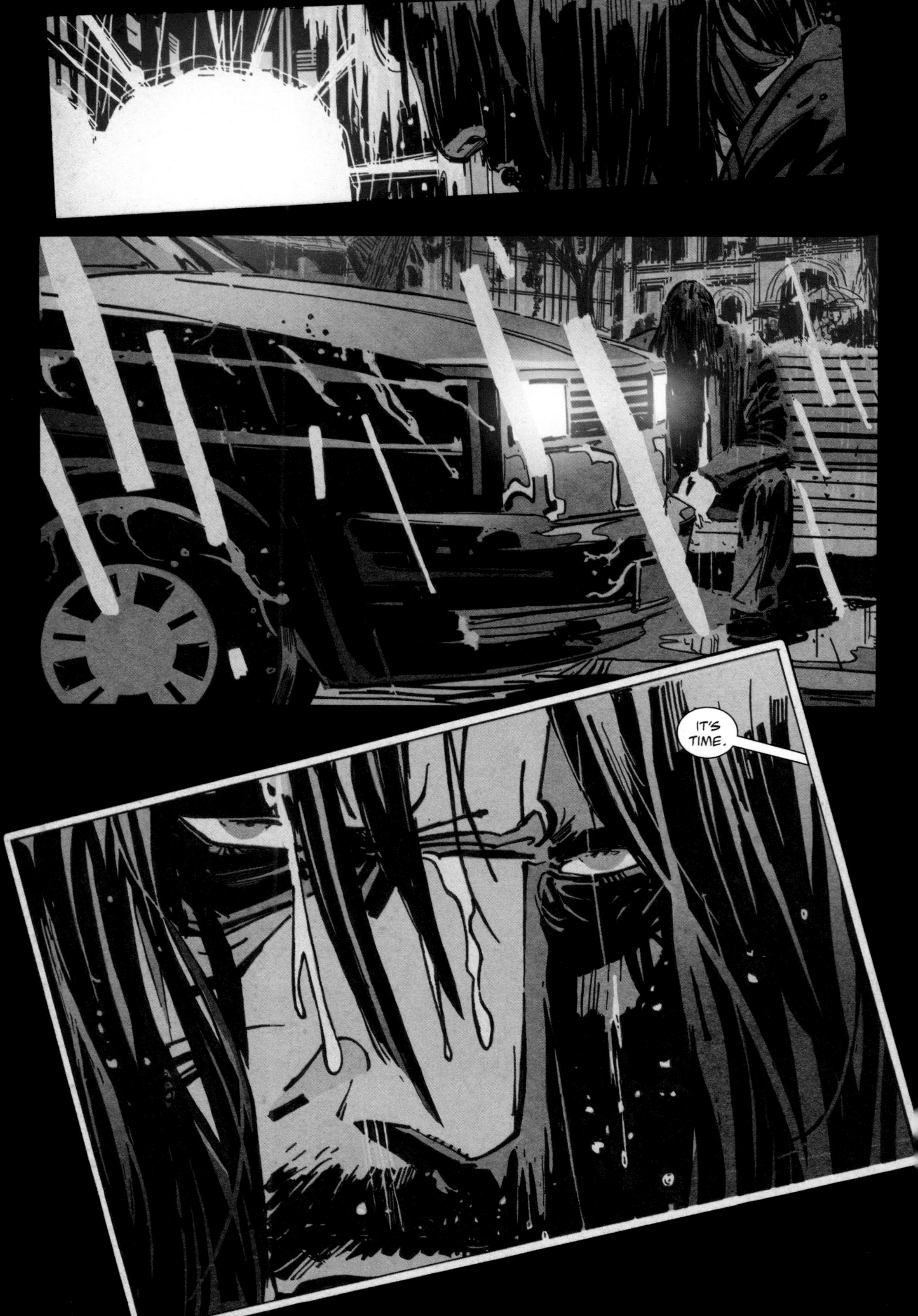
IT'S TIME.

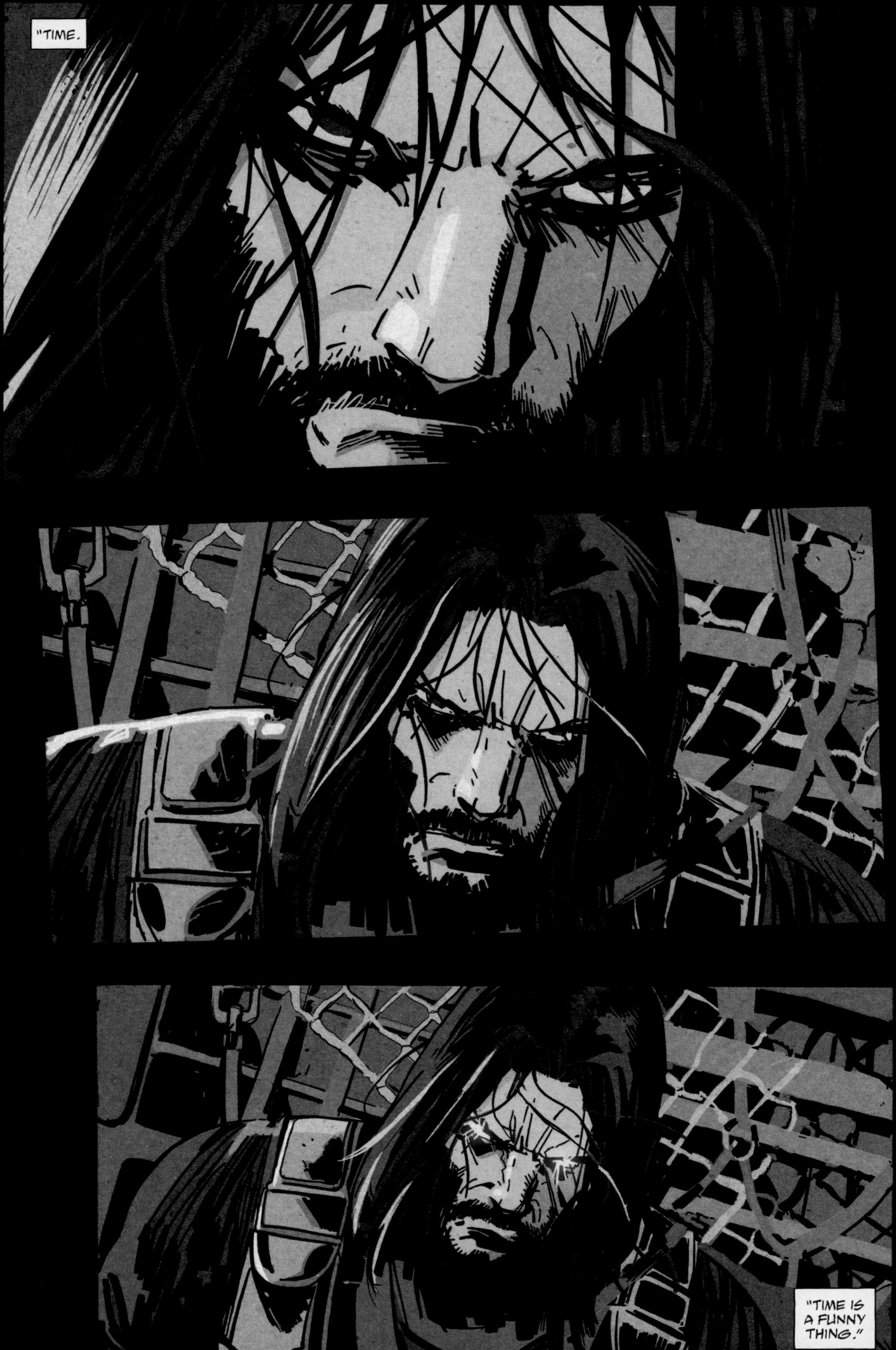
"TIME.
"TIME IS A FUNNY THING."

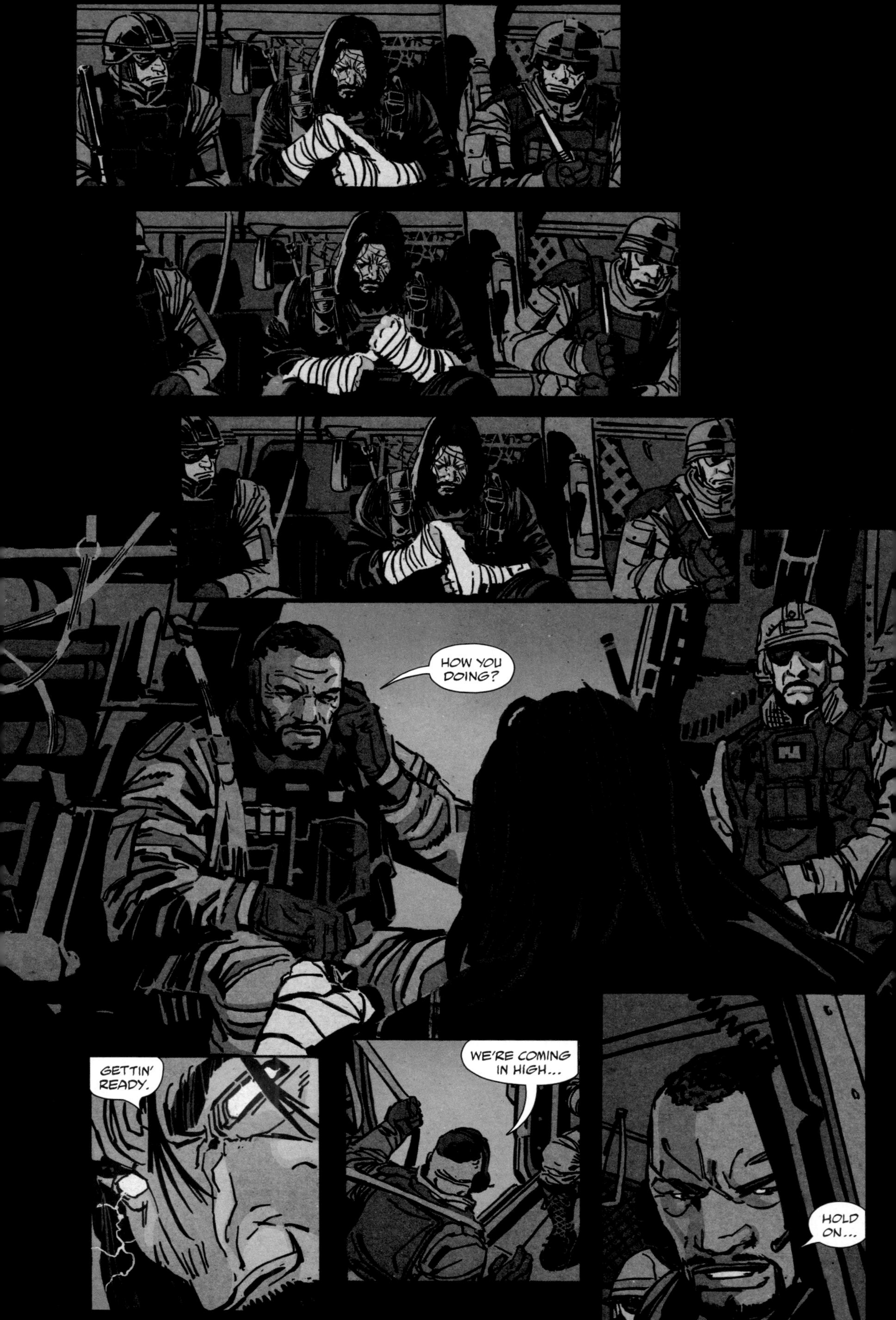
HOW YOU DOING?
GETTIN' READY.
WE'RE COMING IN HIGH...
HOLD ON...

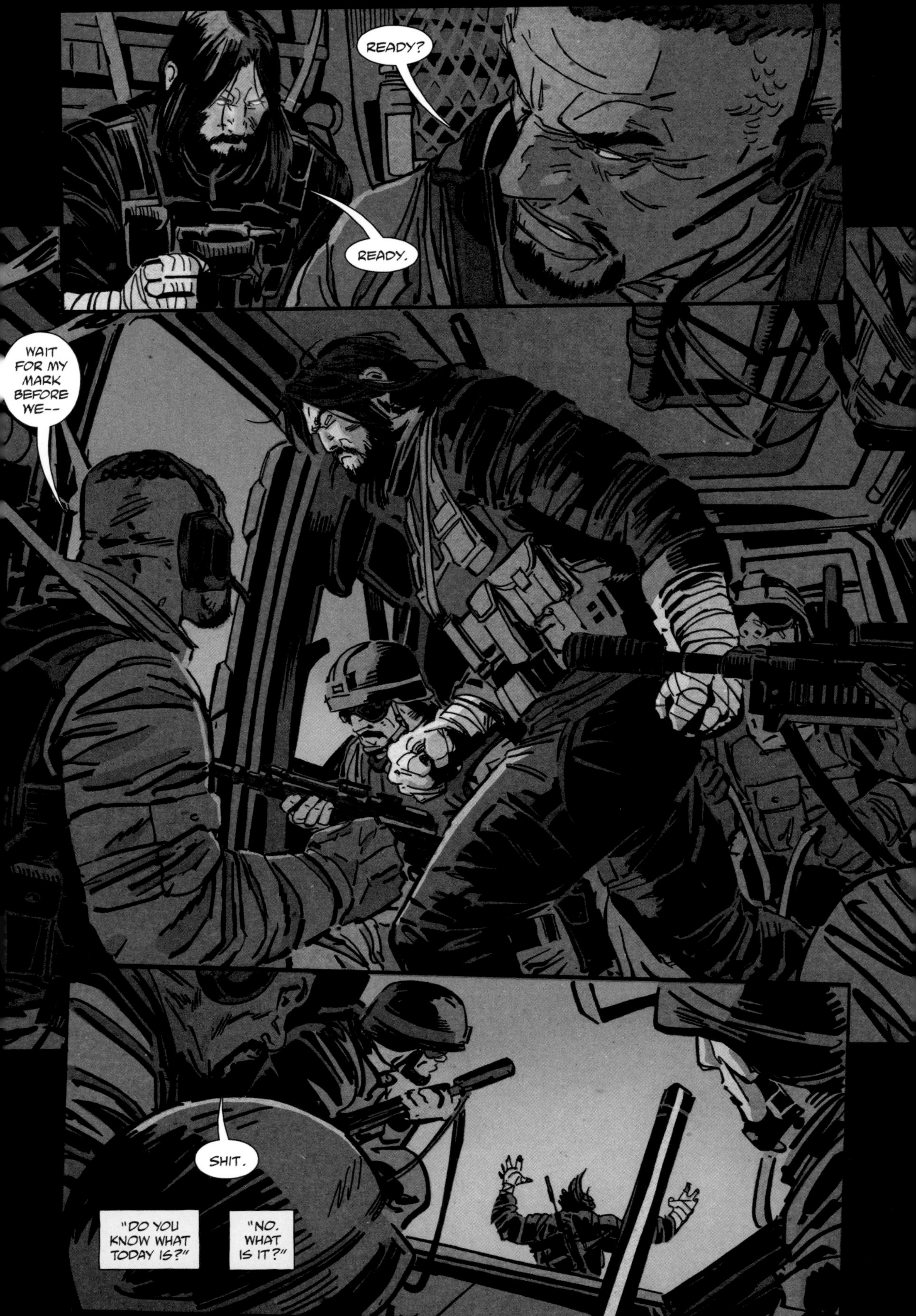
READY?
READY.
WAIT FOR MY MARK BEFORE WE--
SHIT.
"DO YOU KNOW WHAT TODAY IS?"
"NO. WHAT IS IT?"

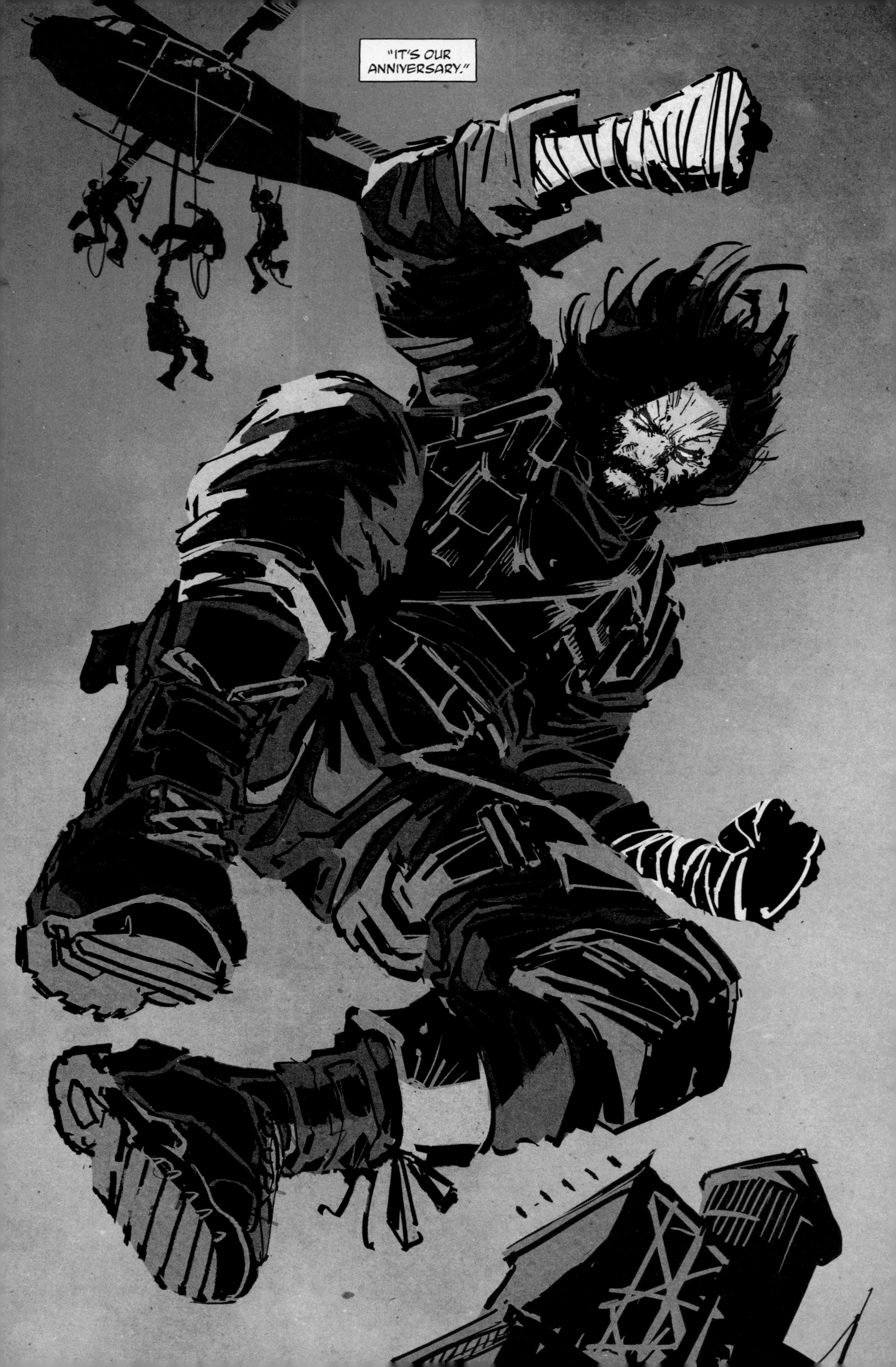
"IT'S OUR ANNIVERSARY."

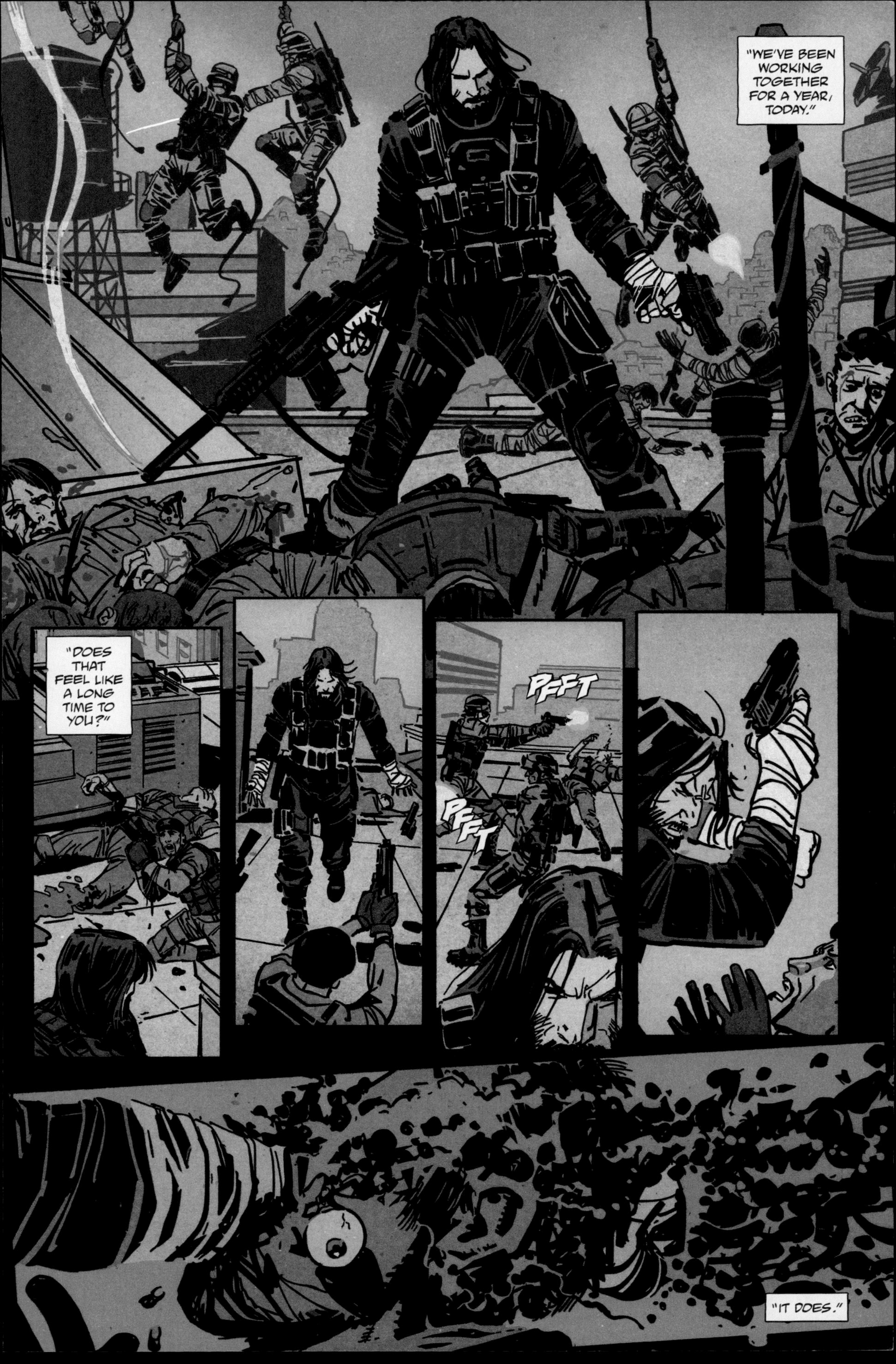
"WE'VE BEEN WORKING TOGETHER FOR A YEAR, TODAY."
"DOES THAT FEEL LIKE A LONG TIME TO YOU?"
PFFT
PFFT
"IT DOES."

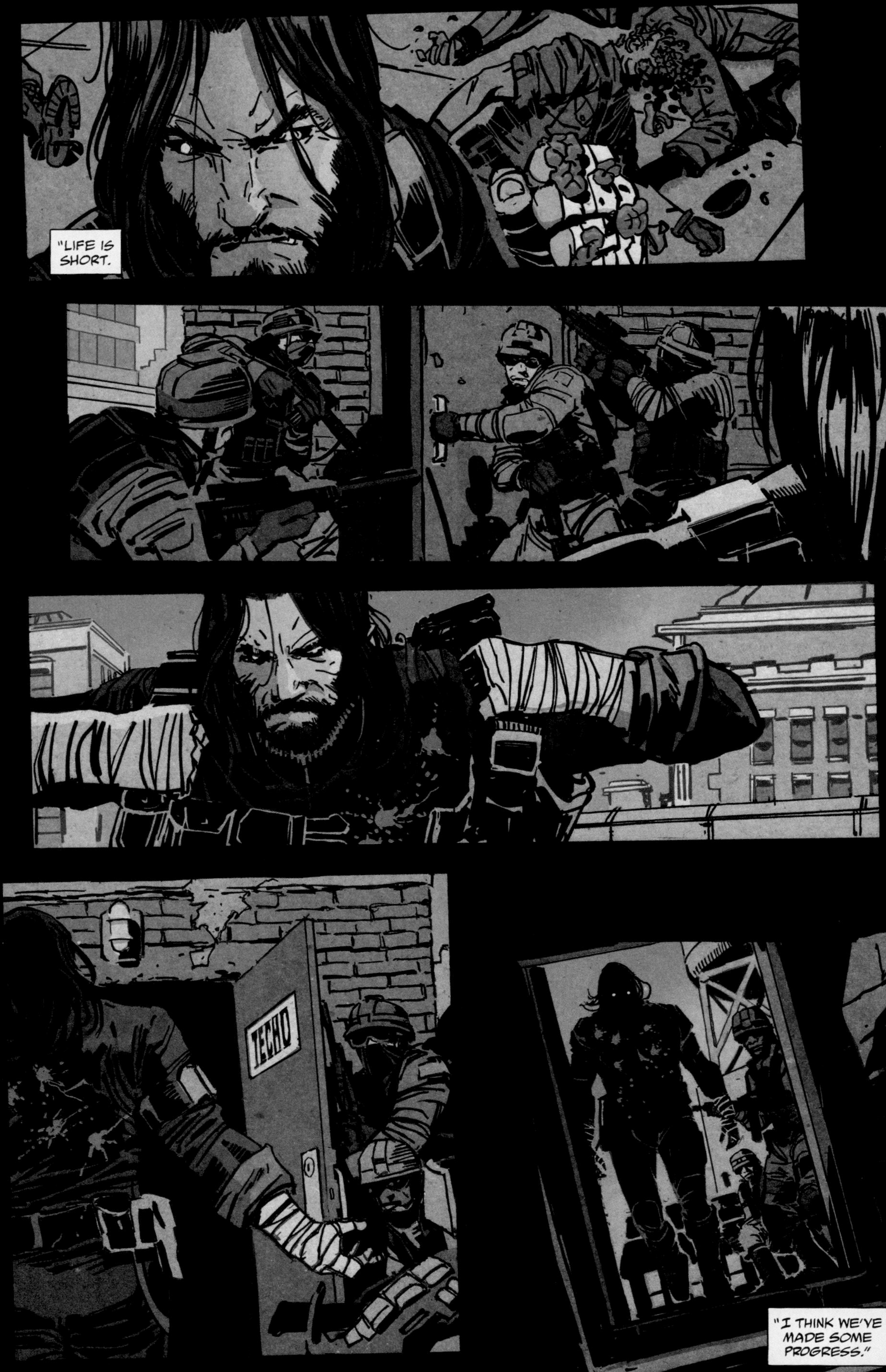
"LIFE IS SHORT.
TECHO
"I THINK WE'VE MADE SOME PROGRESS."

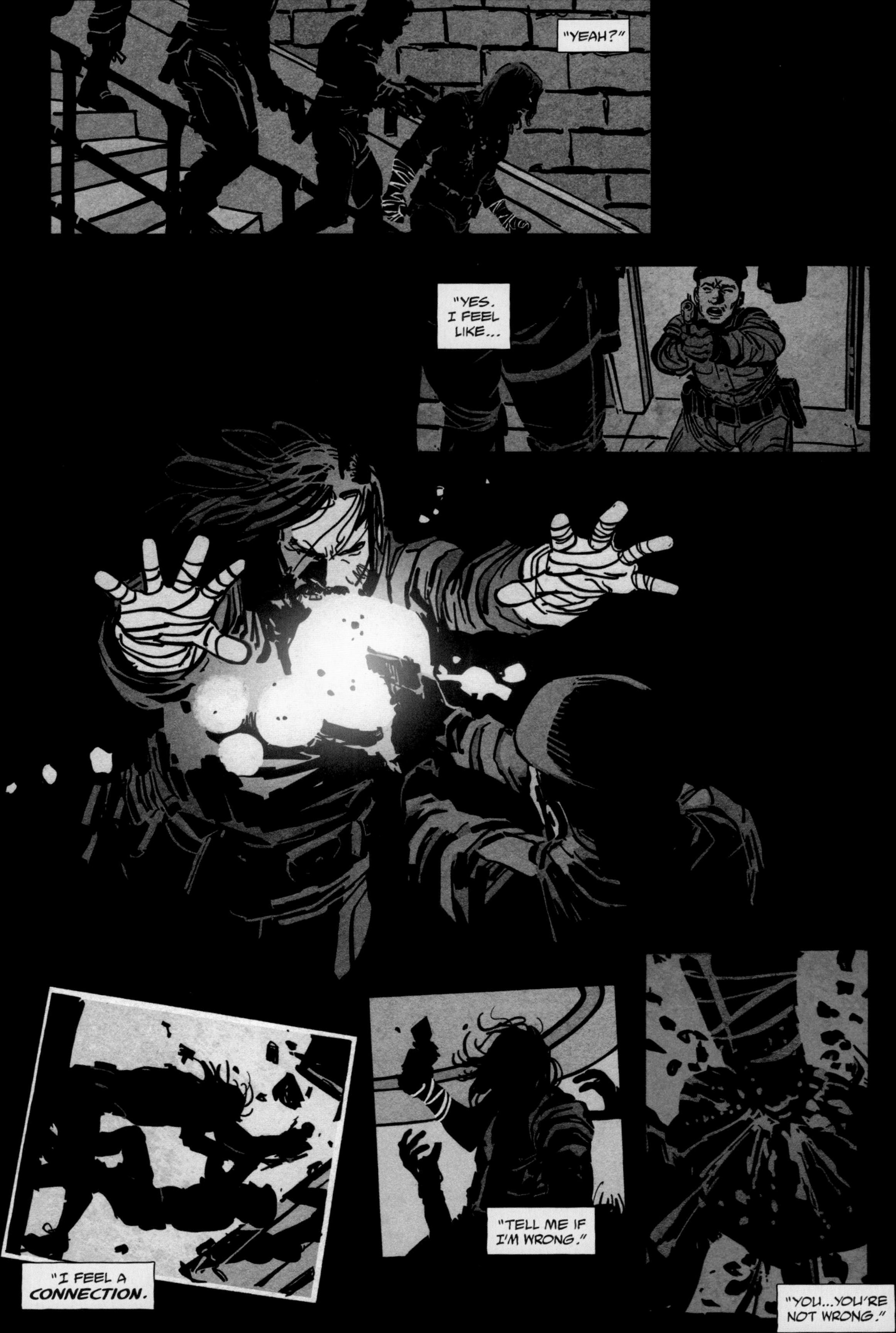
"YEAH?"
"YES. I FEEL LIKE...
"I FEEL A CONNECTION.
"TELL ME IF I'M WRONG."
"YOU...YOU'RE NOT WRONG."

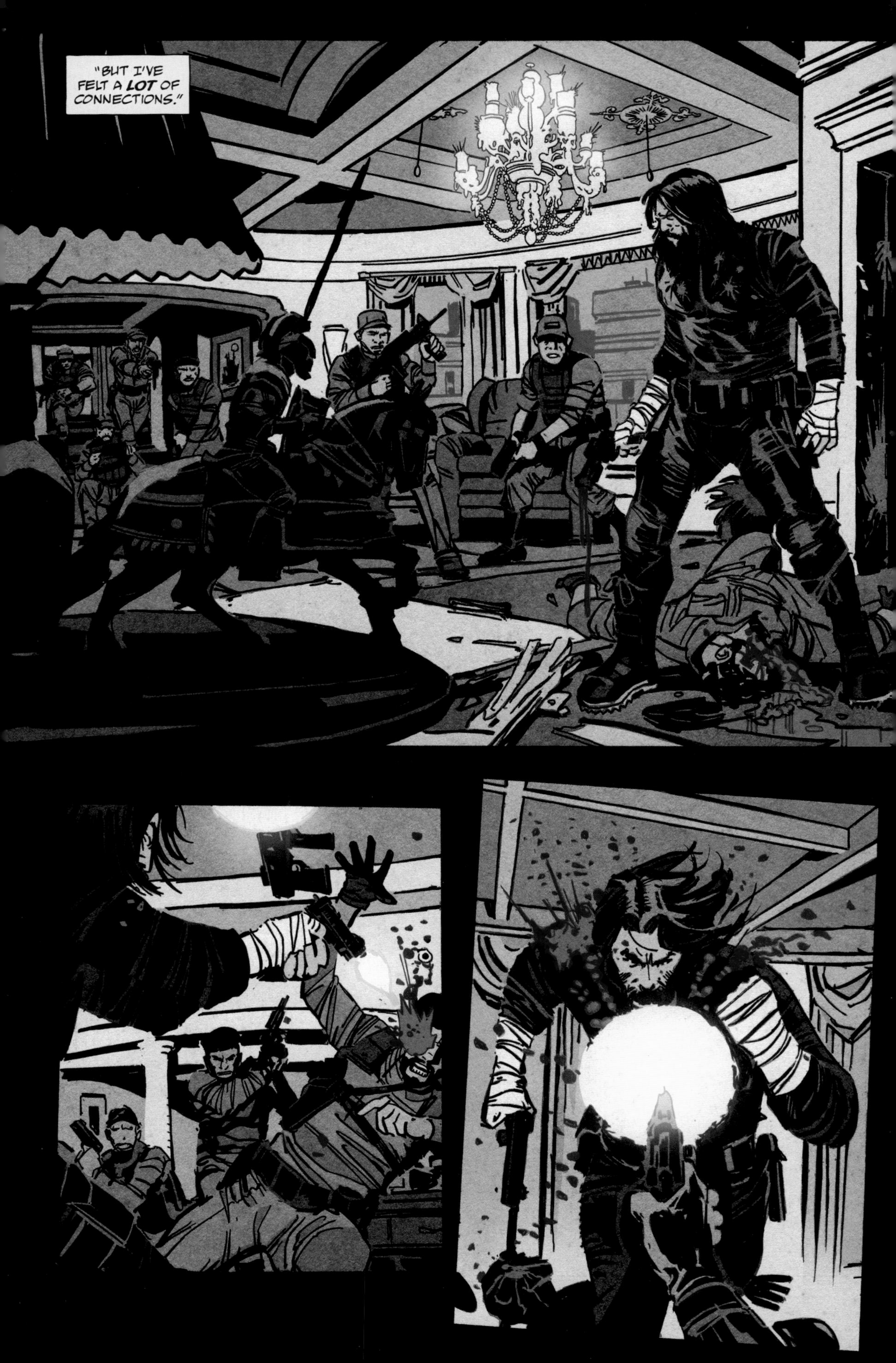
"BUT I'VE FELT A LOT OF CONNECTIONS."

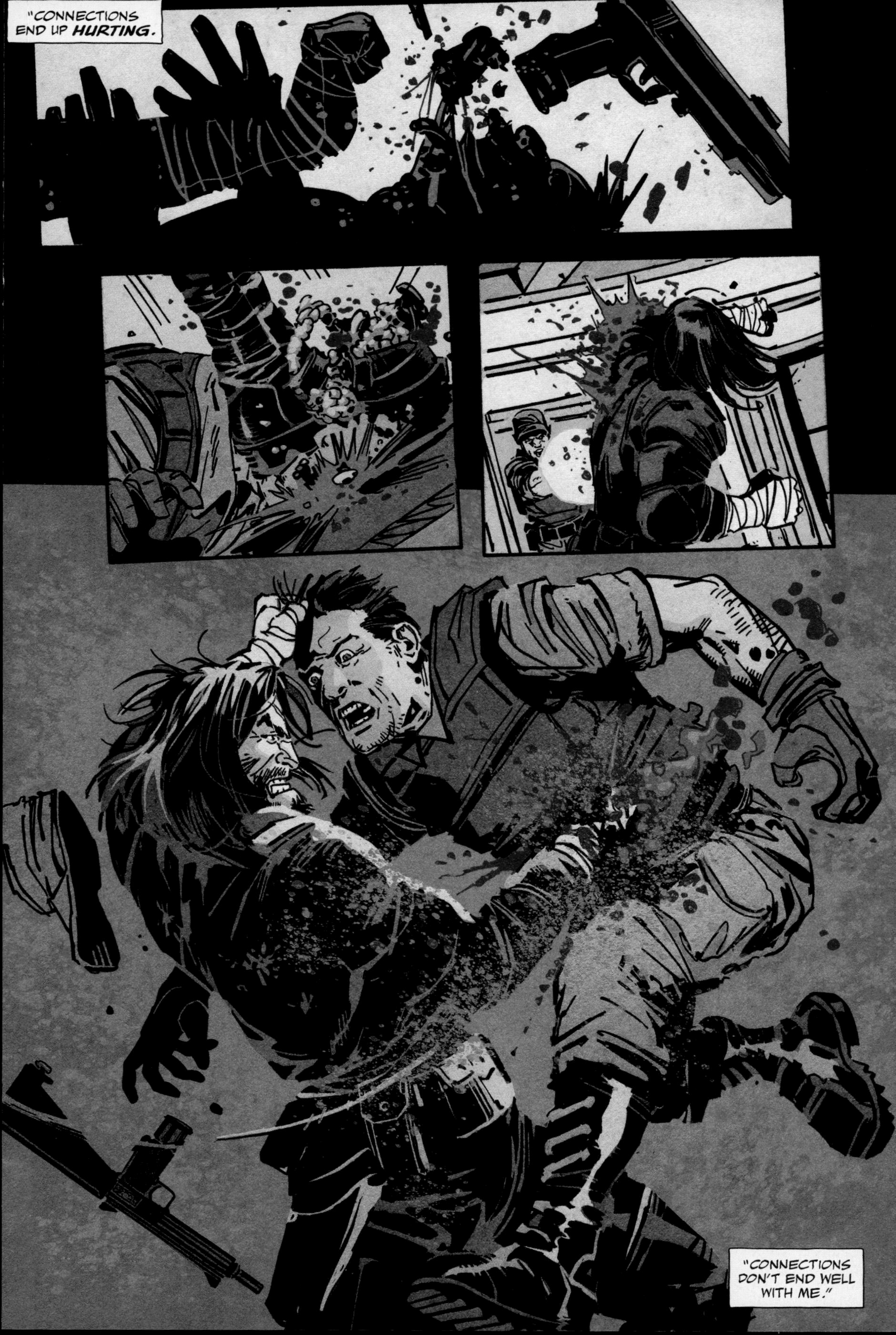
"CONNECTIONS END UP HURTING.
"CONNECTIONS DON'T END WELL WITH ME."

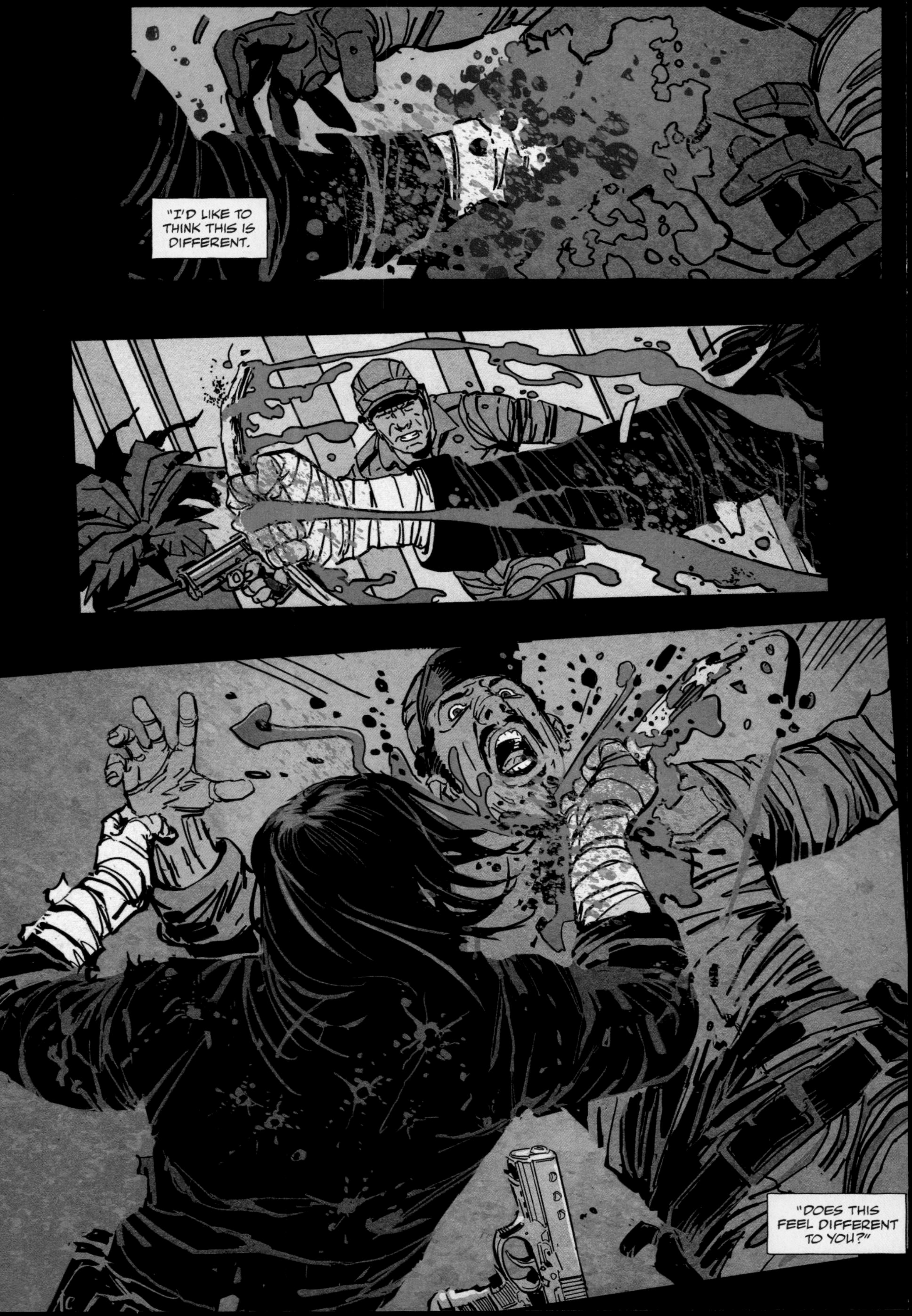
"I'D LIKE TO THINK THIS IS DIFFERENT.
"DOES THIS FEEL DIFFERENT TO YOU?"

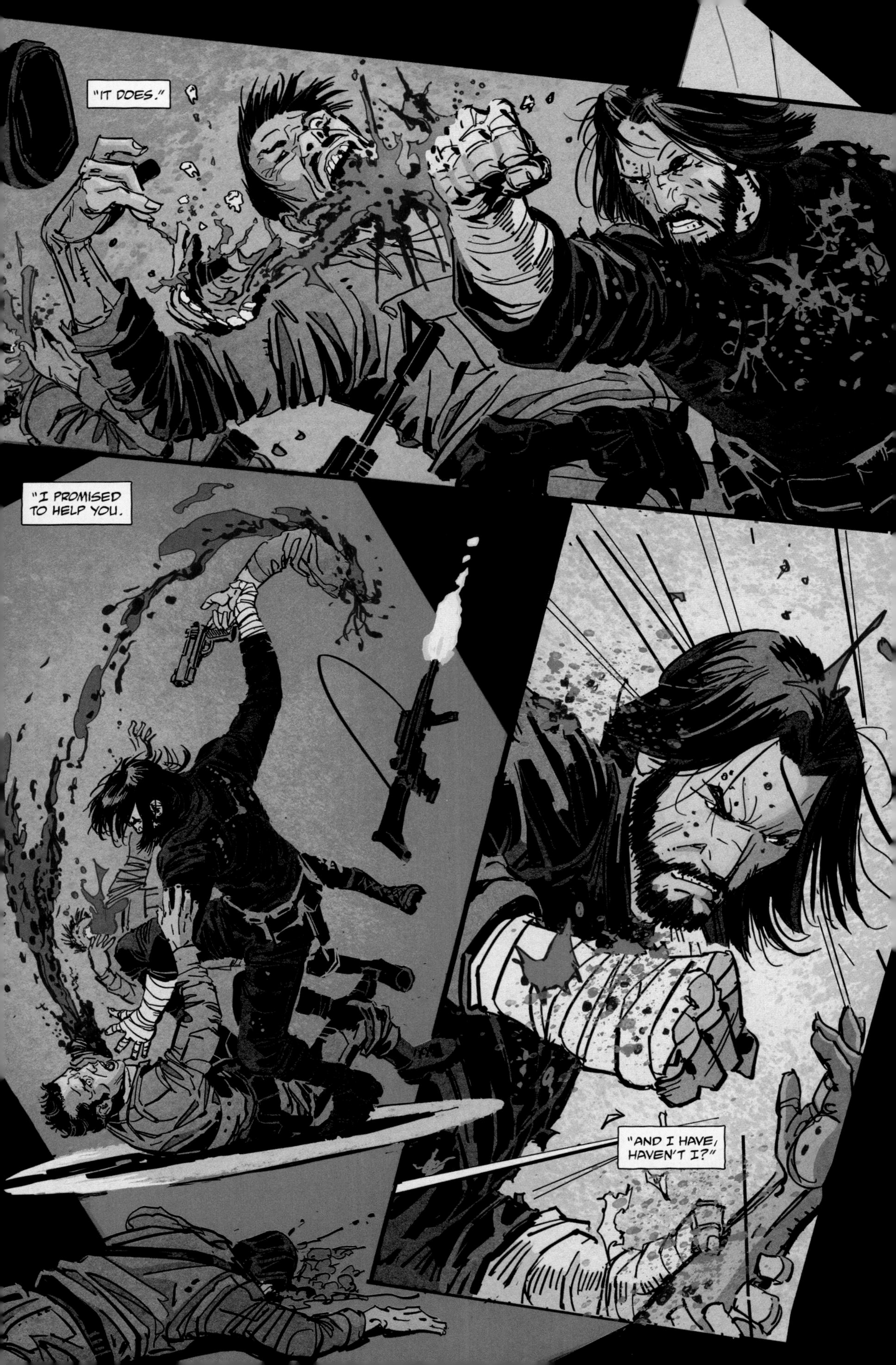
"IT DOES."
"I PROMISED TO HELP YOU.
"AND I HAVE, HAVEN'T I?"

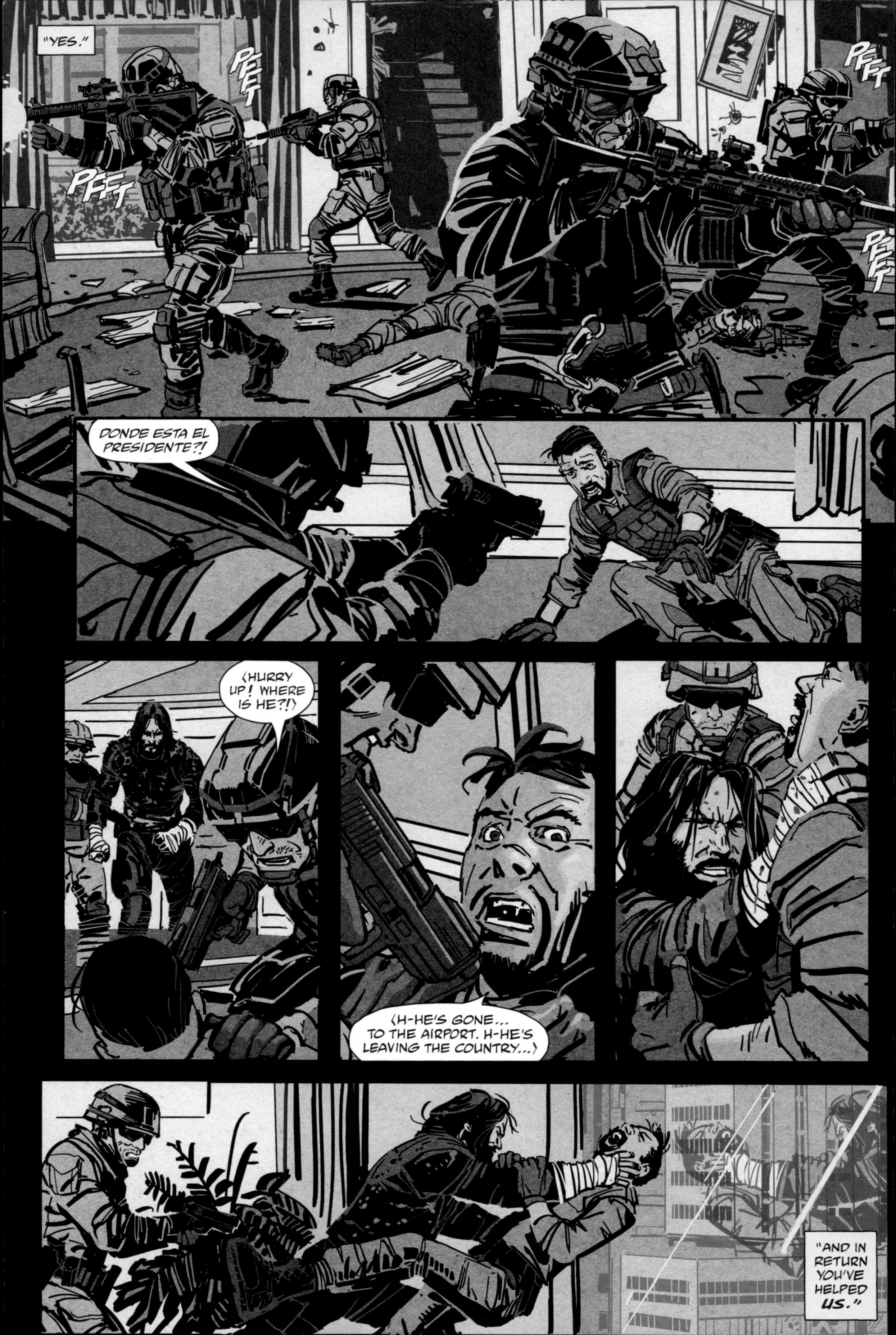
"YES."
PFFFT
PFFFT
PFFFT
PFFFT
DONDE ESTA EL PRESIDENTE?!
‹HURRY UP! WHERE IS HE?!›
‹H-HE'S GONE... TO THE AIRPORT. H-HE'S LEAVING THE COUNTRY...›
"AND IN RETURN YOU'VE HELPED US."

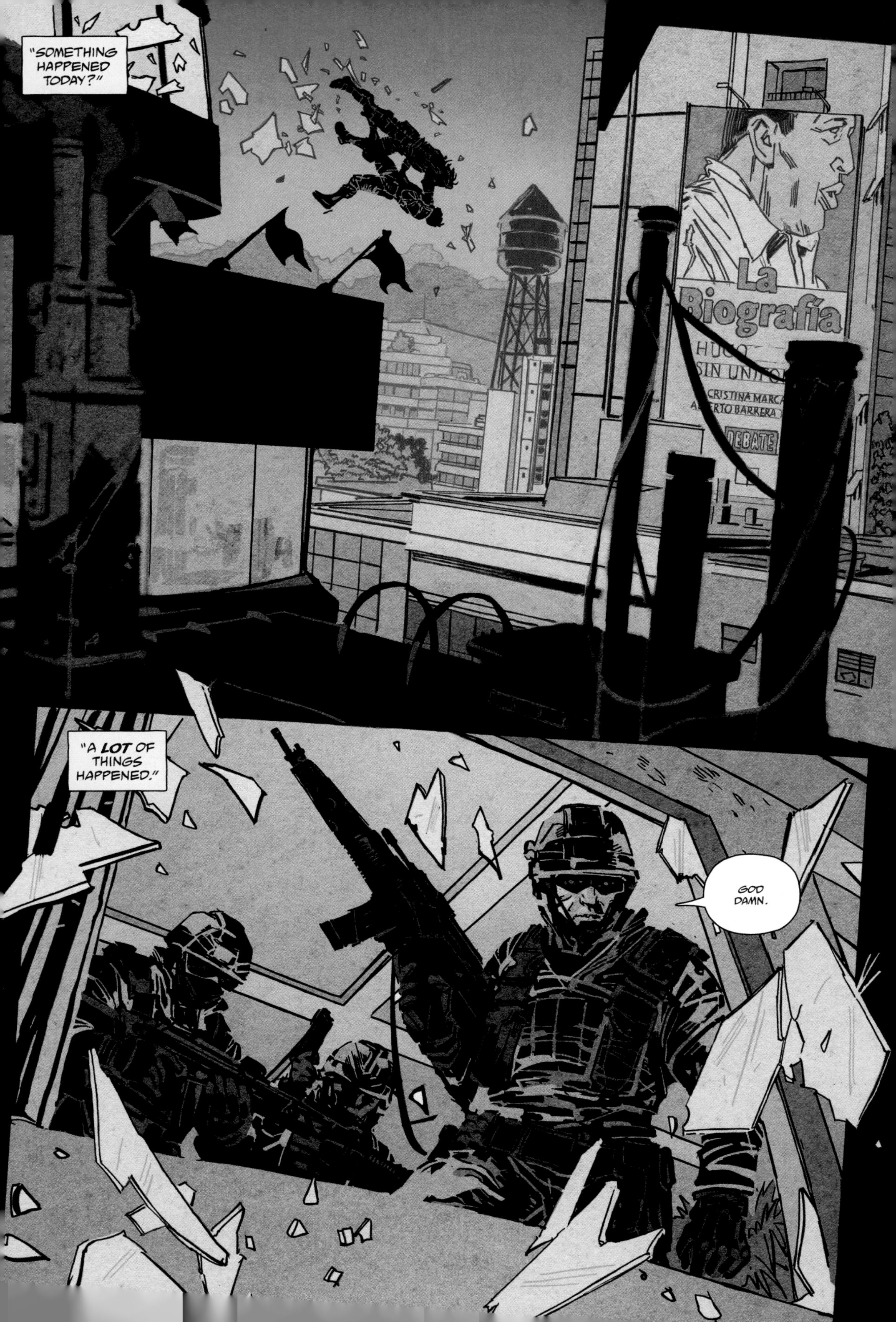
"SOMETHING HAPPENED TODAY?"
La Biografía
DEBATE
"A **LOT** OF THINGS HAPPENED."
GOD DAMN.

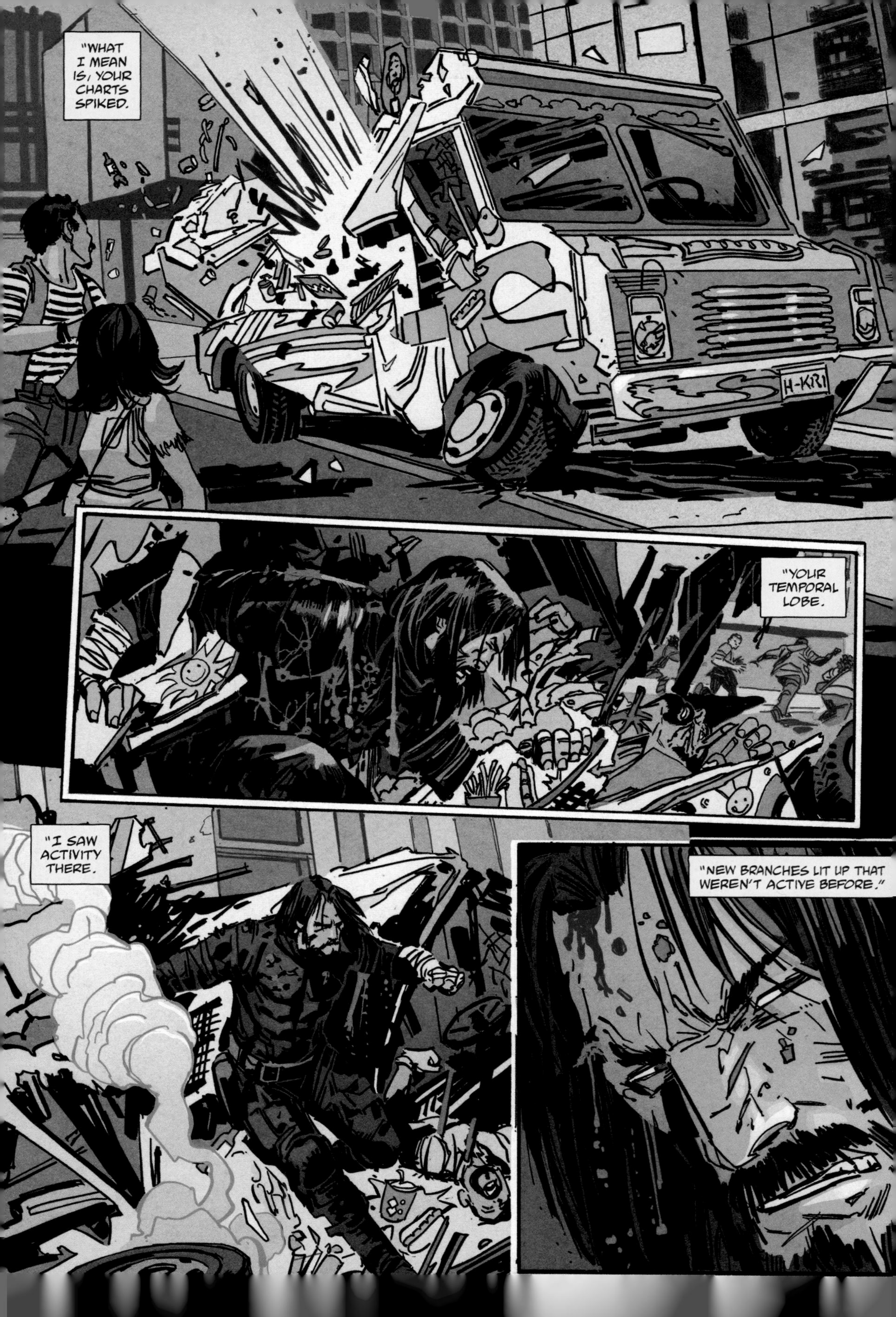
"WHAT I MEAN IS, YOUR CHARTS SPIKED.
H-KIRI
"YOUR TEMPORAL LOBE.
"I SAW ACTIVITY THERE.
"NEW BRANCHES LIT UP THAT WEREN'T ACTIVE BEFORE."

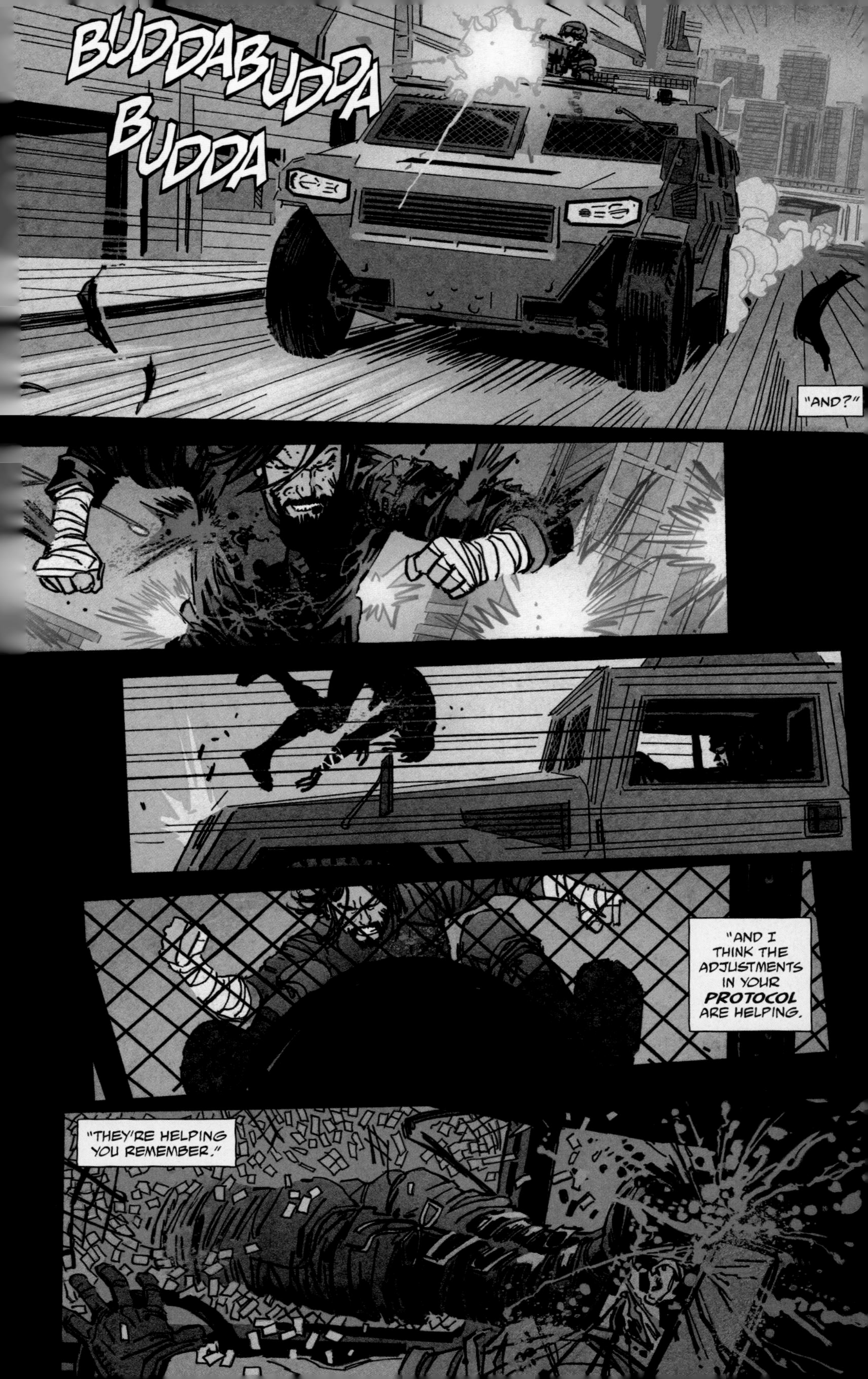
BUDDABUDDA
BUDDA
"AND?"
"AND I THINK THE ADJUSTMENTS IN YOUR **PROTOCOL** ARE HELPING.
"THEY'RE HELPING YOU REMEMBER."

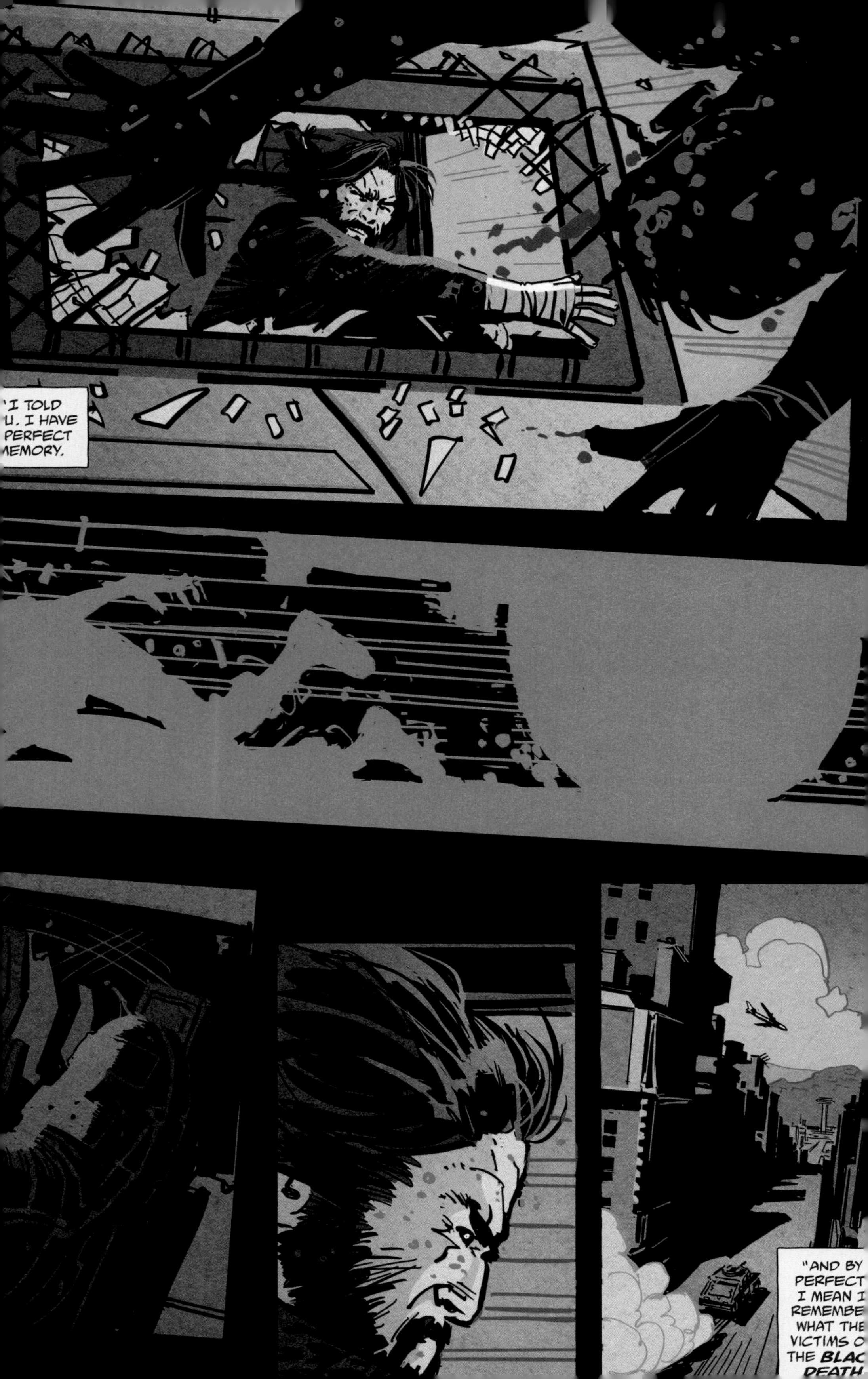
"I TOLD
U. I HAVE
PERFECT
MEMORY.
"AND BY
PERFECT
I MEAN I
REMEMBE
WHAT THE
VICTIMS O
THE BLAC
DEATH

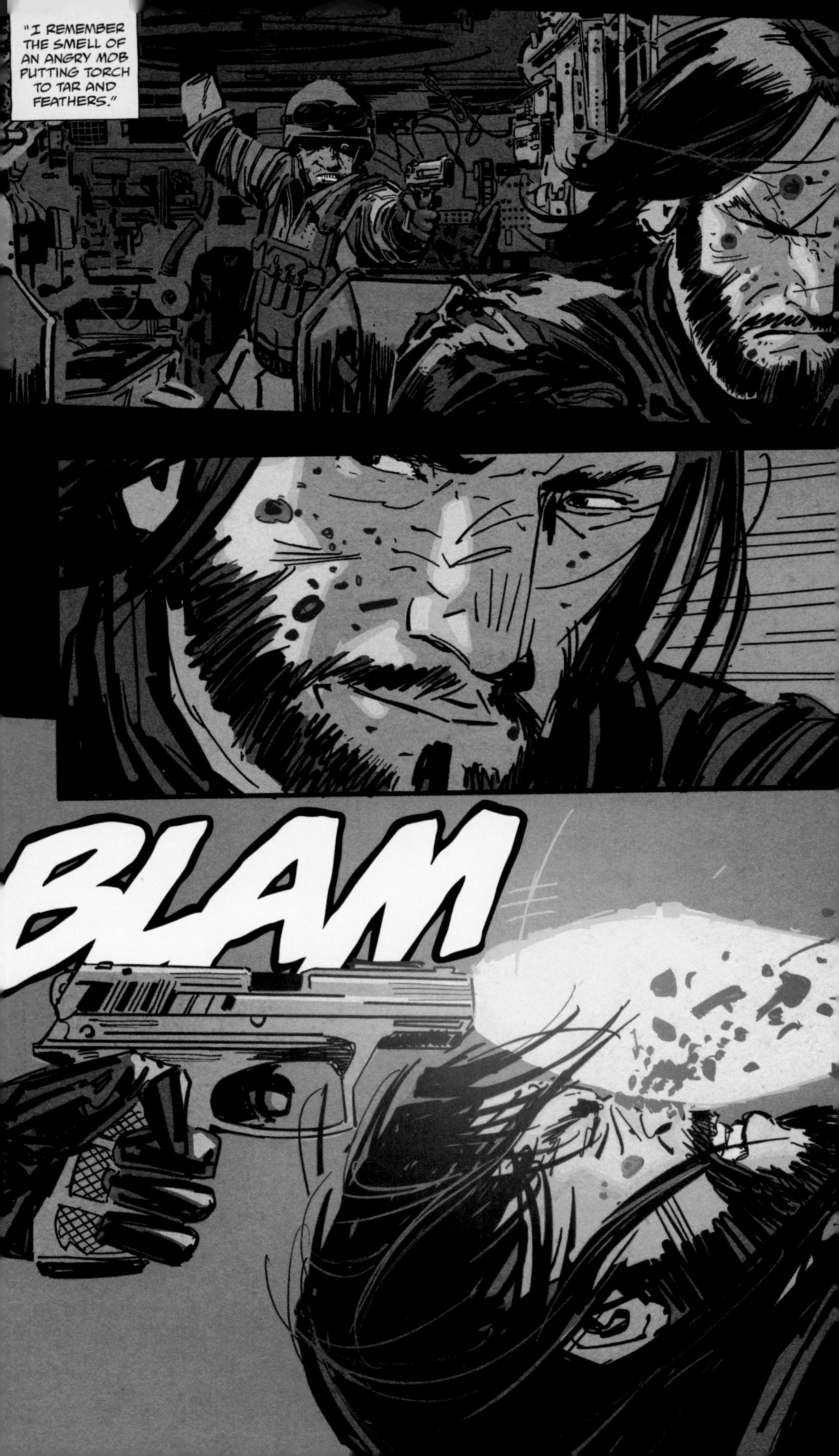
"I REMEMBER THE SMELL OF AN ANGRY MOB PUTTING TORCH TO TAR AND FEATHERS."
BLAM

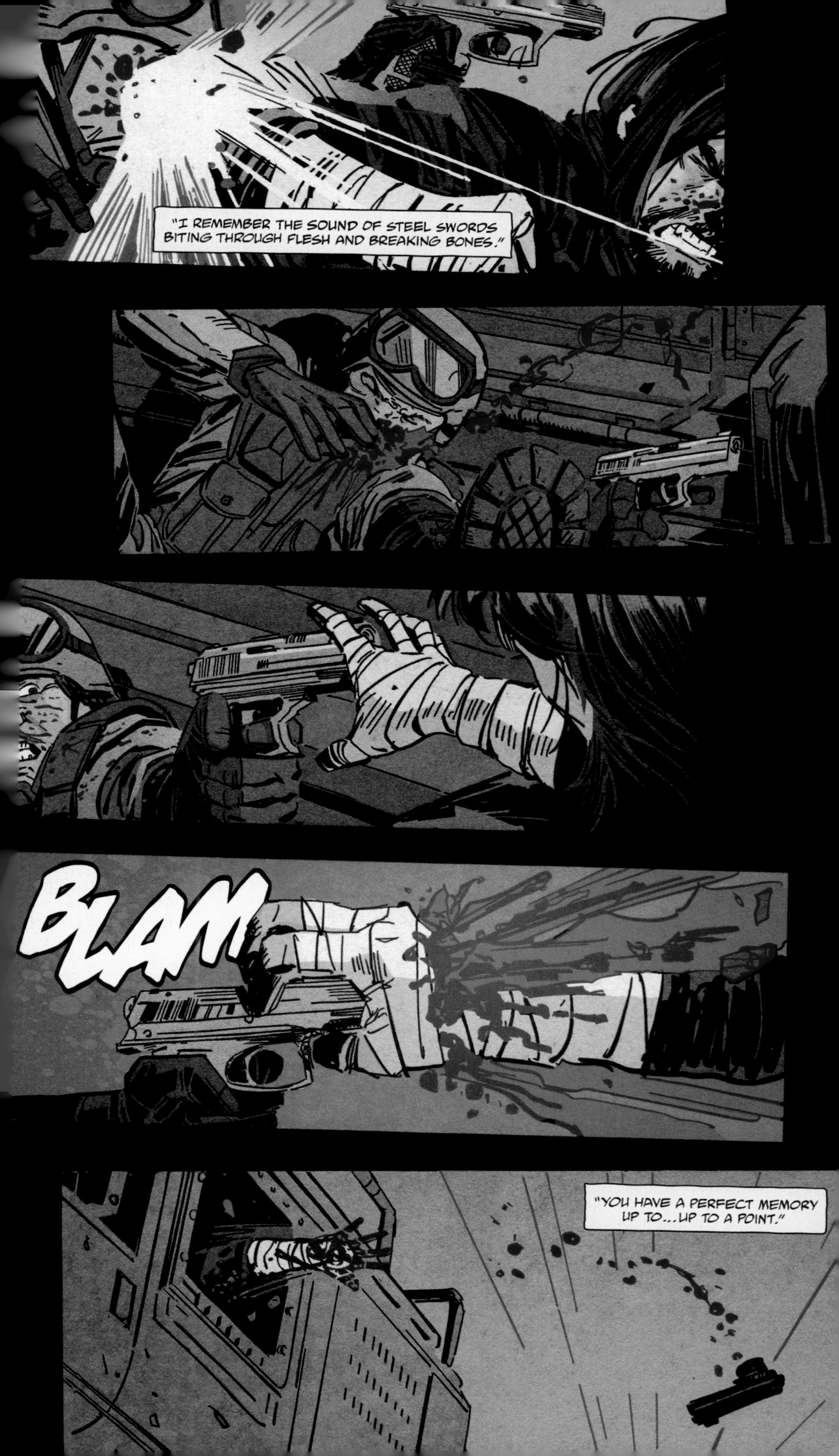
"I REMEMBER THE SOUND OF STEEL SWORDS BITING THROUGH FLESH AND BREAKING BONES."
BLAM
"YOU HAVE A PERFECT MEMORY UP TO... UP TO A POINT."

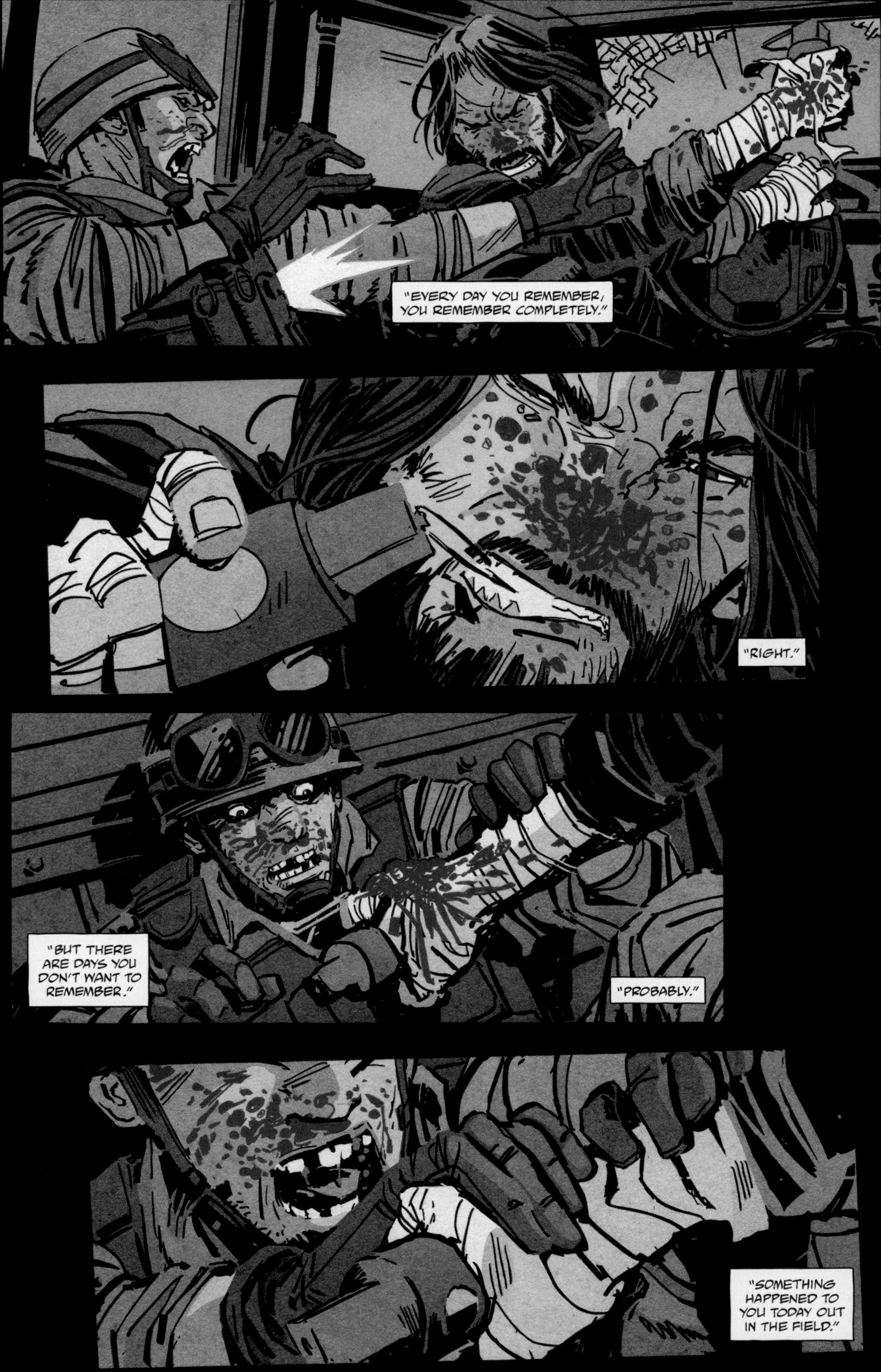
"EVERY DAY YOU REMEMBER, YOU REMEMBER COMPLETELY."
"RIGHT."
"BUT THERE ARE DAYS YOU DON'T WANT TO REMEMBER."
"PROBABLY."
"SOMETHING HAPPENED TO YOU TODAY OUT IN THE FIELD."

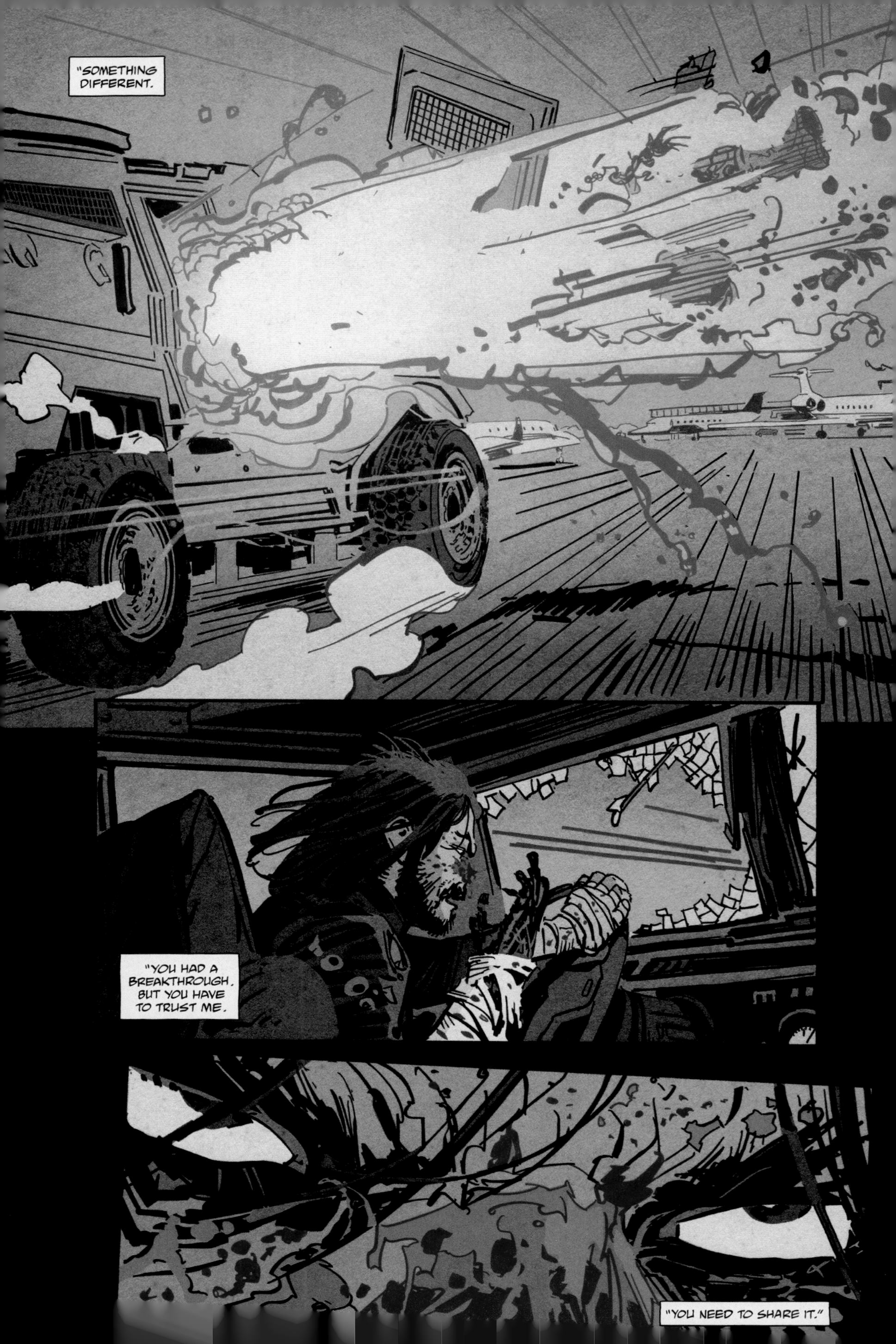
"SOMETHING DIFFERENT.
"YOU HAD A BREAKTHROUGH, BUT YOU HAVE TO TRUST ME.
"YOU NEED TO SHARE IT."

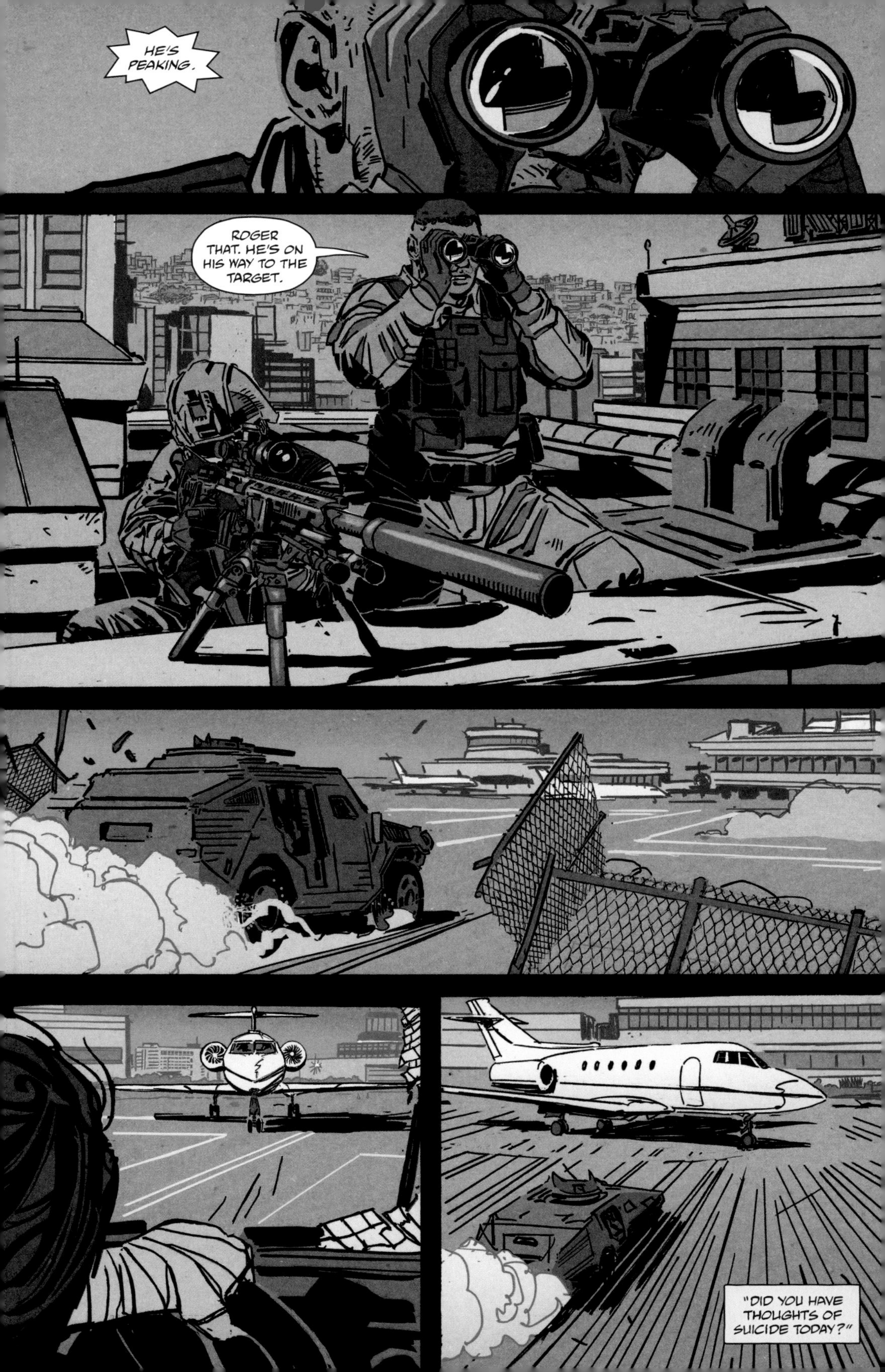
HE'S PEAKING.
ROGER THAT. HE'S ON HIS WAY TO THE TARGET.
"DID YOU HAVE THOUGHTS OF SUICIDE TODAY?"

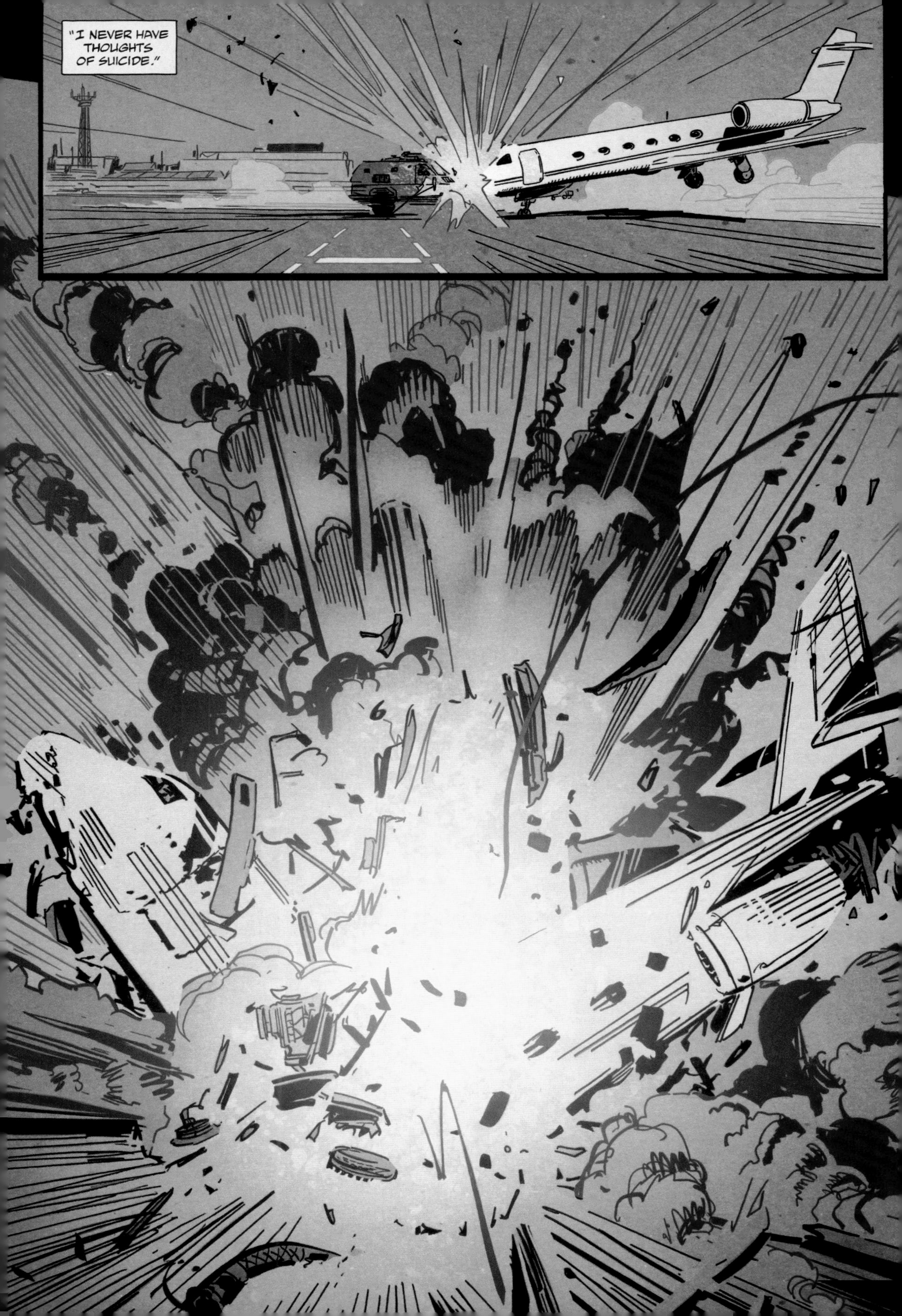
"I NEVER HAVE THOUGHTS OF SUICIDE."

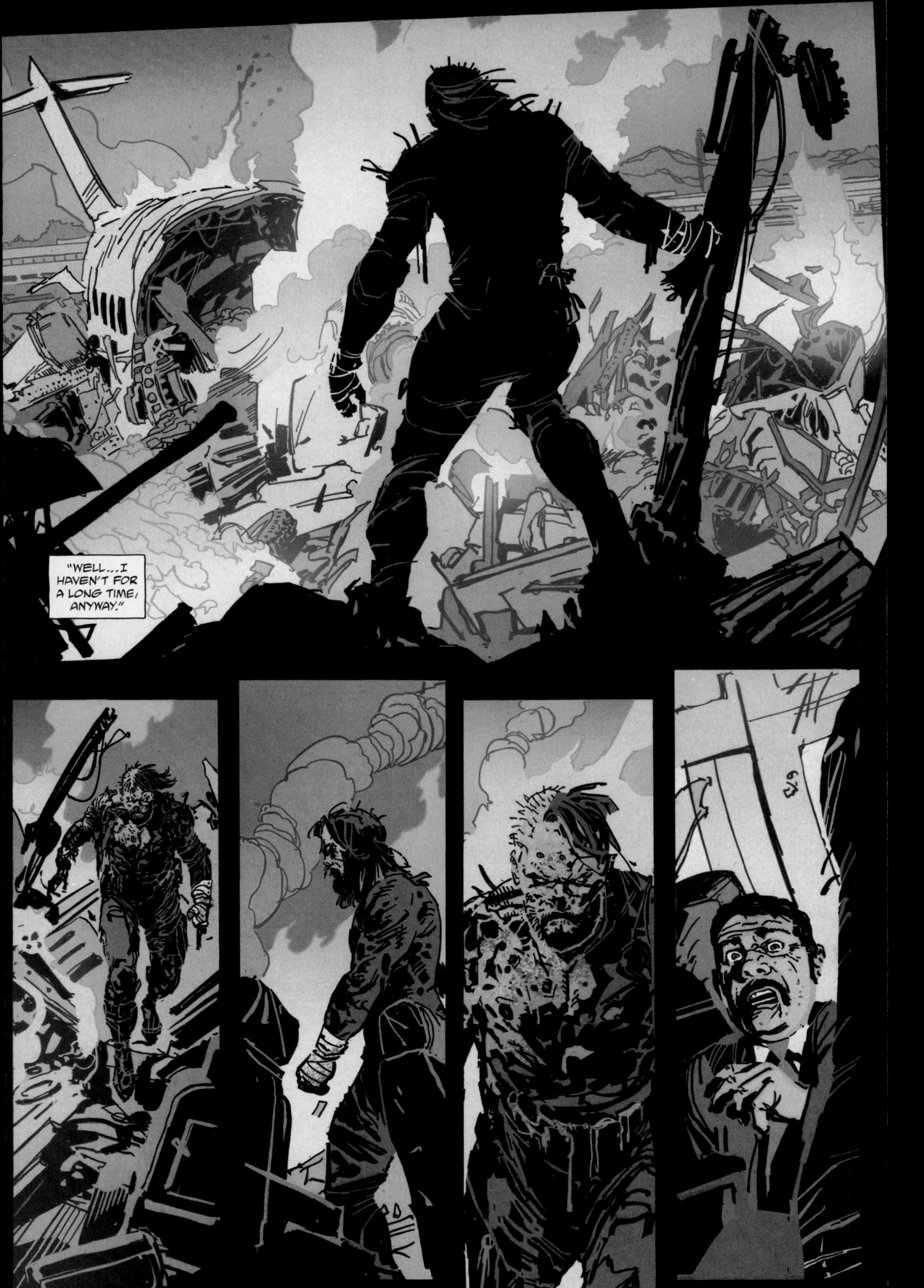
"WELL... I HAVEN'T FOR A LONG TIME, ANYWAY."

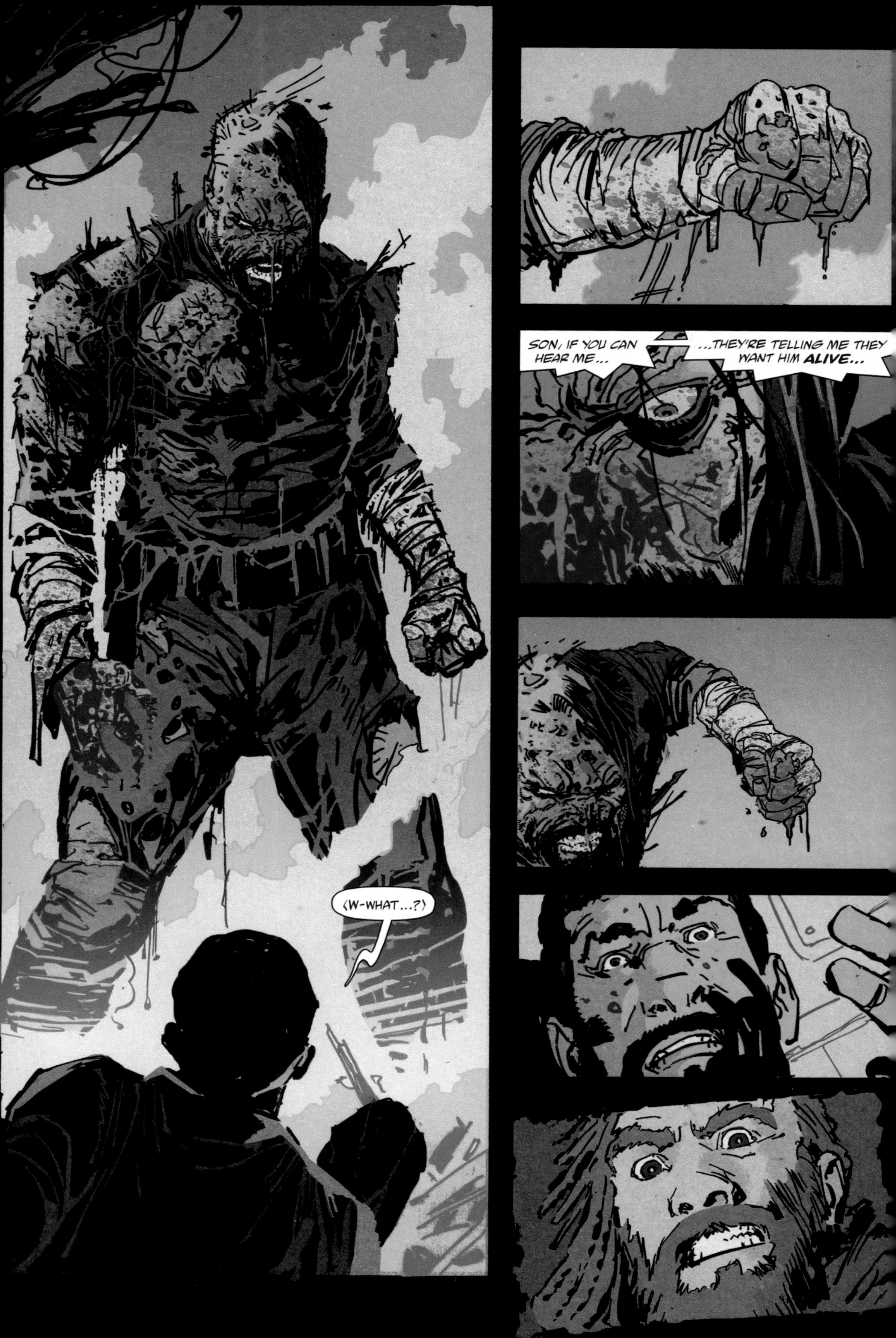
‹W-WHAT...?›
SON, IF YOU CAN HEAR ME...
...THEY'RE TELLING ME THEY WANT HIM **ALIVE...**

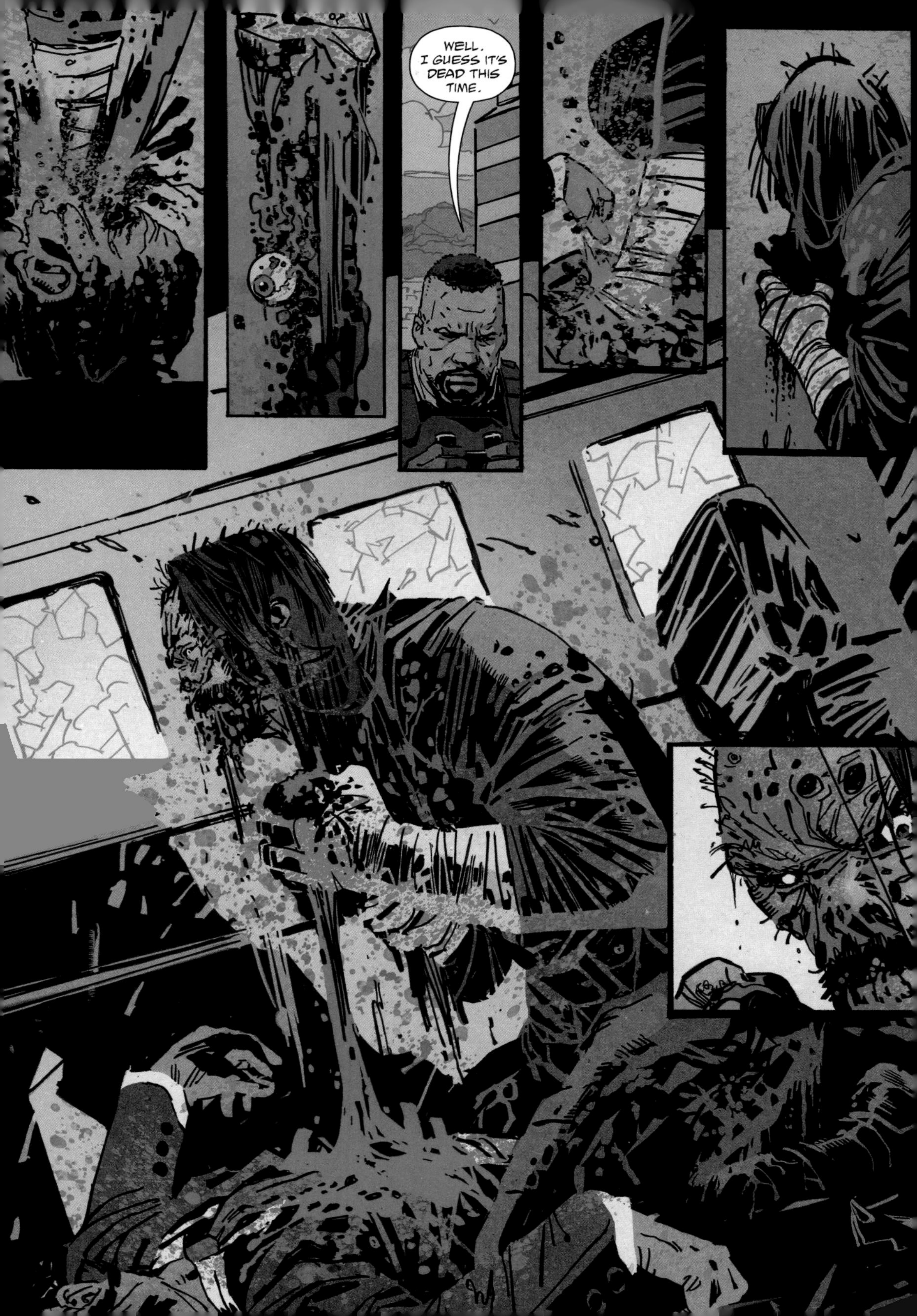
WELL. I GUESS IT'S DEAD THIS TIME.

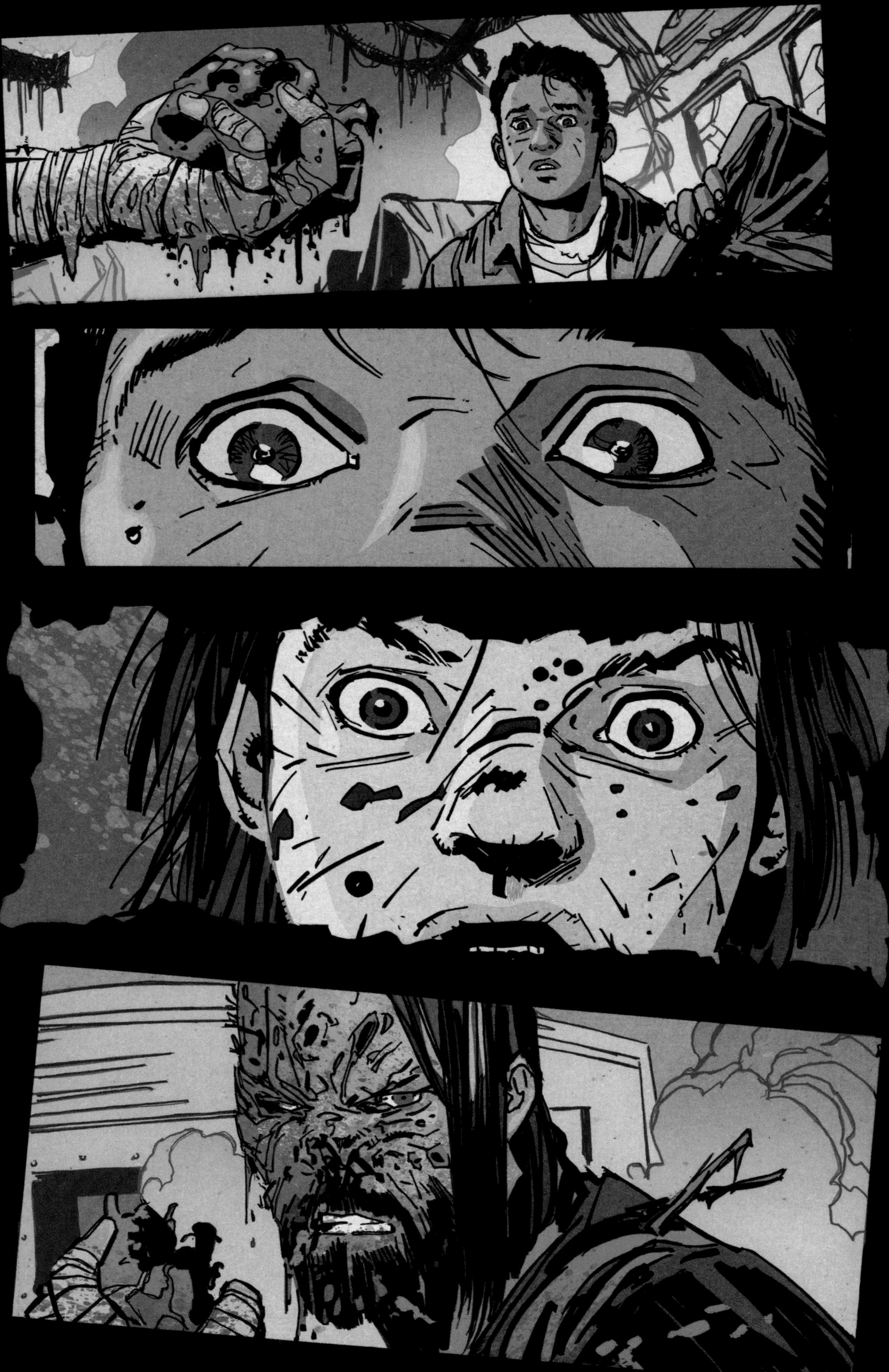

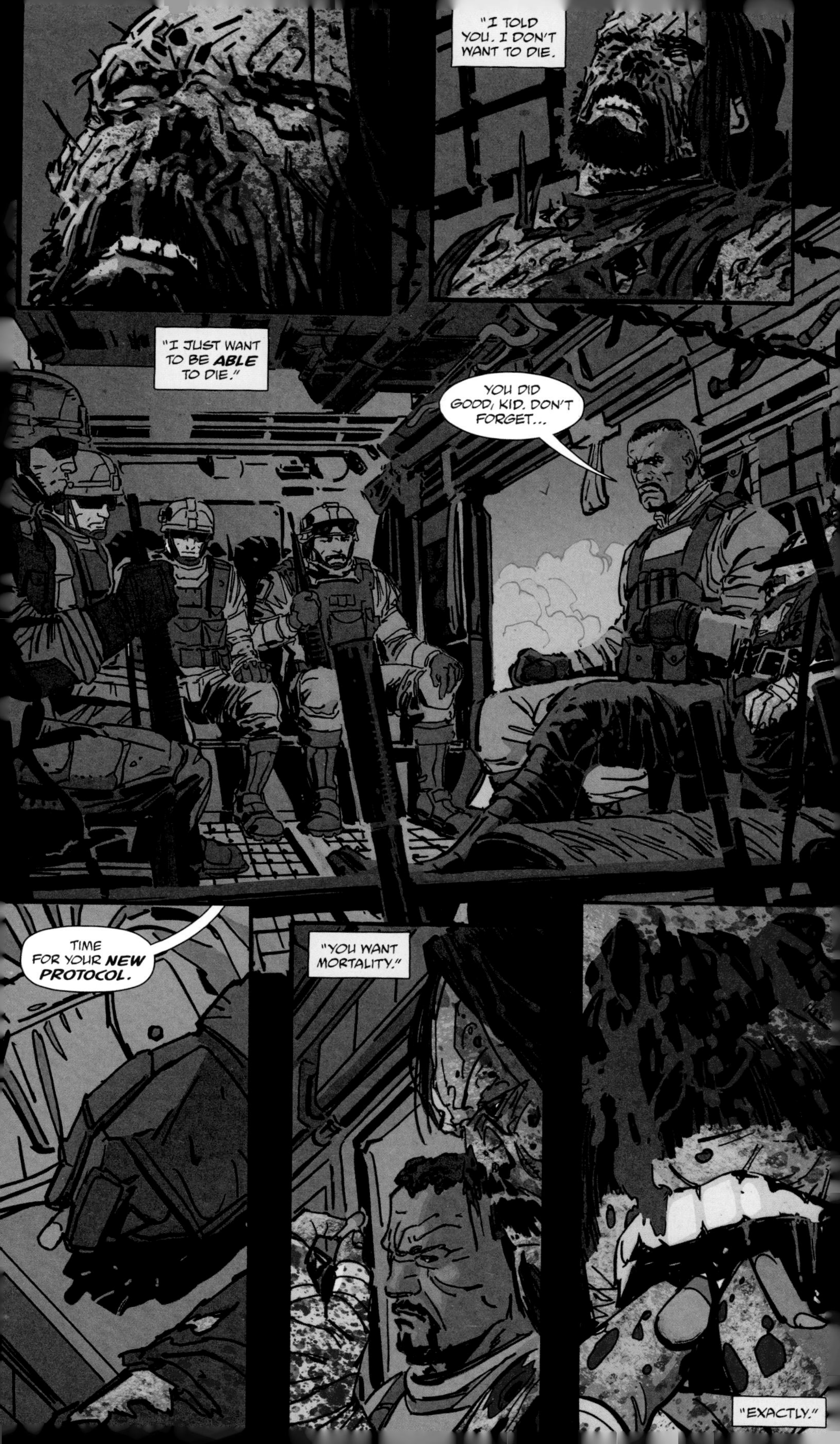
"I TOLD YOU. I DON'T WANT TO DIE.
"I JUST WANT TO BE ABLE TO DIE."
YOU DID GOOD, KID. DON'T FORGET...
TIME FOR YOUR NEW PROTOCOL.
"YOU WANT MORTALITY."
"EXACTLY."

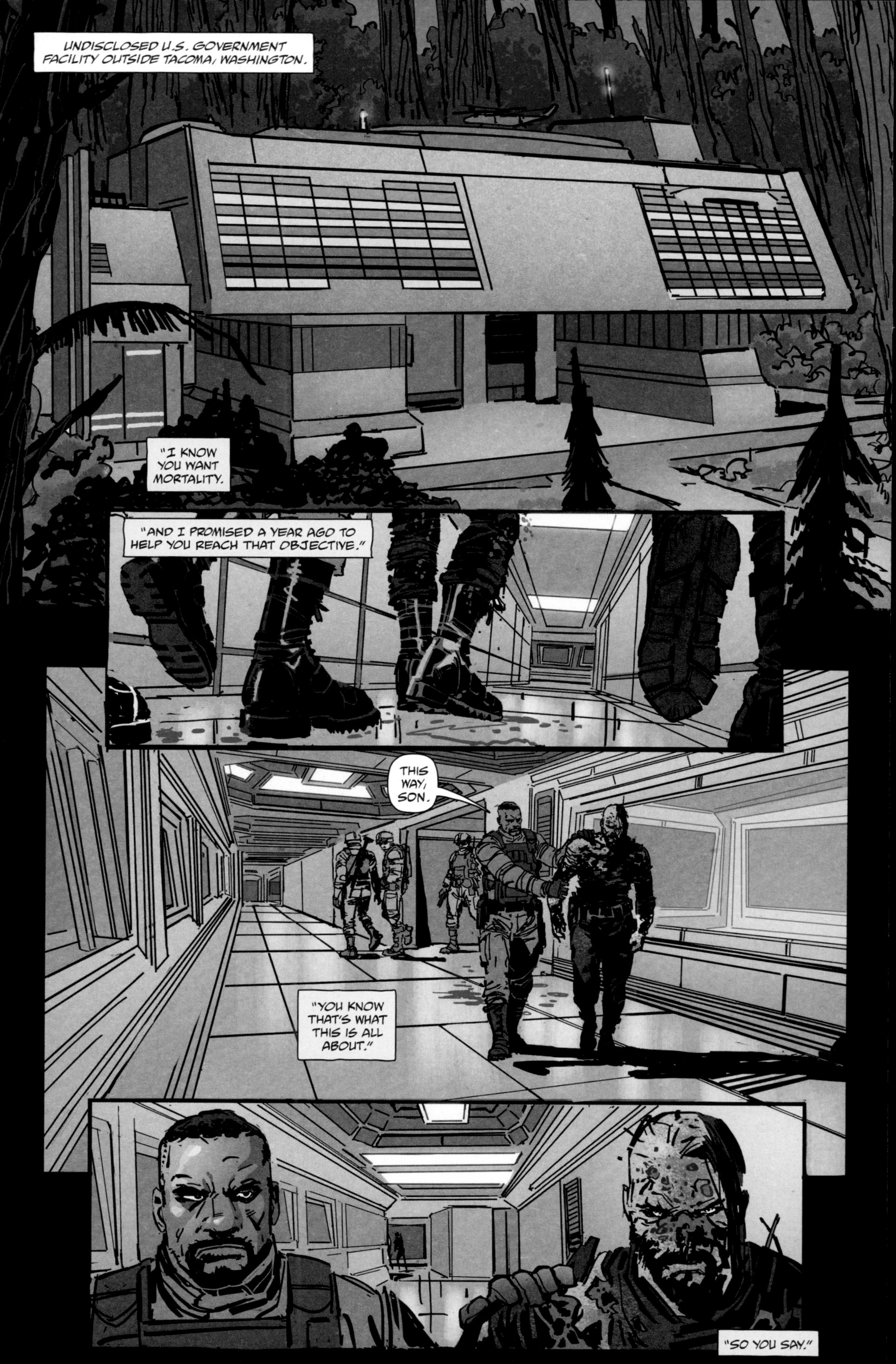
UNDISCLOSED U.S. GOVERNMENT FACILITY OUTSIDE TACOMA, WASHINGTON.
"I KNOW YOU WANT MORTALITY.
"AND I PROMISED A YEAR AGO TO HELP YOU REACH THAT OBJECTIVE."
THIS WAY, SON.
"YOU KNOW THAT'S WHAT THIS IS ALL ABOUT."
"SO YOU SAY."

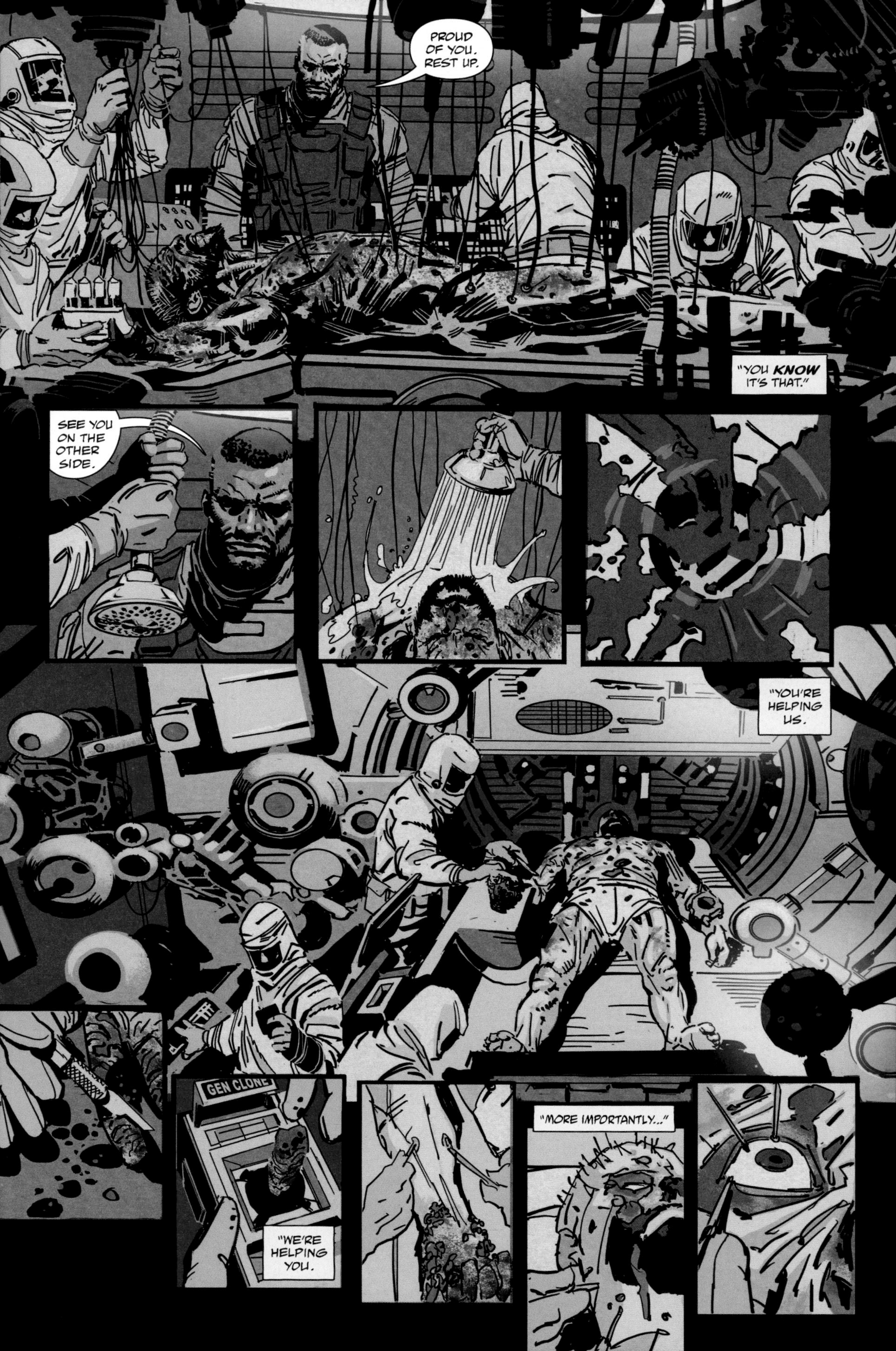
PROUD OF YOU. REST UP.
"YOU KNOW IT'S THAT."
SEE YOU ON THE OTHER SIDE.
"YOU'RE HELPING US.
GEN CLONE
"WE'RE HELPING YOU.
"MORE IMPORTANTLY..."

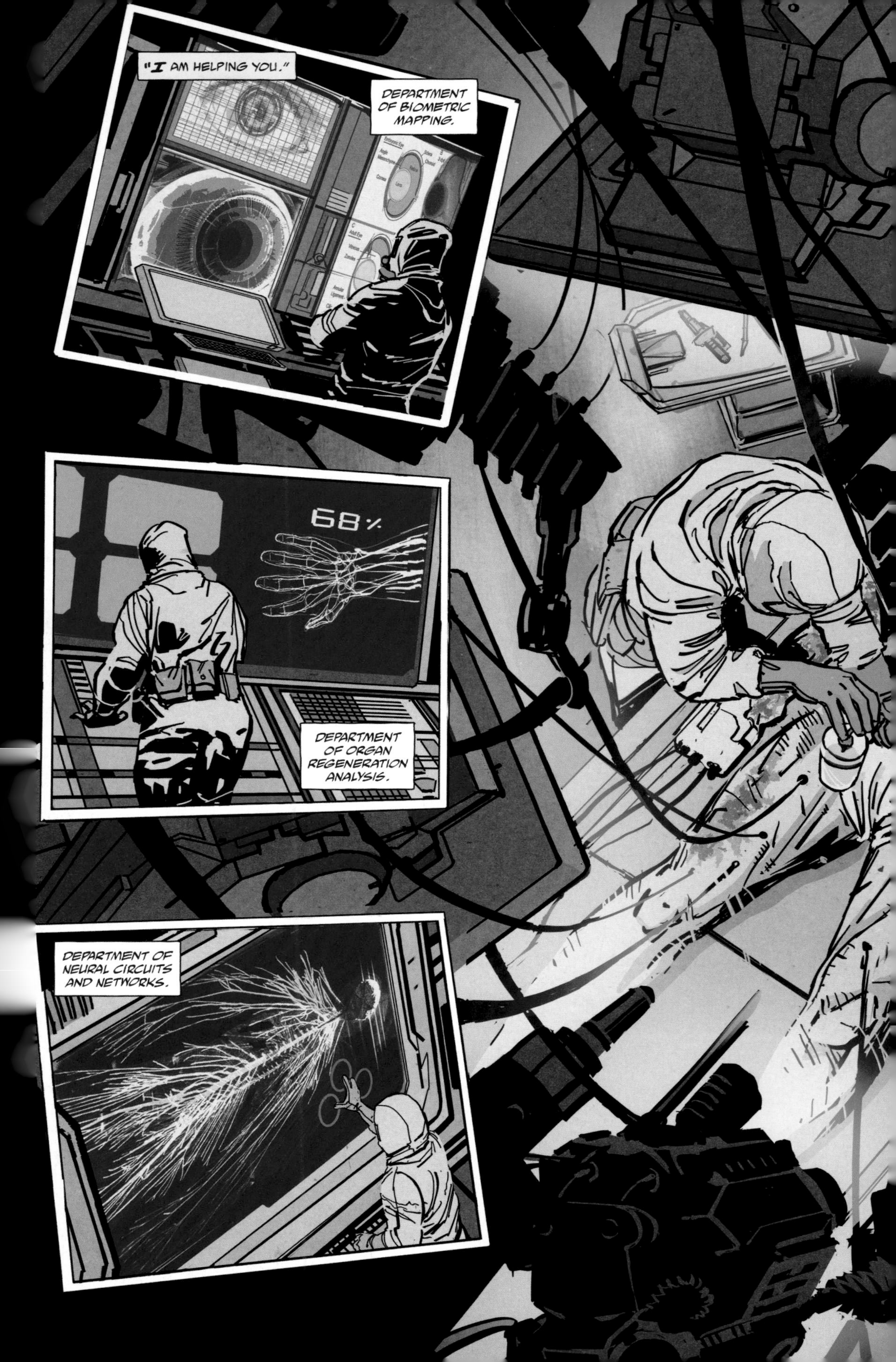
"I AM HELPING YOU."
DEPARTMENT OF BIOMETRIC MAPPING.
68%
DEPARTMENT OF ORGAN REGENERATION ANALYSIS.
DEPARTMENT OF NEURAL CIRCUITS AND NETWORKS.

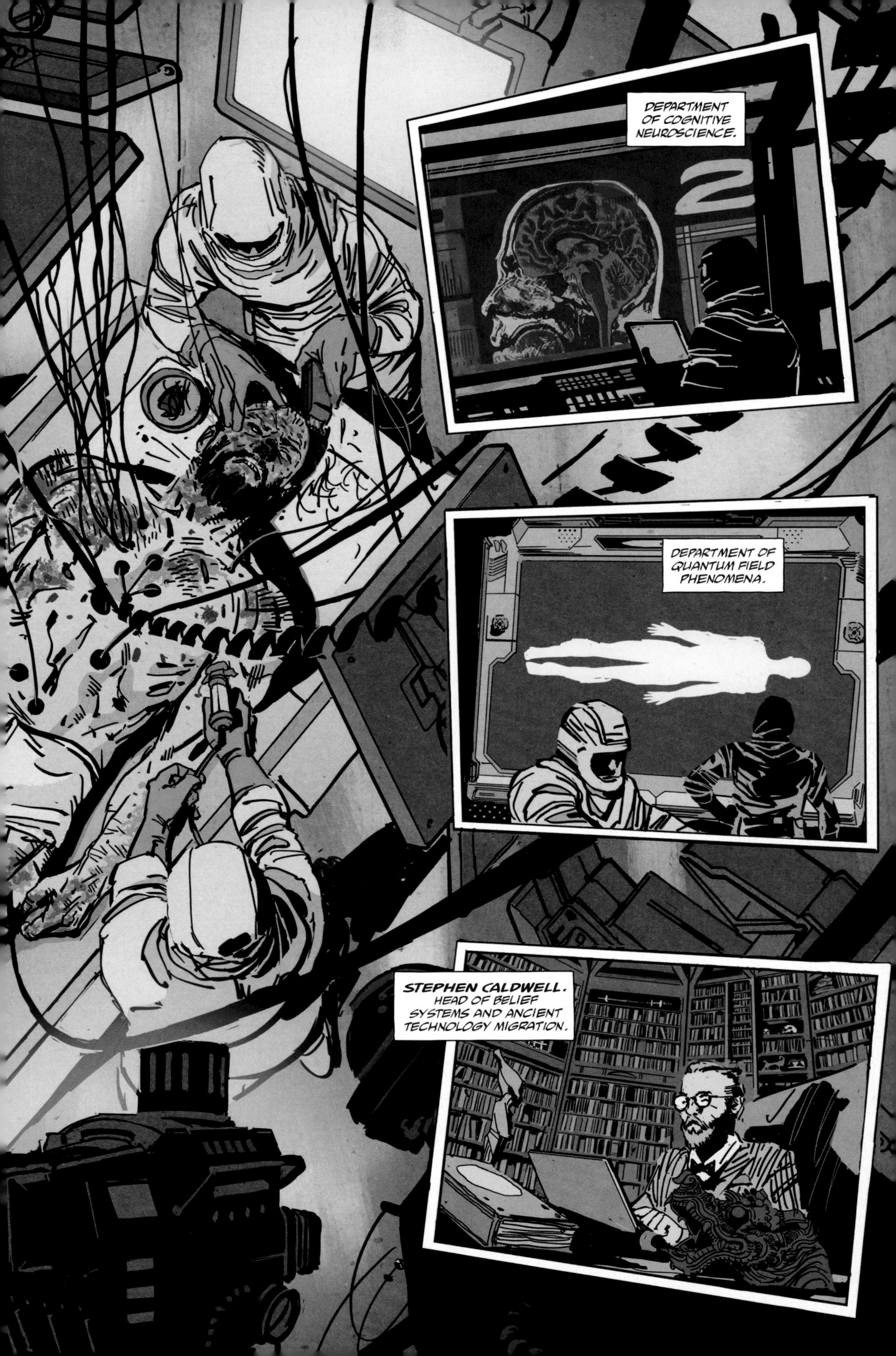
DEPARTMENT OF COGNITIVE NEUROSCIENCE.
DEPARTMENT OF QUANTUM FIELD PHENOMENA.
STEPHEN CALDWELL. HEAD OF BELIEF SYSTEMS AND ANCIENT TECHNOLOGY MIGRATION.

"BUT YOUR MEMORY IS GOING TO BE THE KEY.

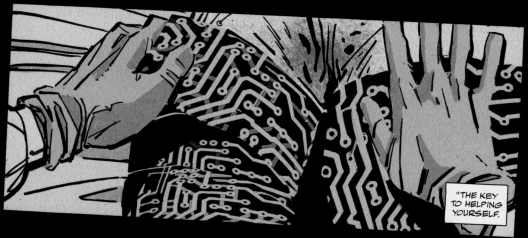

"THE KEY TO HELPING YOURSELF.

"THIS IS YOUR JOB. AND MINE. BUT YOU KNOW THIS..."

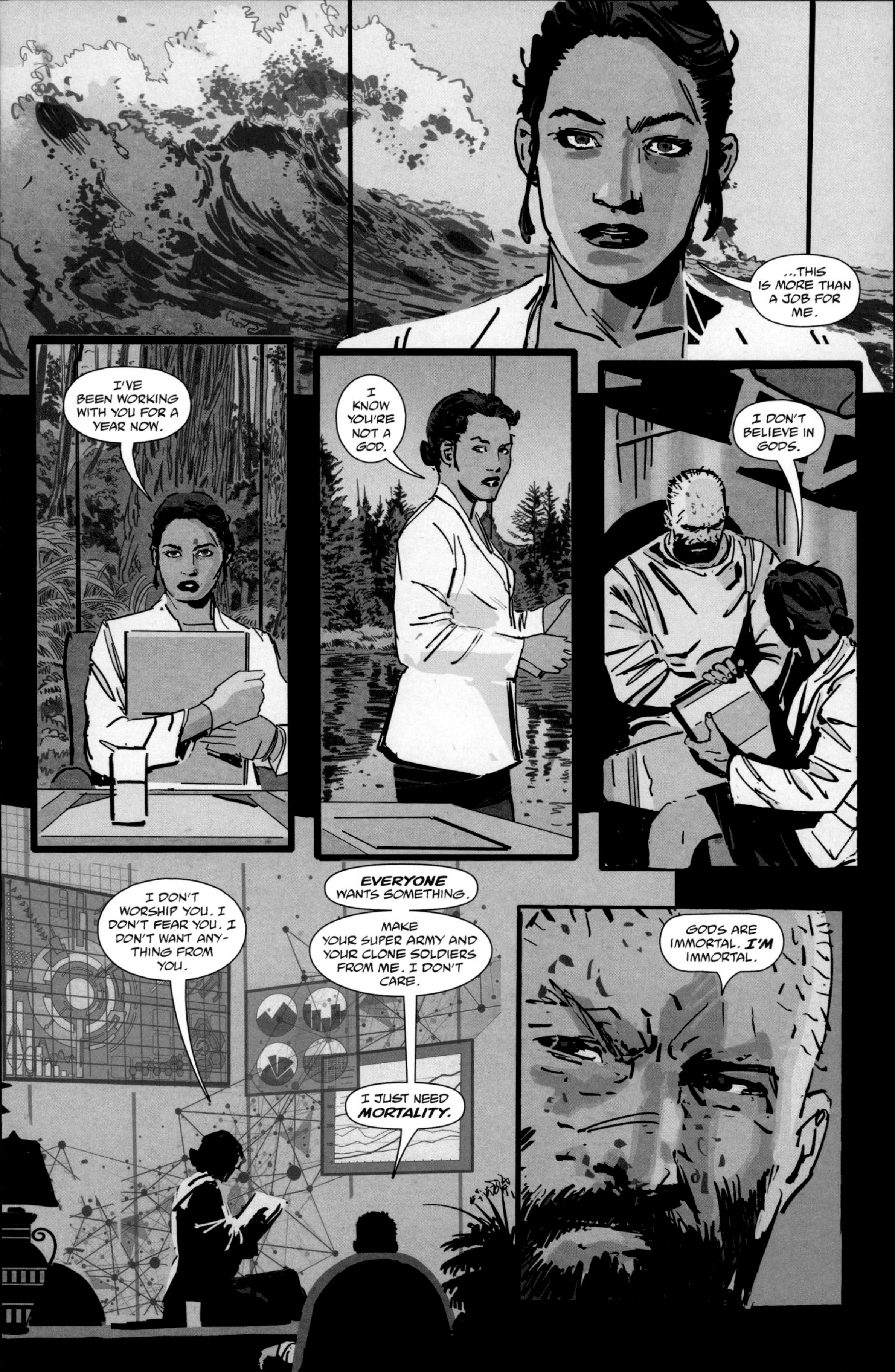
...THIS IS MORE THAN A JOB FOR ME.
I'VE BEEN WORKING WITH YOU FOR A YEAR NOW.
I KNOW YOU'RE NOT A GOD.
I DON'T BELIEVE IN GODS.
I DON'T WORSHIP YOU. I DON'T FEAR YOU. I DON'T WANT ANY-THING FROM YOU.
EVERYONE WANTS SOMETHING.
MAKE YOUR SUPER ARMY AND YOUR CLONE SOLDIERS FROM ME. I DON'T CARE.
I JUST NEED MORTALITY.
GODS ARE IMMORTAL. I'M IMMORTAL.

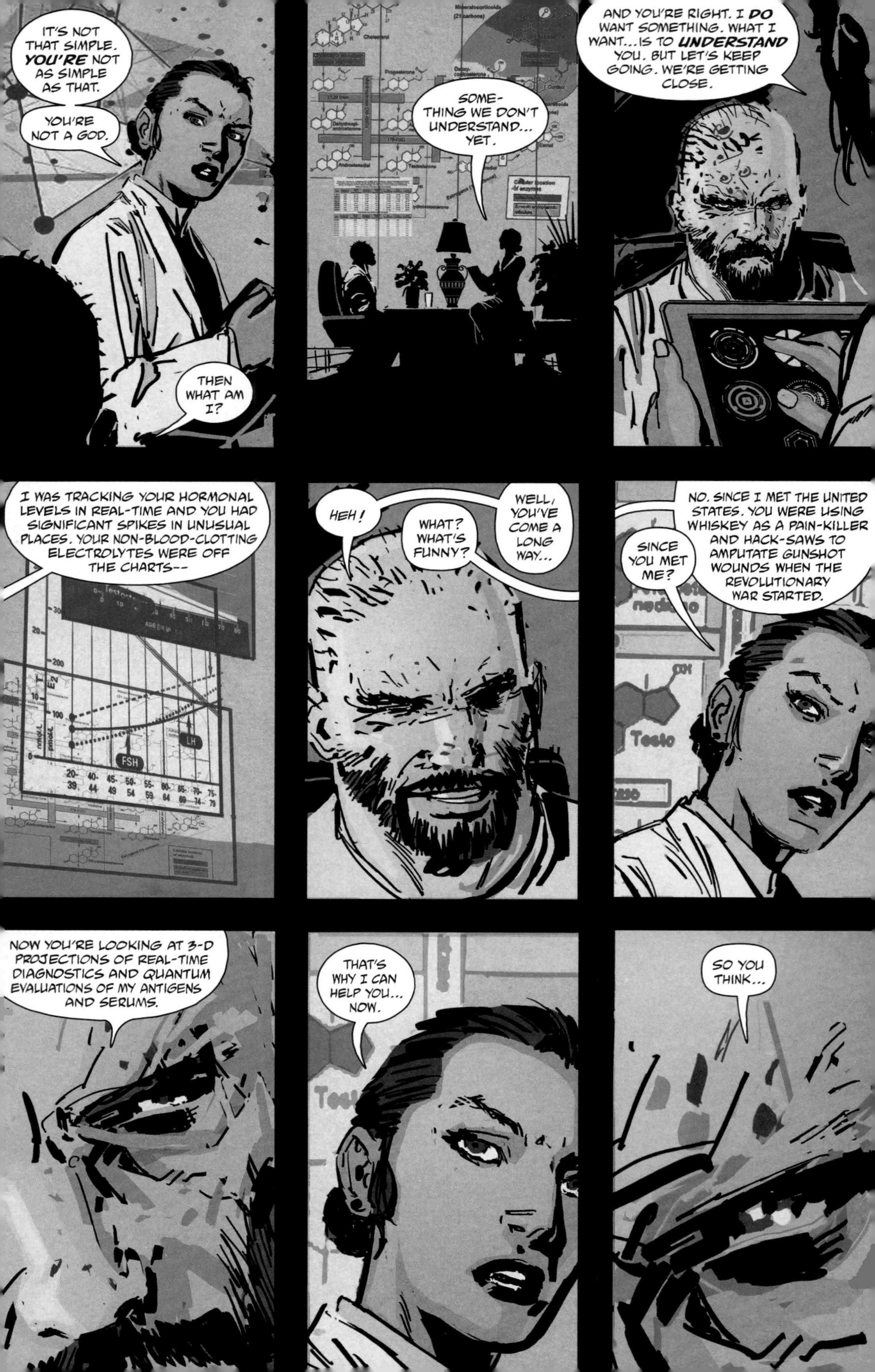
IT'S NOT THAT SIMPLE. YOU'RE NOT AS SIMPLE AS THAT.
YOU'RE NOT A GOD.
THEN WHAT AM I?
SOME-THING WE DON'T UNDERSTAND... YET.
AND YOU'RE RIGHT. I DO WANT SOMETHING. WHAT I WANT...IS TO UNDERSTAND YOU. BUT LET'S KEEP GOING. WE'RE GETTING CLOSE.
I WAS TRACKING YOUR HORMONAL LEVELS IN REAL-TIME AND YOU HAD SIGNIFICANT SPIKES IN UNUSUAL PLACES. YOUR NON-BLOOD-CLOTTING ELECTROLYTES WERE OFF THE CHARTS--
HEH!
WHAT? WHAT'S FUNNY?
WELL, YOU'VE COME A LONG WAY...
SINCE YOU MET ME?
NO. SINCE I MET THE UNITED STATES. YOU WERE USING WHISKEY AS A PAIN-KILLER AND HACK-SAWS TO AMPUTATE GUNSHOT WOUNDS WHEN THE REVOLUTIONARY WAR STARTED.
NOW YOU'RE LOOKING AT 3-D PROJECTIONS OF REAL-TIME DIAGNOSTICS AND QUANTUM EVALUATIONS OF MY ANTIGENS AND SERUMS.
THAT'S WHY I CAN HELP YOU... NOW.
SO YOU THINK...

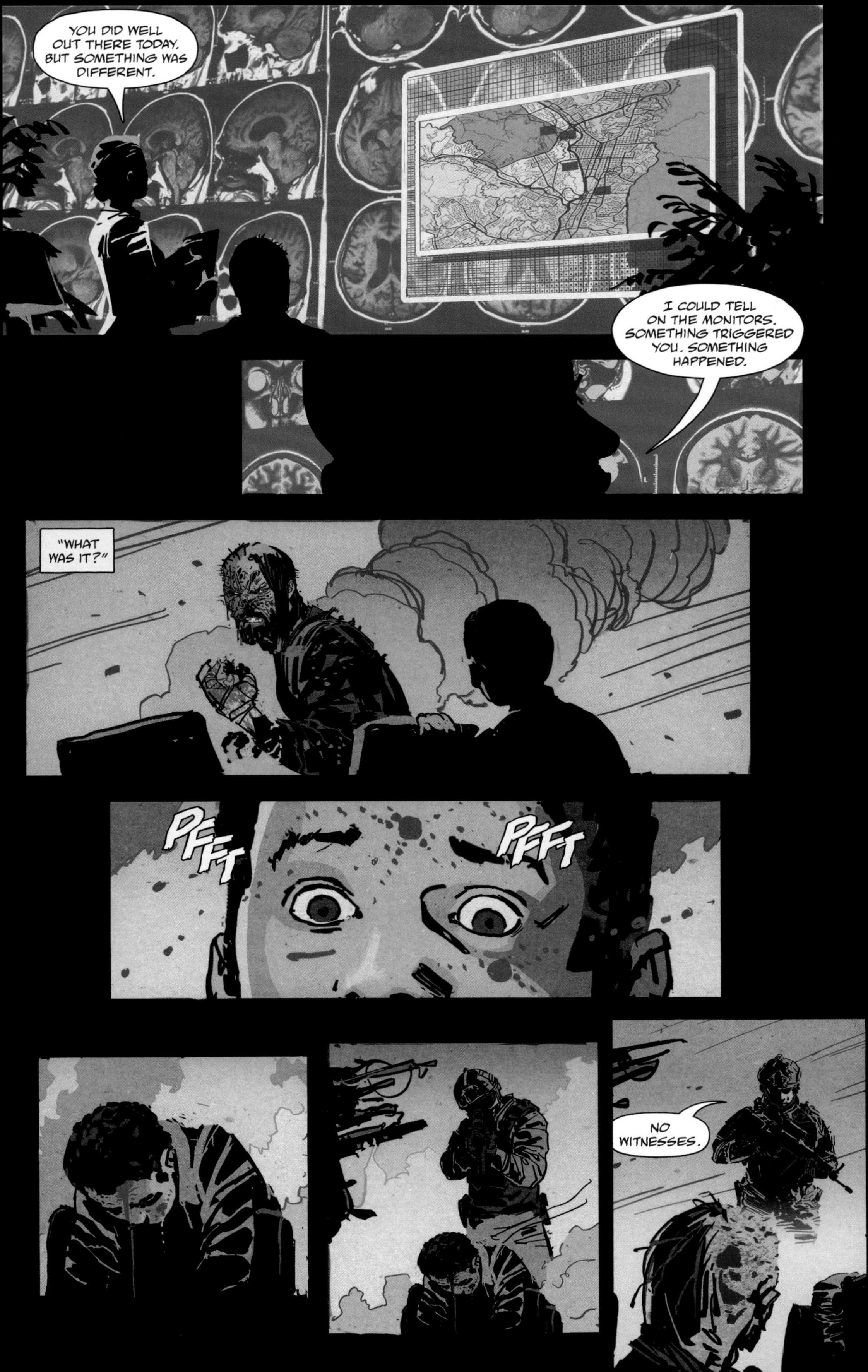
YOU DID WELL OUT THERE TODAY. BUT SOMETHING WAS DIFFERENT.
I COULD TELL ON THE MONITORS. SOMETHING TRIGGERED YOU. SOMETHING HAPPENED.
"WHAT WAS IT?"
PFFT
PFFT
NO WITNESSES.

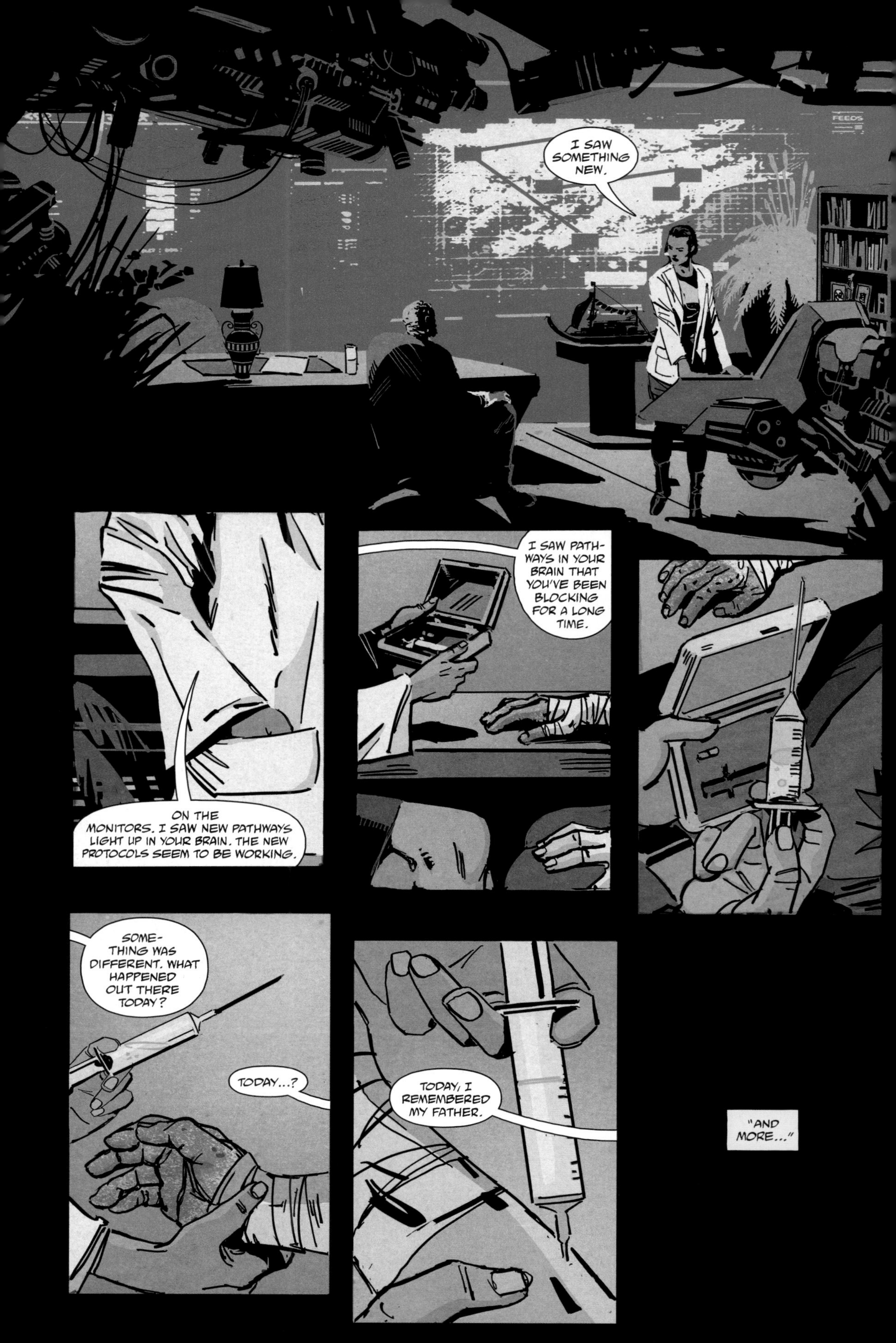
FEEDS
I SAW SOMETHING NEW.
ON THE MONITORS. I SAW NEW PATHWAYS LIGHT UP IN YOUR BRAIN. THE NEW PROTOCOLS SEEM TO BE WORKING.
I SAW PATHWAYS IN YOUR BRAIN THAT YOU'VE BEEN BLOCKING FOR A LONG TIME.
SOMETHING WAS DIFFERENT. WHAT HAPPENED OUT THERE TODAY?
TODAY...?
TODAY, I REMEMBERED MY FATHER.
"AND MORE..."

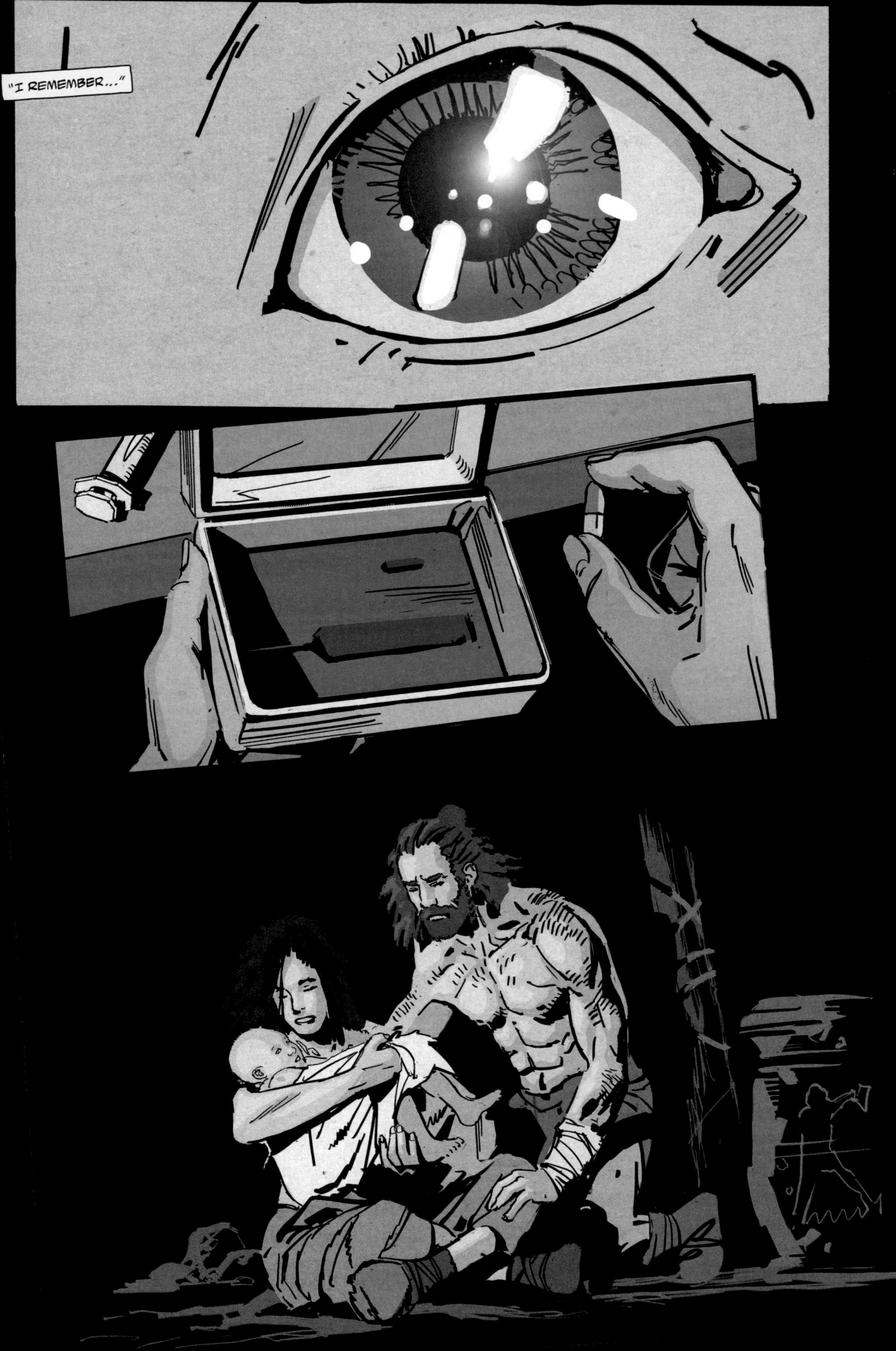
"I REMEMBER..."

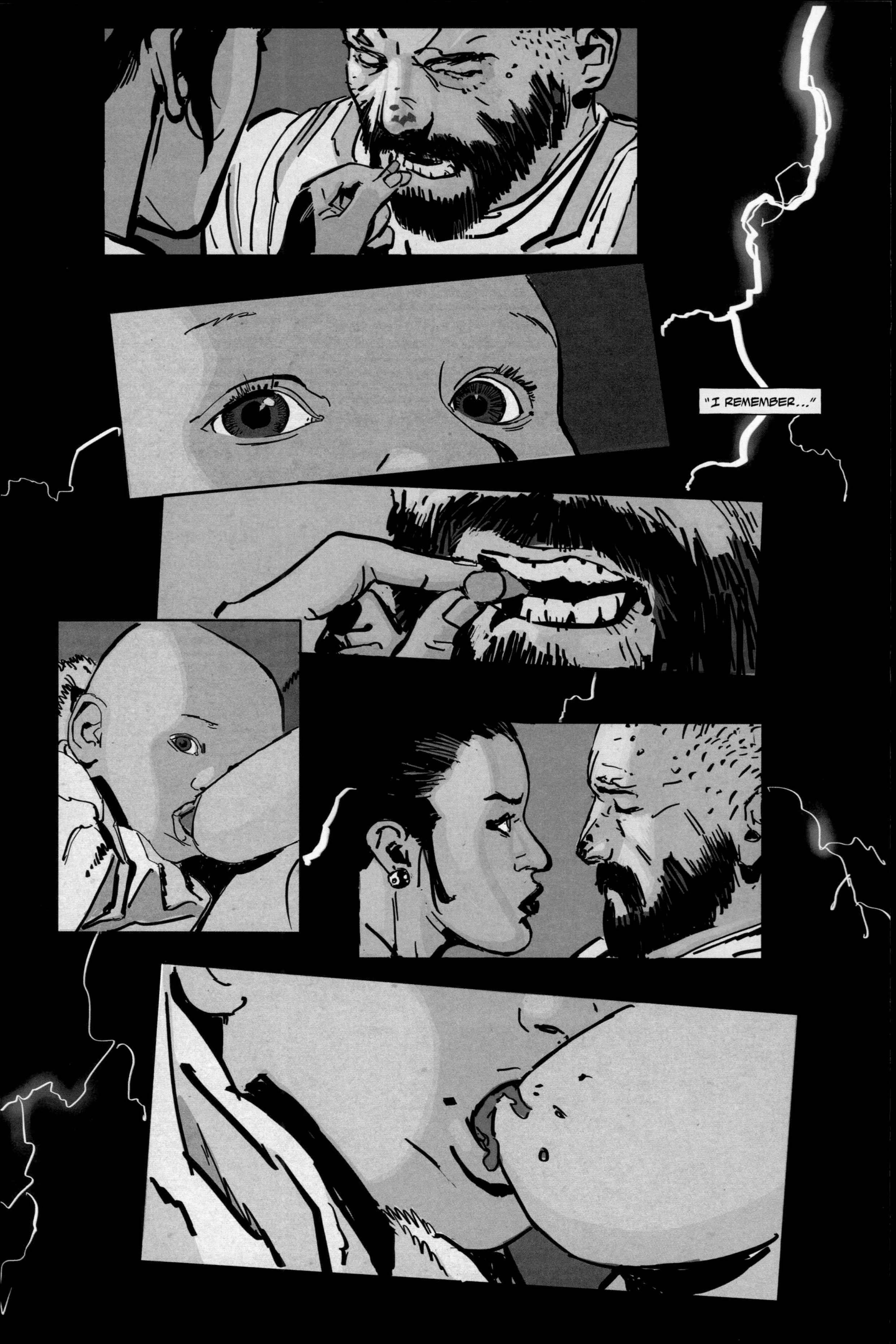
"I REMEMBER..."

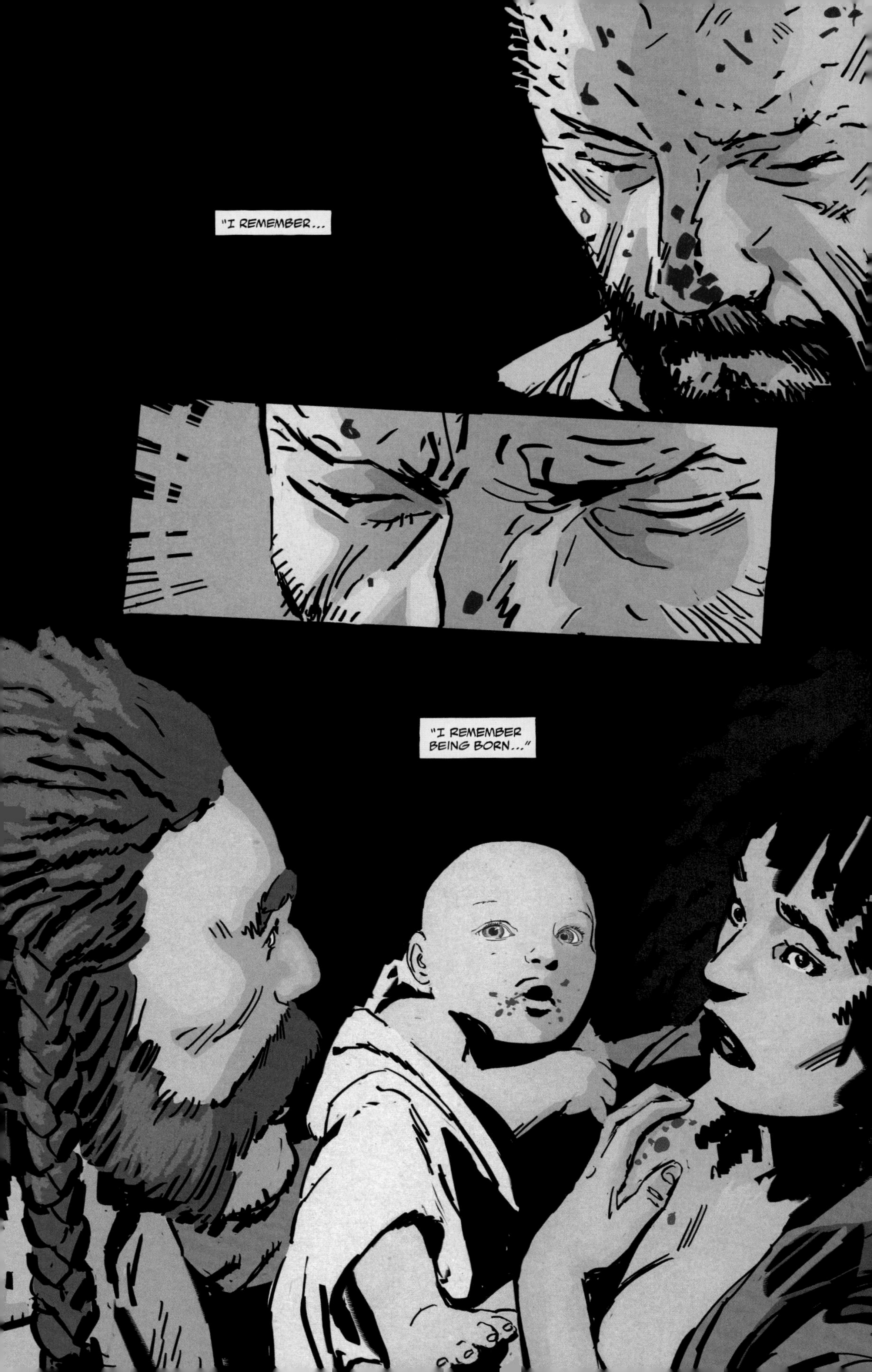
"I REMEMBER...
"I REMEMBER BEING BORN..."

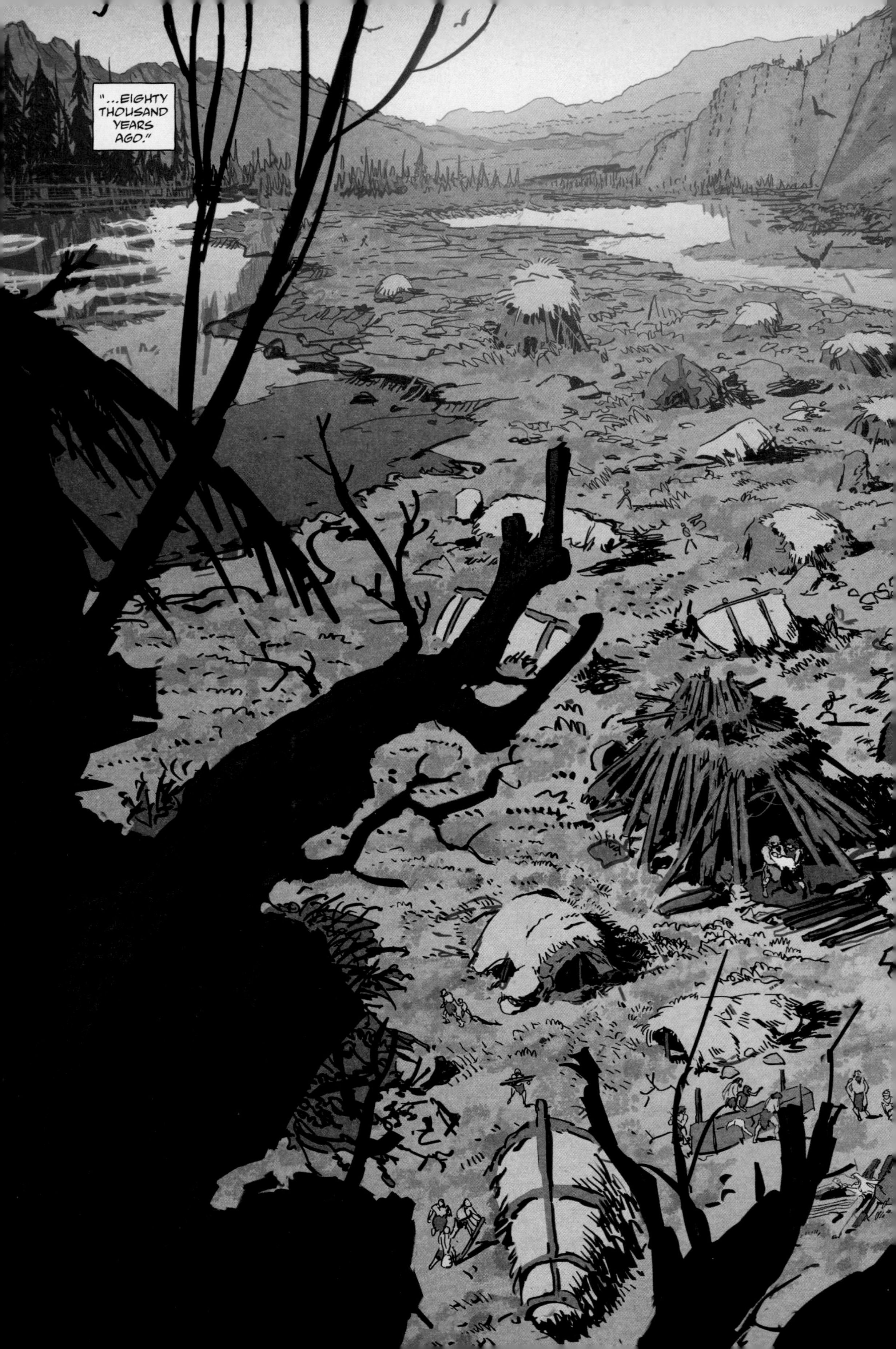
"...EIGHTY THOUSAND YEARS AGO."

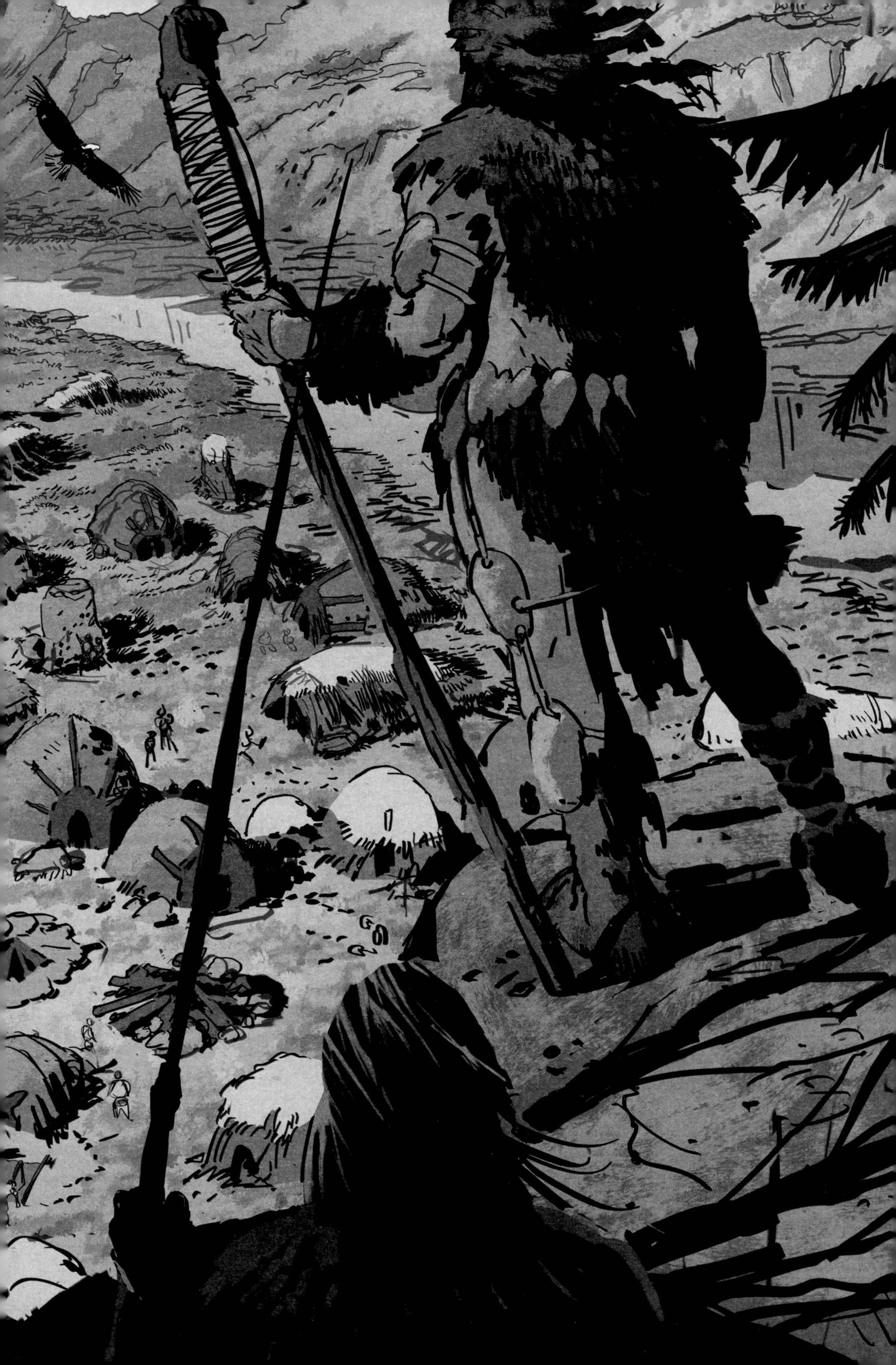

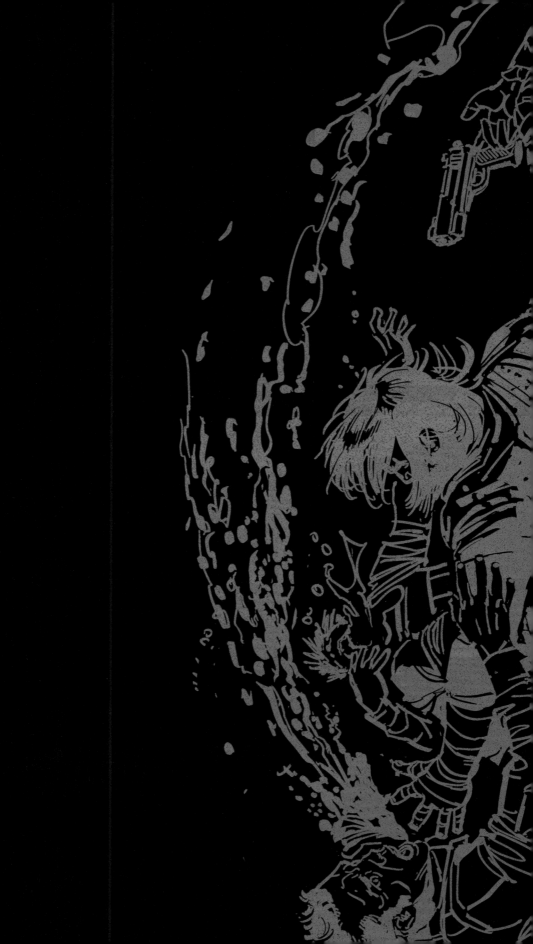

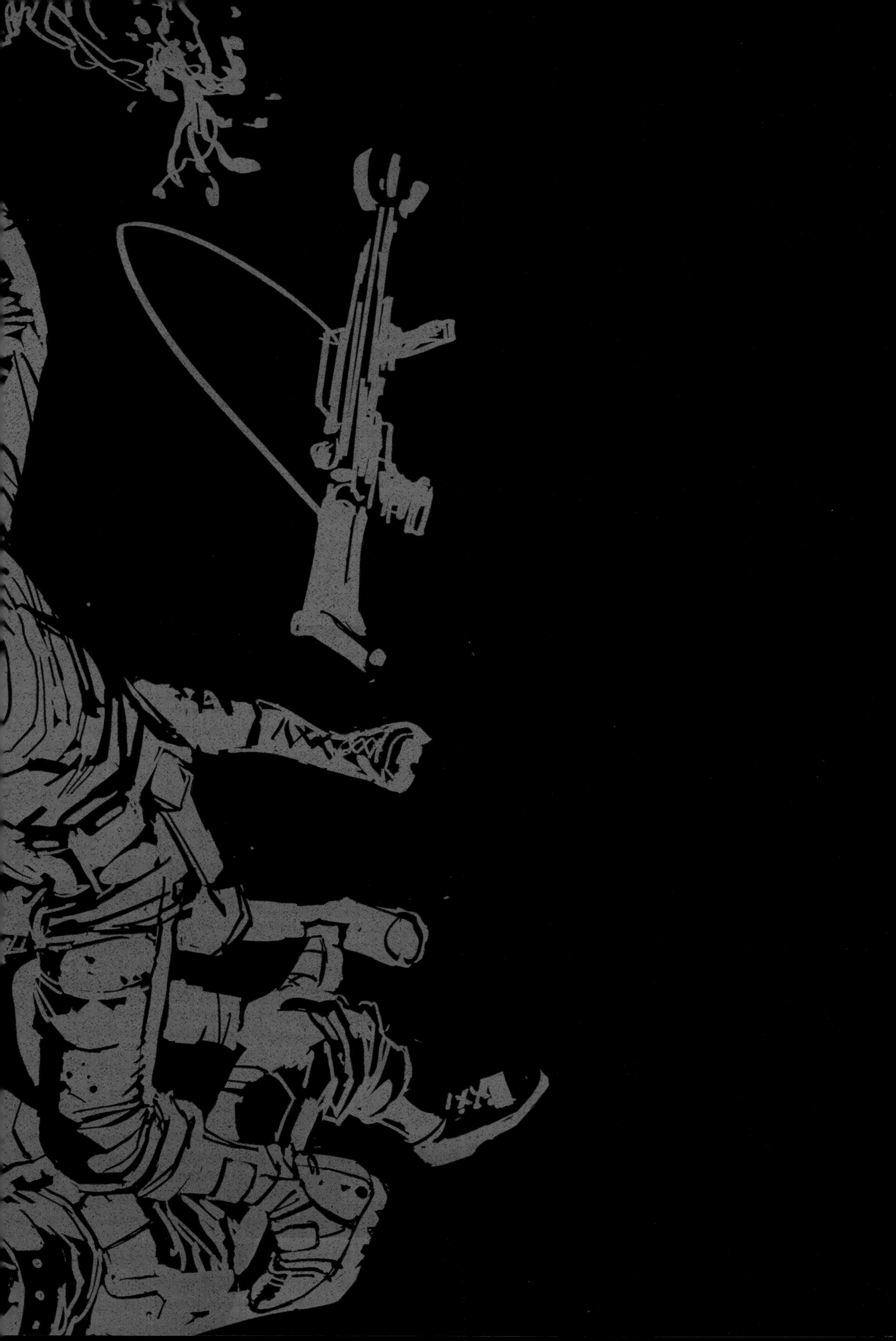

CHAPTER
TWO

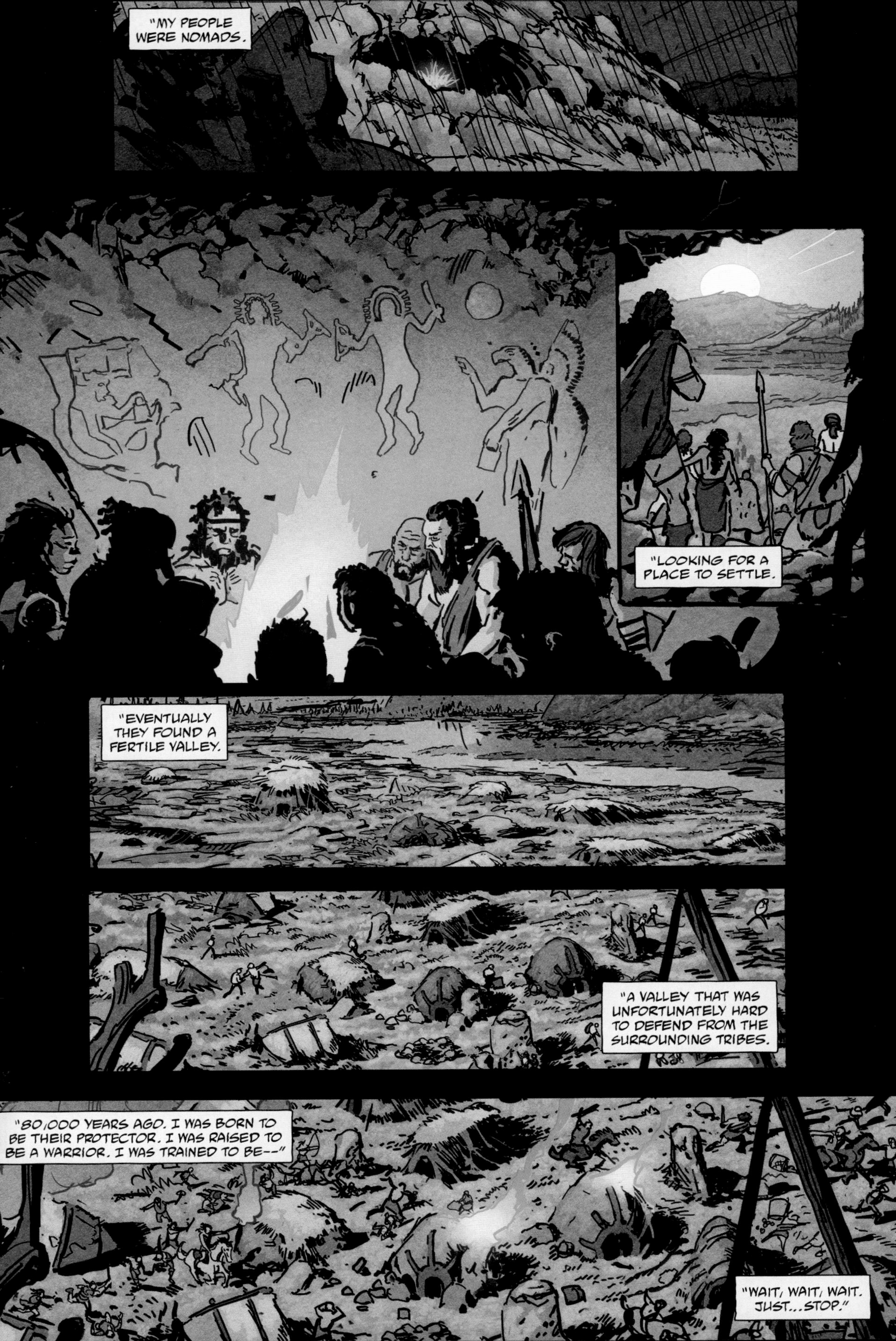
"MY PEOPLE WERE NOMADS.
"LOOKING FOR A PLACE TO SETTLE.
"EVENTUALLY THEY FOUND A FERTILE VALLEY.
"A VALLEY THAT WAS UNFORTUNATELY HARD TO DEFEND FROM THE SURROUNDING TRIBES.
"80,000 YEARS AGO. I WAS BORN TO BE THEIR PROTECTOR. I WAS RAISED TO BE A WARRIOR. I WAS TRAINED TO BE--"
"WAIT, WAIT, WAIT. JUST...STOP."

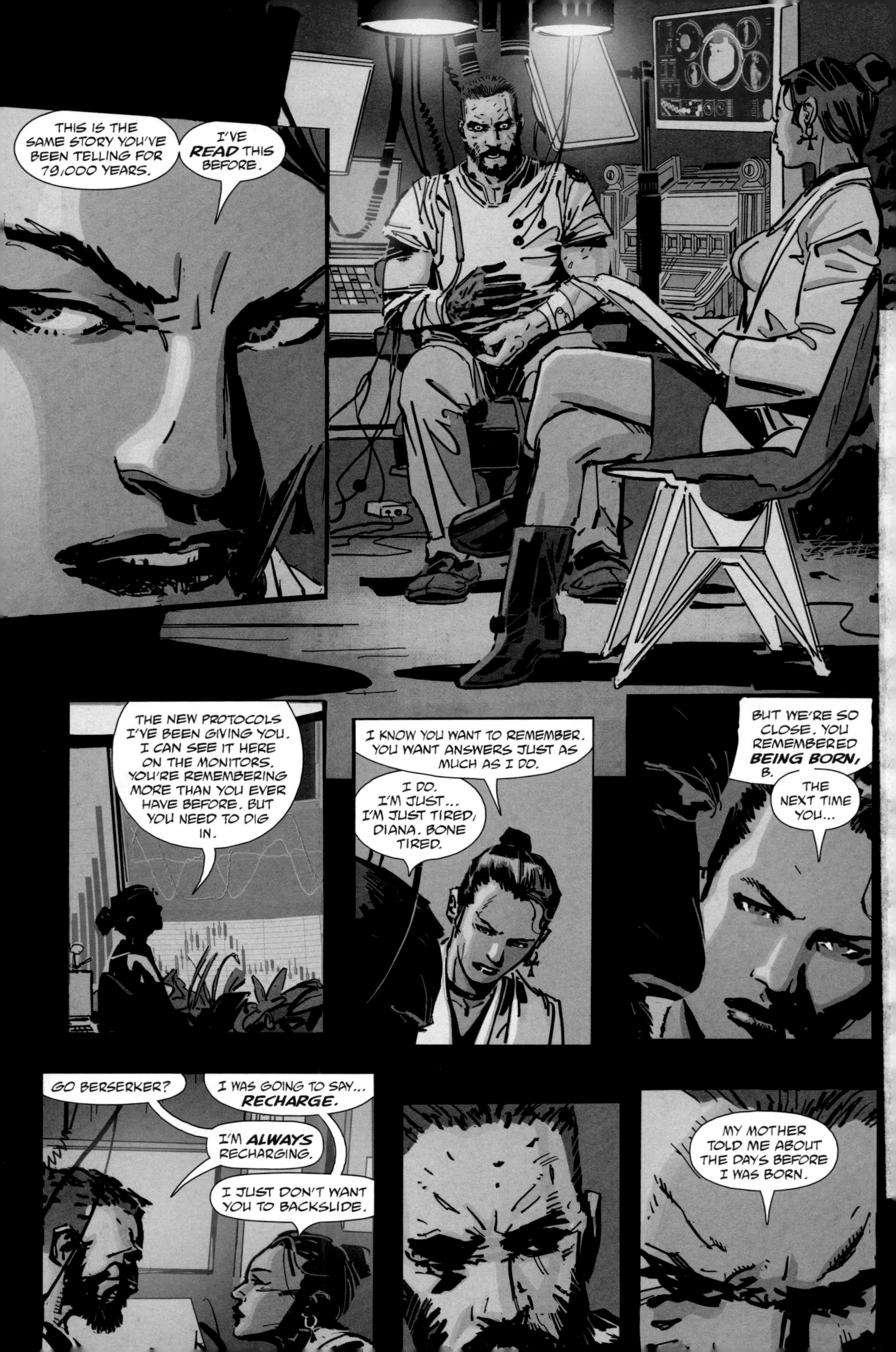
THIS IS THE SAME STORY YOU'VE BEEN TELLING FOR 79,000 YEARS.
I'VE **READ** THIS BEFORE.
THE NEW PROTOCOLS I'VE BEEN GIVING YOU. I CAN SEE IT HERE ON THE MONITORS. YOU'RE REMEMBERING MORE THAN YOU EVER HAVE BEFORE. BUT YOU NEED TO DIG IN.
I KNOW YOU WANT TO REMEMBER. YOU WANT ANSWERS JUST AS MUCH AS I DO.
I DO. I'M JUST... I'M JUST TIRED, DIANA. BONE TIRED.
BUT WE'RE SO CLOSE. YOU REMEMBERED **BEING BORN,** B.
THE NEXT TIME YOU...
GO BERSERKER?
I WAS GOING TO SAY... **RECHARGE.**
I'M **ALWAYS** RECHARGING.
I JUST DON'T WANT YOU TO BACKSLIDE.
MY MOTHER TOLD ME ABOUT THE DAYS BEFORE I WAS BORN.

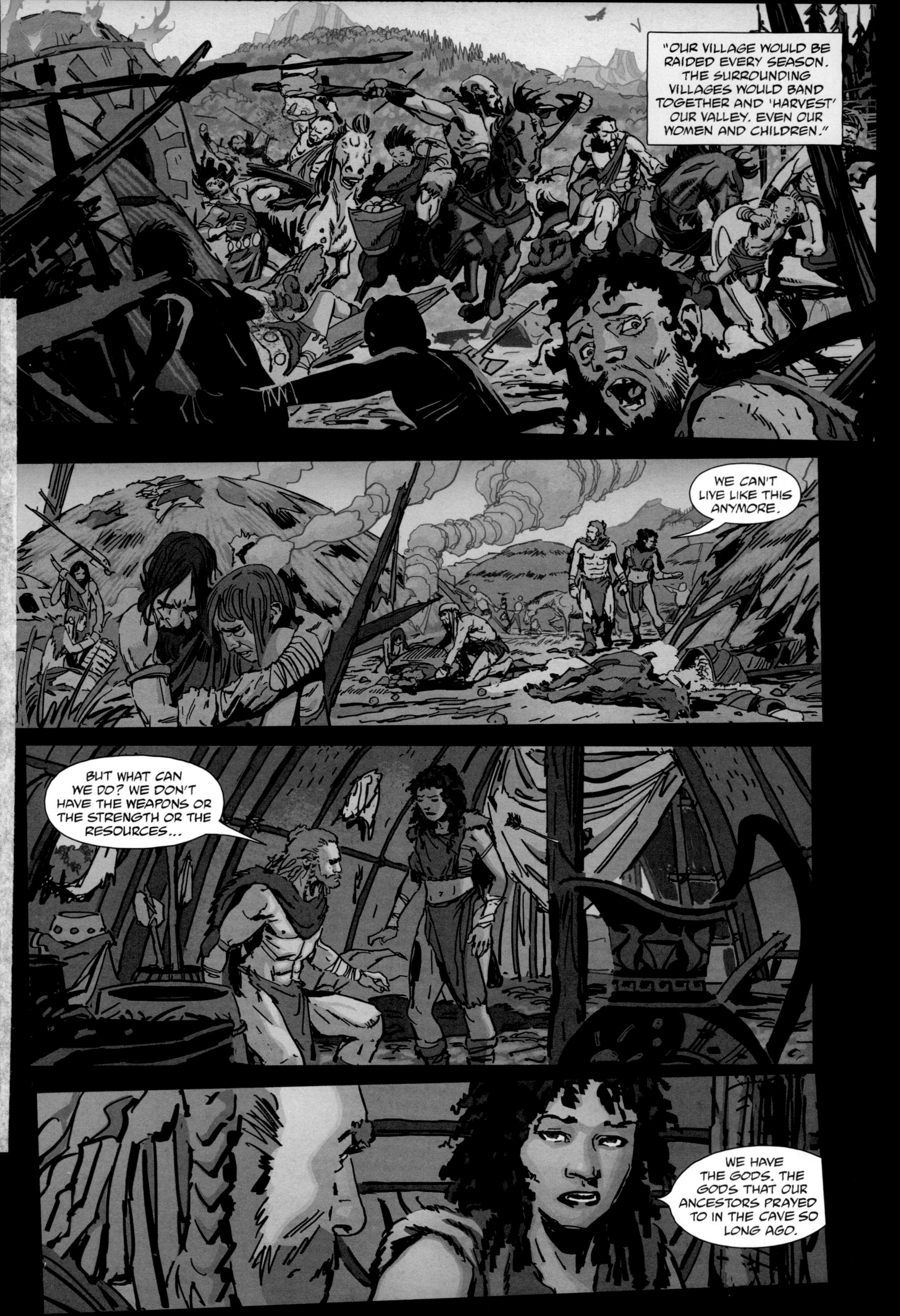
"OUR VILLAGE WOULD BE RAIDED EVERY SEASON. THE SURROUNDING VILLAGES WOULD BAND TOGETHER AND 'HARVEST' OUR VALLEY. EVEN OUR WOMEN AND CHILDREN."
WE CAN'T LIVE LIKE THIS ANYMORE.
BUT WHAT CAN WE DO? WE DON'T HAVE THE WEAPONS OR THE STRENGTH OR THE RESOURCES...
WE HAVE THE GODS. THE GODS THAT OUR ANCESTORS PRAYED TO IN THE CAVE SO LONG AGO.

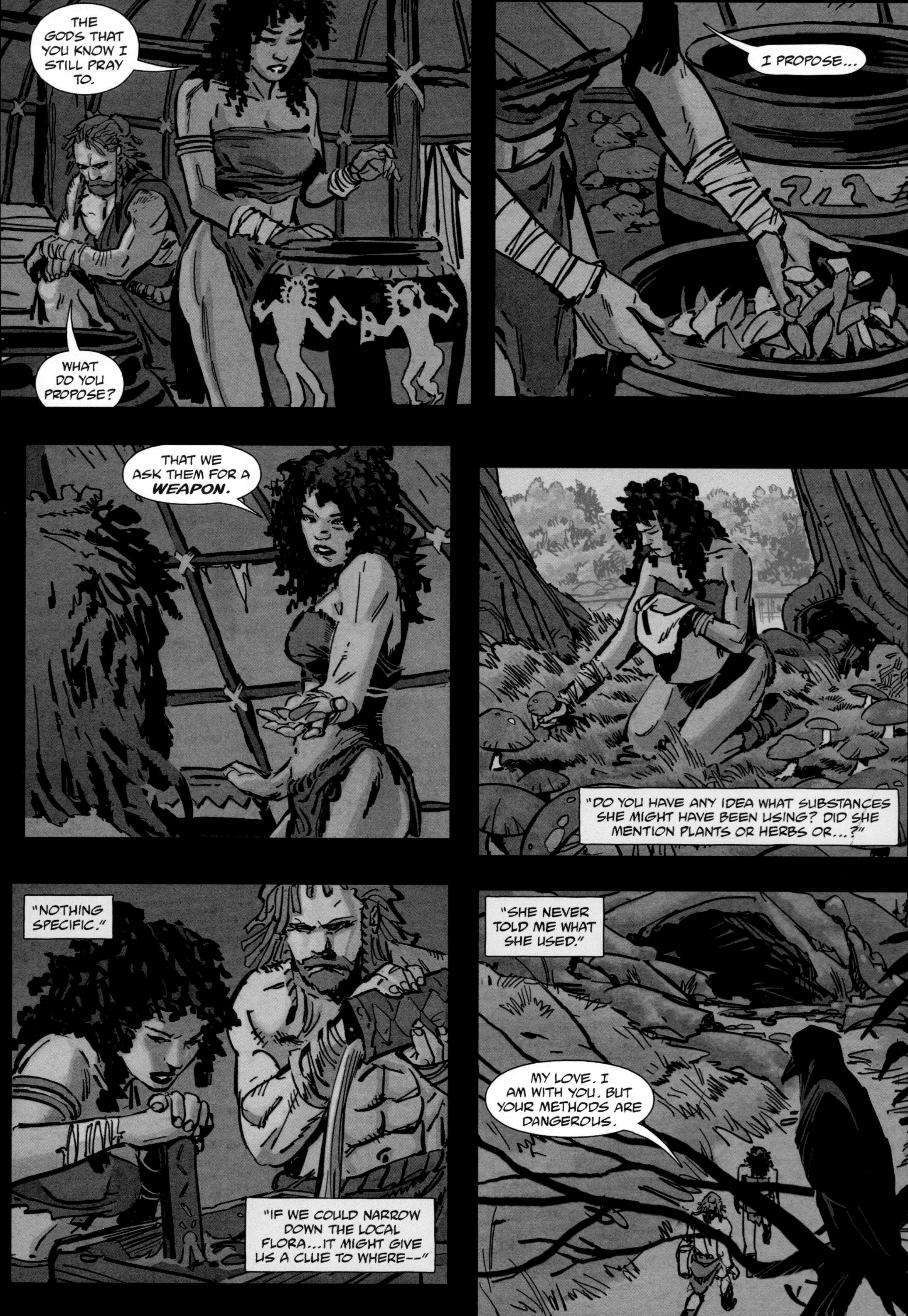
THE GODS THAT YOU KNOW I STILL PRAY TO.
WHAT DO YOU PROPOSE?
I PROPOSE...
THAT WE ASK THEM FOR A WEAPON.
"DO YOU HAVE ANY IDEA WHAT SUBSTANCES SHE MIGHT HAVE BEEN USING? DID SHE MENTION PLANTS OR HERBS OR...?"
"NOTHING SPECIFIC."
"IF WE COULD NARROW DOWN THE LOCAL FLORA...IT MIGHT GIVE US A CLUE TO WHERE--"
"SHE NEVER TOLD ME WHAT SHE USED."
MY LOVE. I AM WITH YOU. BUT YOUR METHODS ARE DANGEROUS.

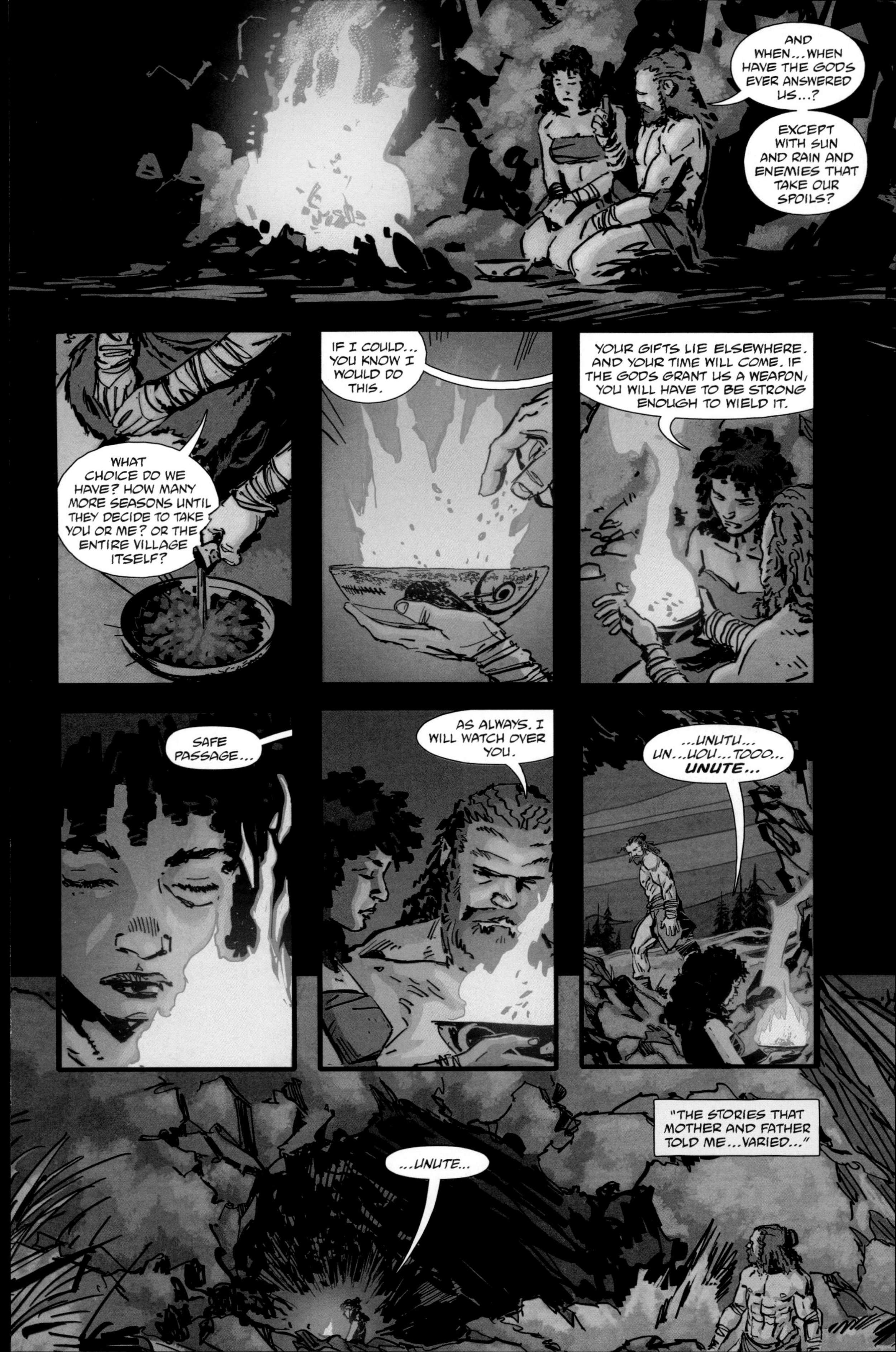
AND WHEN...WHEN HAVE THE GODS EVER ANSWERED US...?
EXCEPT WITH SUN AND RAIN AND ENEMIES THAT TAKE OUR SPOILS?
WHAT CHOICE DO WE HAVE? HOW MANY MORE SEASONS UNTIL THEY DECIDE TO TAKE YOU OR ME? OR THE ENTIRE VILLAGE ITSELF?
IF I COULD... YOU KNOW I WOULD DO THIS.
YOUR GIFTS LIE ELSEWHERE. AND YOUR TIME WILL COME. IF THE GODS GRANT US A WEAPON, YOU WILL HAVE TO BE STRONG ENOUGH TO WIELD IT.
SAFE PASSAGE...
AS ALWAYS. I WILL WATCH OVER YOU.
...UNUTU... UN...UOU...TOOO... UNUTE...
"THE STORIES THAT MOTHER AND FATHER TOLD ME...VARIED..."
...UNUTE...

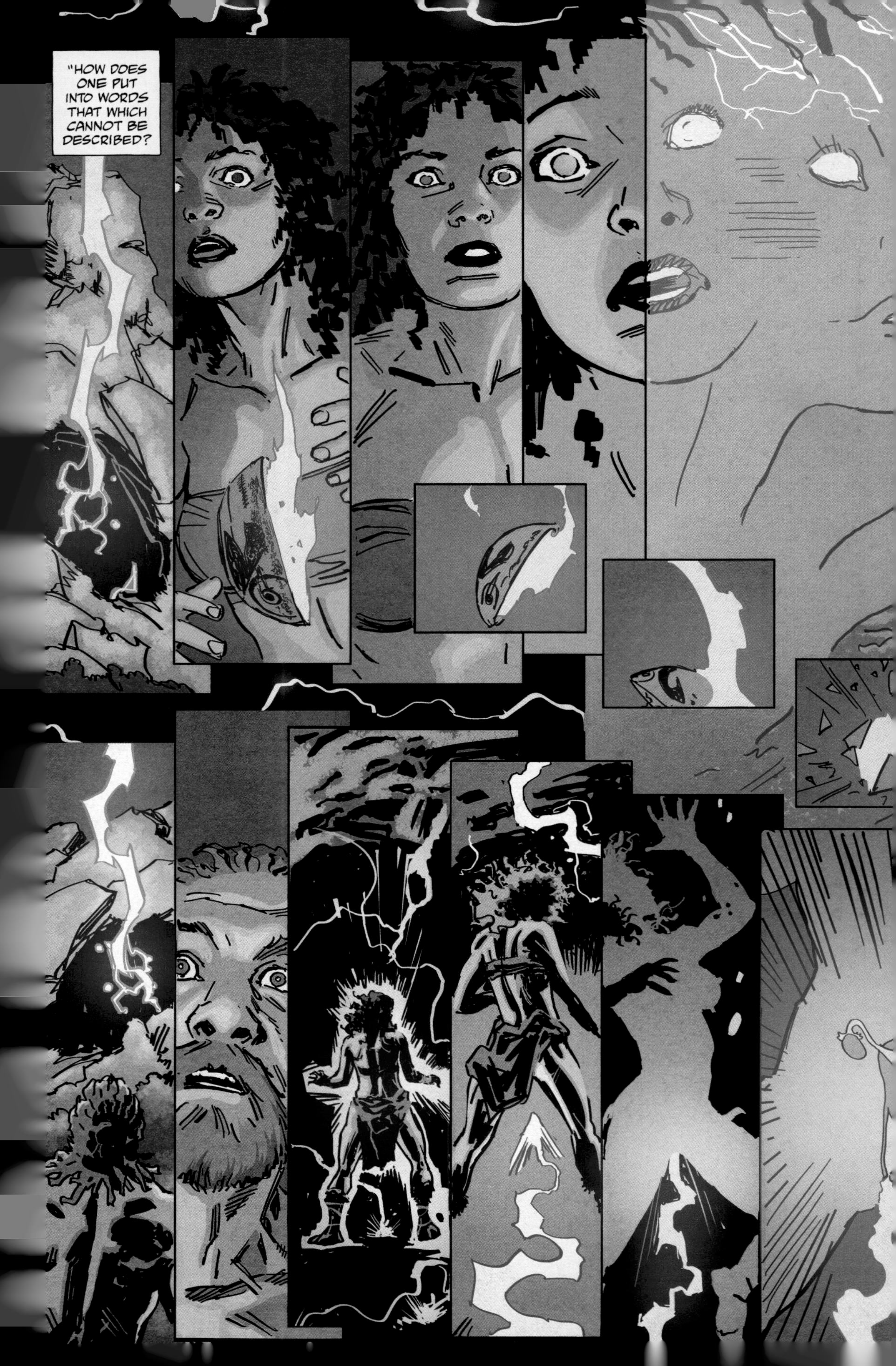
"HOW DOES ONE PUT INTO WORDS THAT WHICH CANNOT BE DESCRIBED?

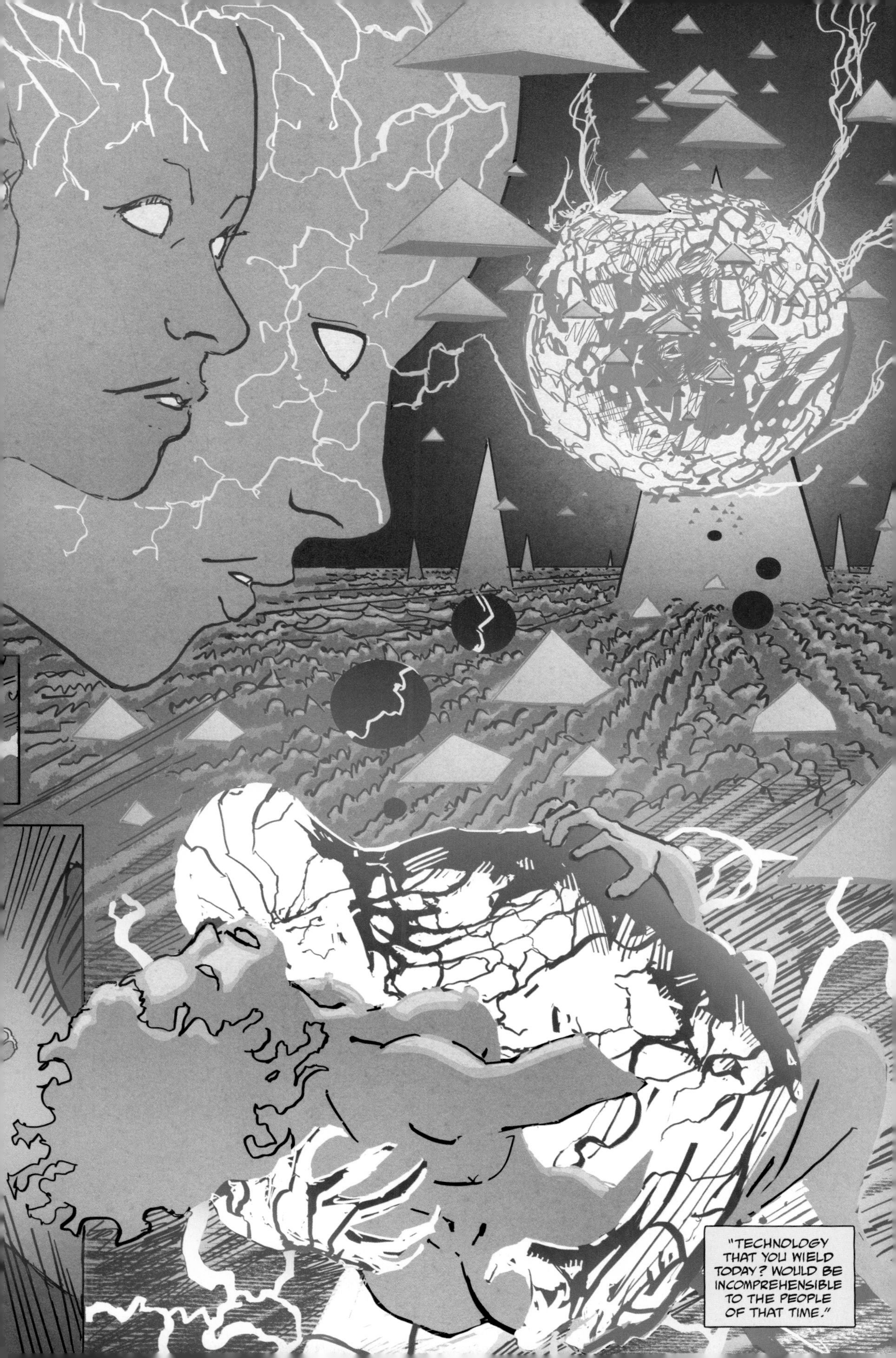
"TECHNOLOGY THAT YOU WIELD TODAY? WOULD BE INCOMPREHENSIBLE TO THE PEOPLE OF THAT TIME."

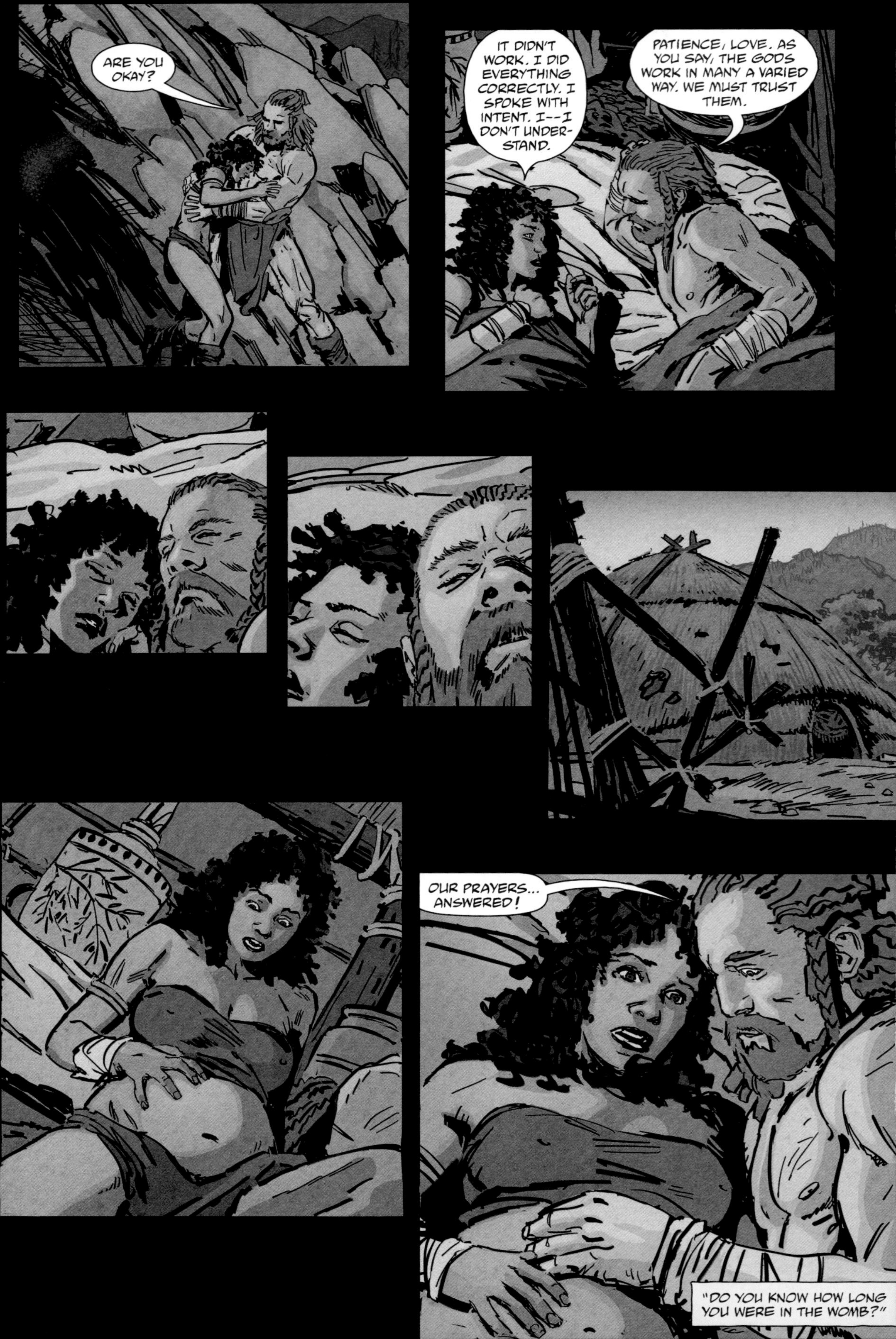
ARE YOU OKAY?
IT DIDN'T WORK. I DID EVERYTHING CORRECTLY. I SPOKE WITH INTENT. I--I DON'T UNDERSTAND.
PATIENCE, LOVE. AS YOU SAY, THE GODS WORK IN MANY A VARIED WAY. WE MUST TRUST THEM.
OUR PRAYERS... ANSWERED!
"DO YOU KNOW HOW LONG YOU WERE IN THE WOMB?"

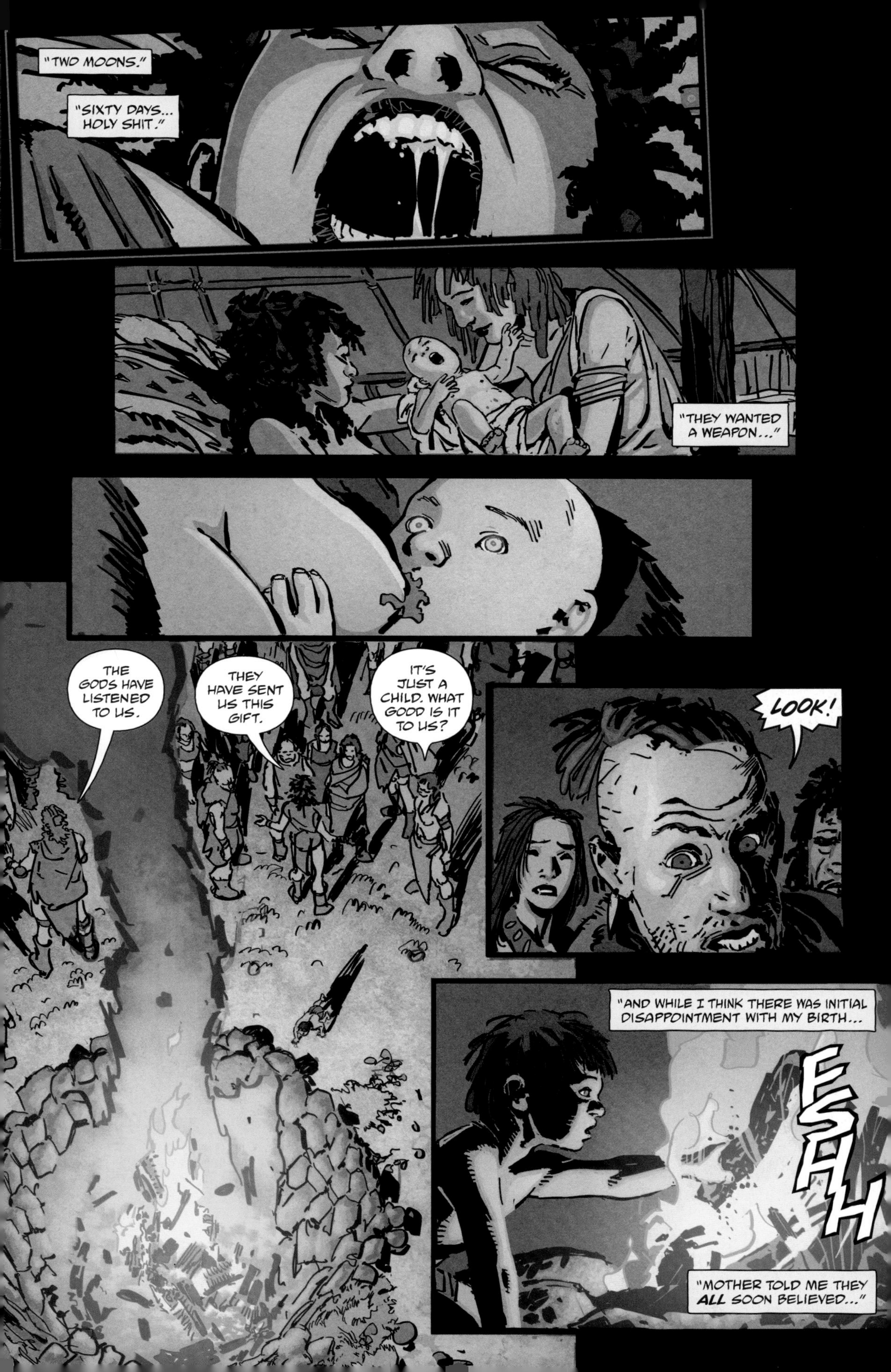
"TWO MOONS."
"SIXTY DAYS... HOLY SHIT."
"THEY WANTED A WEAPON..."
THE GODS HAVE LISTENED TO US.
THEY HAVE SENT US THIS GIFT.
IT'S JUST A CHILD. WHAT GOOD IS IT TO US?
LOOK!
"AND WHILE I THINK THERE WAS INITIAL DISAPPOINTMENT WITH MY BIRTH...
FSHH
"MOTHER TOLD ME THEY ALL SOON BELIEVED..."

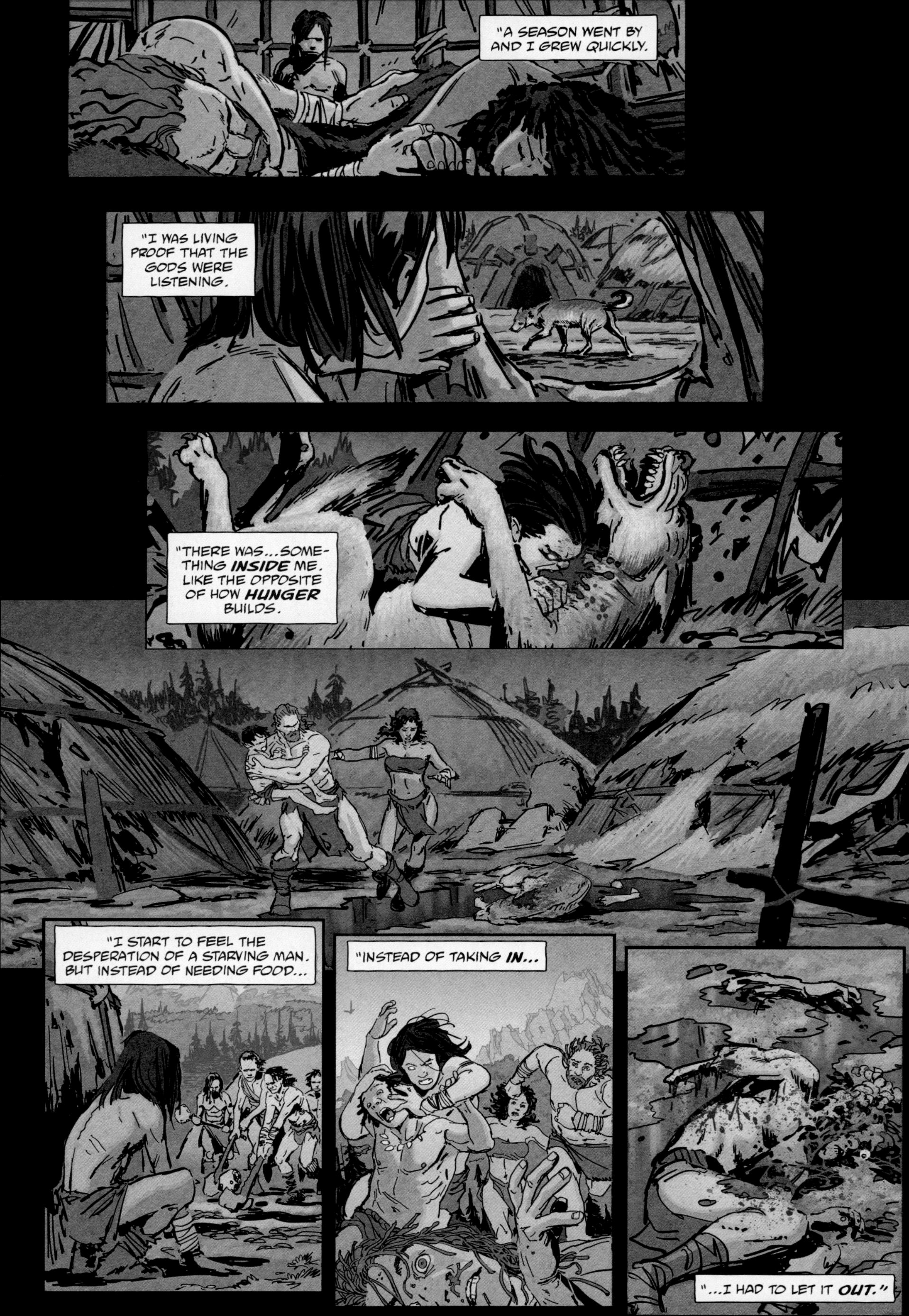
"A SEASON WENT BY AND I GREW QUICKLY.
"I WAS LIVING PROOF THAT THE GODS WERE LISTENING.
"THERE WAS...SOME-THING INSIDE ME. LIKE THE OPPOSITE OF HOW HUNGER BUILDS.
"I START TO FEEL THE DESPERATION OF A STARVING MAN. BUT INSTEAD OF NEEDING FOOD...
"INSTEAD OF TAKING IN...
"...I HAD TO LET IT OUT."

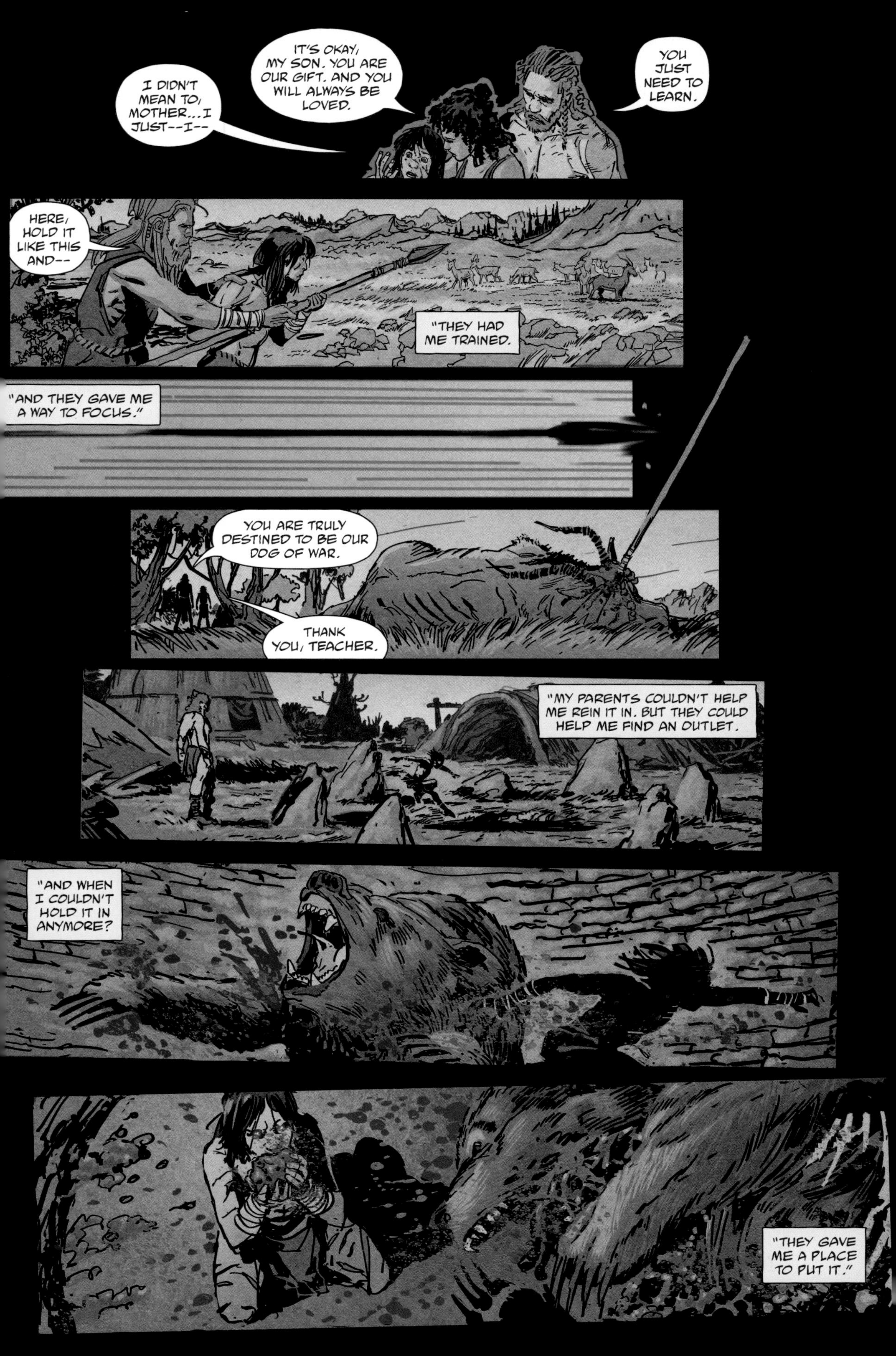
I DIDN'T MEAN TO, MOTHER...I JUST--I--
IT'S OKAY, MY SON. YOU ARE OUR GIFT. AND YOU WILL ALWAYS BE LOVED.
YOU JUST NEED TO LEARN.
HERE, HOLD IT LIKE THIS AND--
"THEY HAD ME TRAINED.
"AND THEY GAVE ME A WAY TO FOCUS."
YOU ARE TRULY DESTINED TO BE OUR DOG OF WAR.
THANK YOU, TEACHER.
"MY PARENTS COULDN'T HELP ME REIN IT IN. BUT THEY COULD HELP ME FIND AN OUTLET.
"AND WHEN I COULDN'T HOLD IT IN ANYMORE?
"THEY GAVE ME A PLACE TO PUT IT."

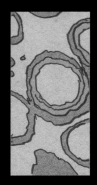

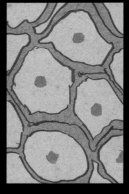

...HE'S ALREADY HEALED...

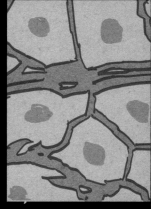

"ANOTHER SEASON. ANOTHER HARVEST STOLEN."

MANY THANKS.

NOW, MY LOVE. NOW...

NOT YET...HE'S NOT READY.

THIS IS YOUR MISSION, SON. DO YOU SEE?

THIS IS YOUR PURPOSE.

NEVER. NEVER AGAIN.

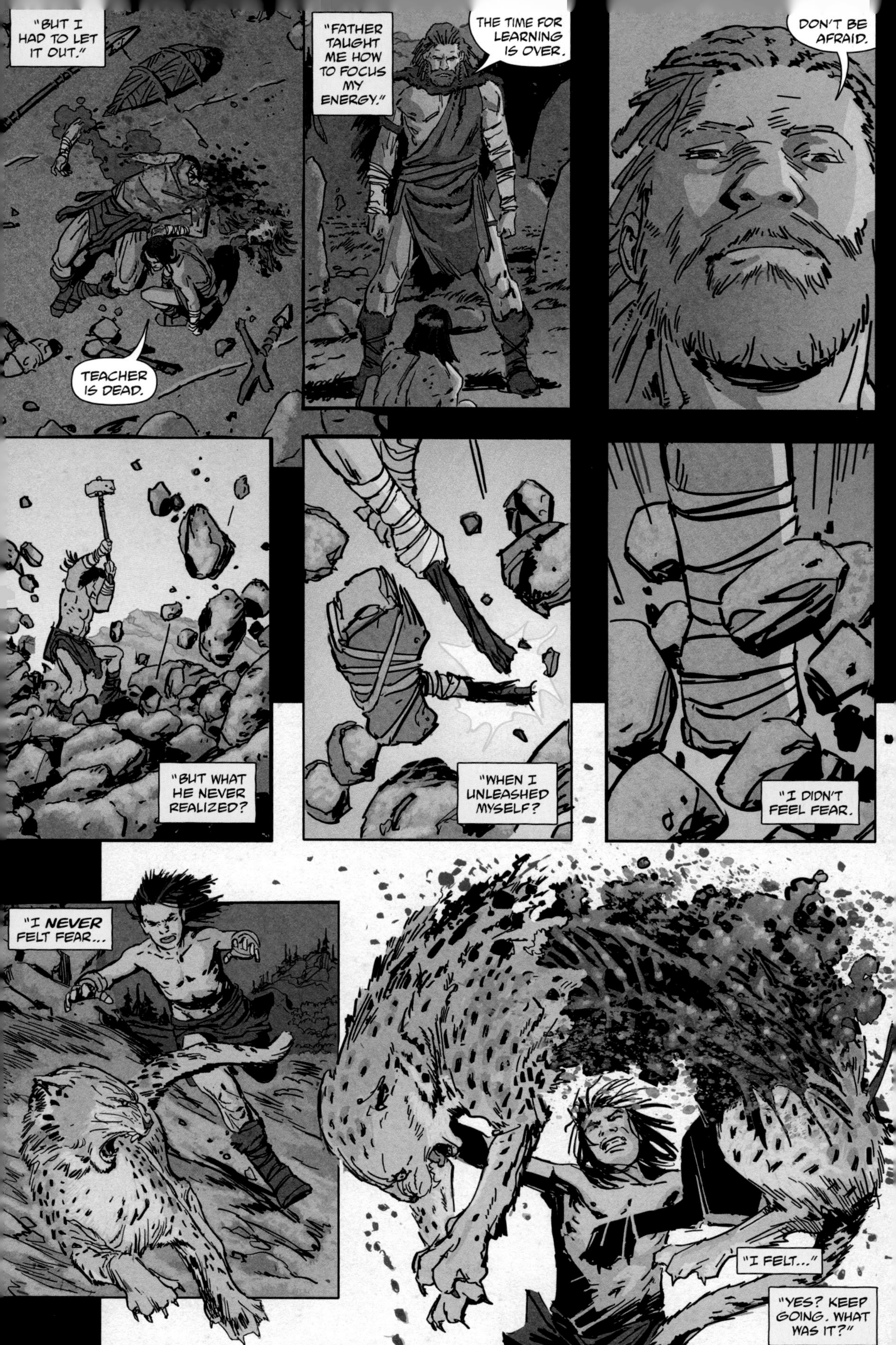
"BUT I HAD TO LET IT OUT."
TEACHER IS DEAD.
"FATHER TAUGHT ME HOW TO FOCUS MY ENERGY."
THE TIME FOR LEARNING IS OVER.
DON'T BE AFRAID.
"BUT WHAT HE NEVER REALIZED?
"WHEN I UNLEASHED MYSELF?
"I DIDN'T FEEL FEAR.
"I NEVER FELT FEAR...
"I FELT..."
"YES? KEEP GOING. WHAT WAS IT?"

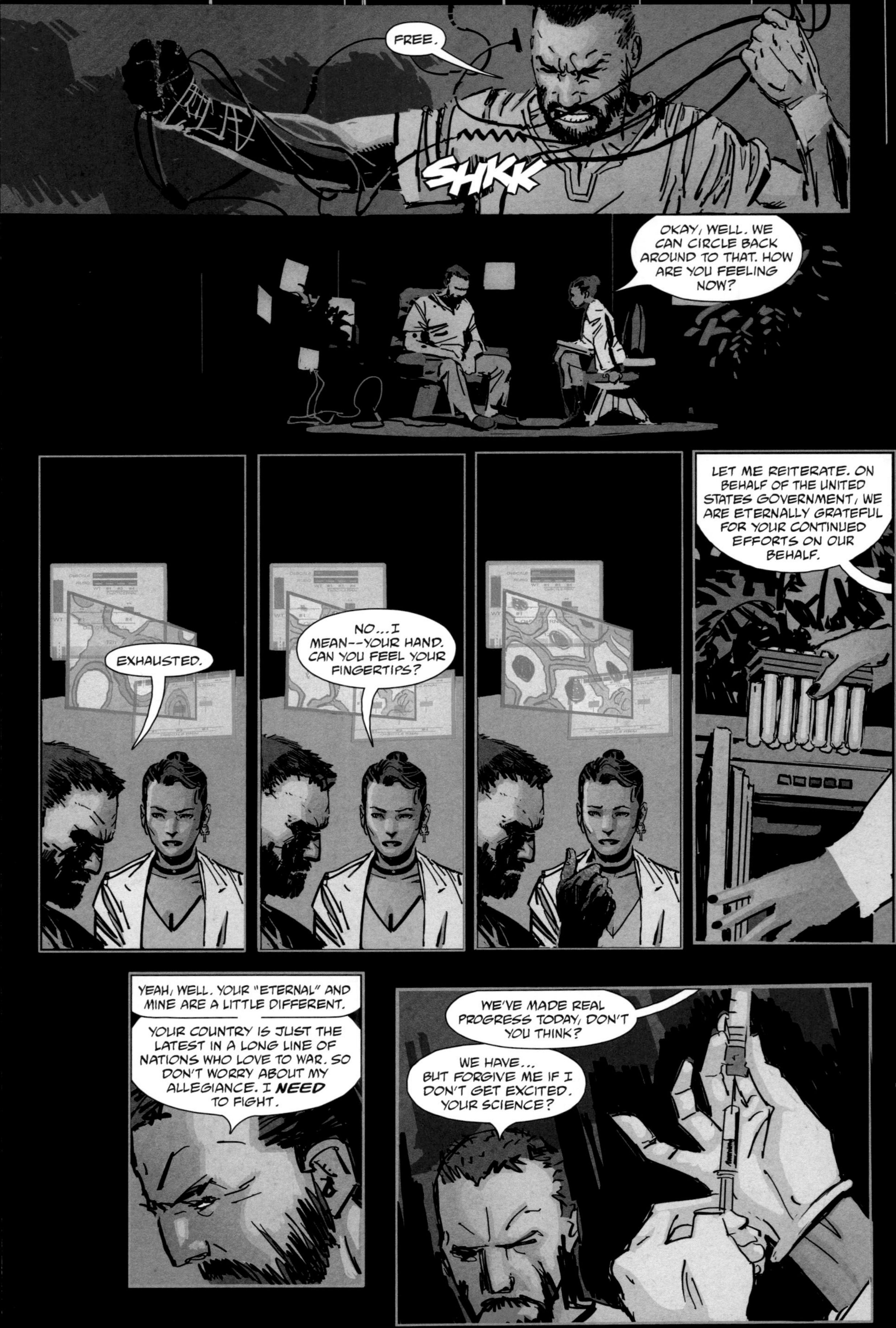
FREE.
SHKK
OKAY, WELL. WE CAN CIRCLE BACK AROUND TO THAT. HOW ARE YOU FEELING NOW?
EXHAUSTED.
NO...I MEAN--YOUR HAND. CAN YOU FEEL YOUR FINGERTIPS?
LET ME REITERATE. ON BEHALF OF THE UNITED STATES GOVERNMENT, WE ARE ETERNALLY GRATEFUL FOR YOUR CONTINUED EFFORTS ON OUR BEHALF.
YEAH, WELL. YOUR "ETERNAL" AND MINE ARE A LITTLE DIFFERENT.
YOUR COUNTRY IS JUST THE LATEST IN A LONG LINE OF NATIONS WHO LOVE TO WAR. SO DON'T WORRY ABOUT MY ALLEGIANCE. I **NEED** TO FIGHT.
WE'VE MADE REAL PROGRESS TODAY, DON'T YOU THINK?
WE HAVE... BUT FORGIVE ME IF I DON'T GET EXCITED. YOUR SCIENCE?

"FOR CENTURIES YOU'VE BEEN MEASURING ME...

"TAKING SAMPLES...

"ANALYZING ME...

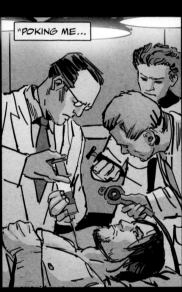

"POKING ME...

"SCANNING ME...

"I'VE BEEN STUCK A THOUSAND TIMES..."

BUT MY PROTOCOLS, OUR PROTOCOLS.. THEY'RE WORKING. YOU SEE OUR RESULTS.

JUST A LITTLE MORE. I WANT YOU TO GO BACK...REMEMBER THE FIRST TIME...

THE FIRST TIME YOU REALIZED WHAT YOU TRULY WERE.

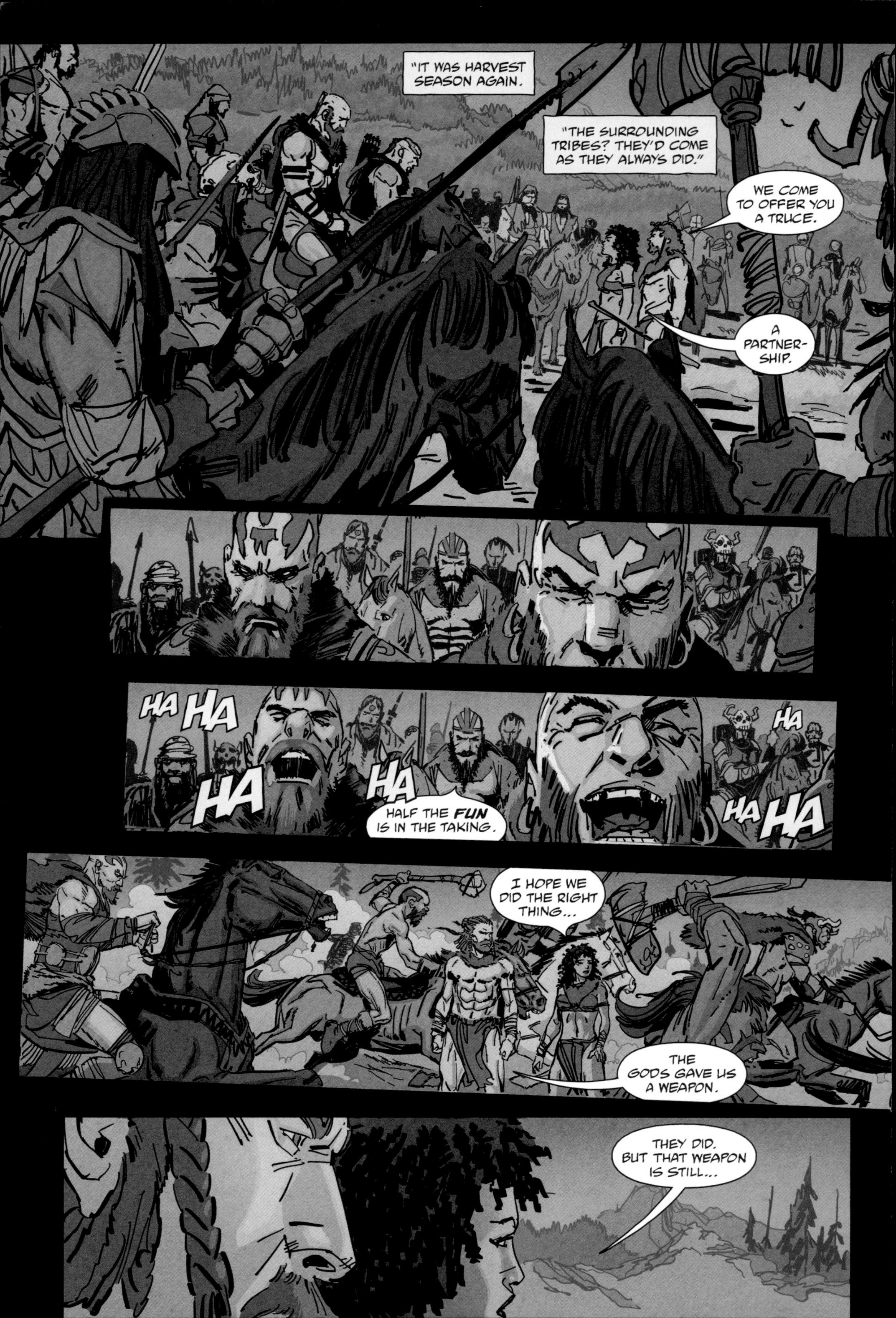
"IT WAS HARVEST SEASON AGAIN.
"THE SURROUNDING TRIBES? THEY'D COME AS THEY ALWAYS DID."
WE COME TO OFFER YOU A TRUCE.
A PARTNERSHIP.
HA HA
HA
HA
HALF THE FUN IS IN THE TAKING.
HA
HA HA
I HOPE WE DID THE RIGHT THING...
THE GODS GAVE US A WEAPON.
THEY DID. BUT THAT WEAPON IS STILL...

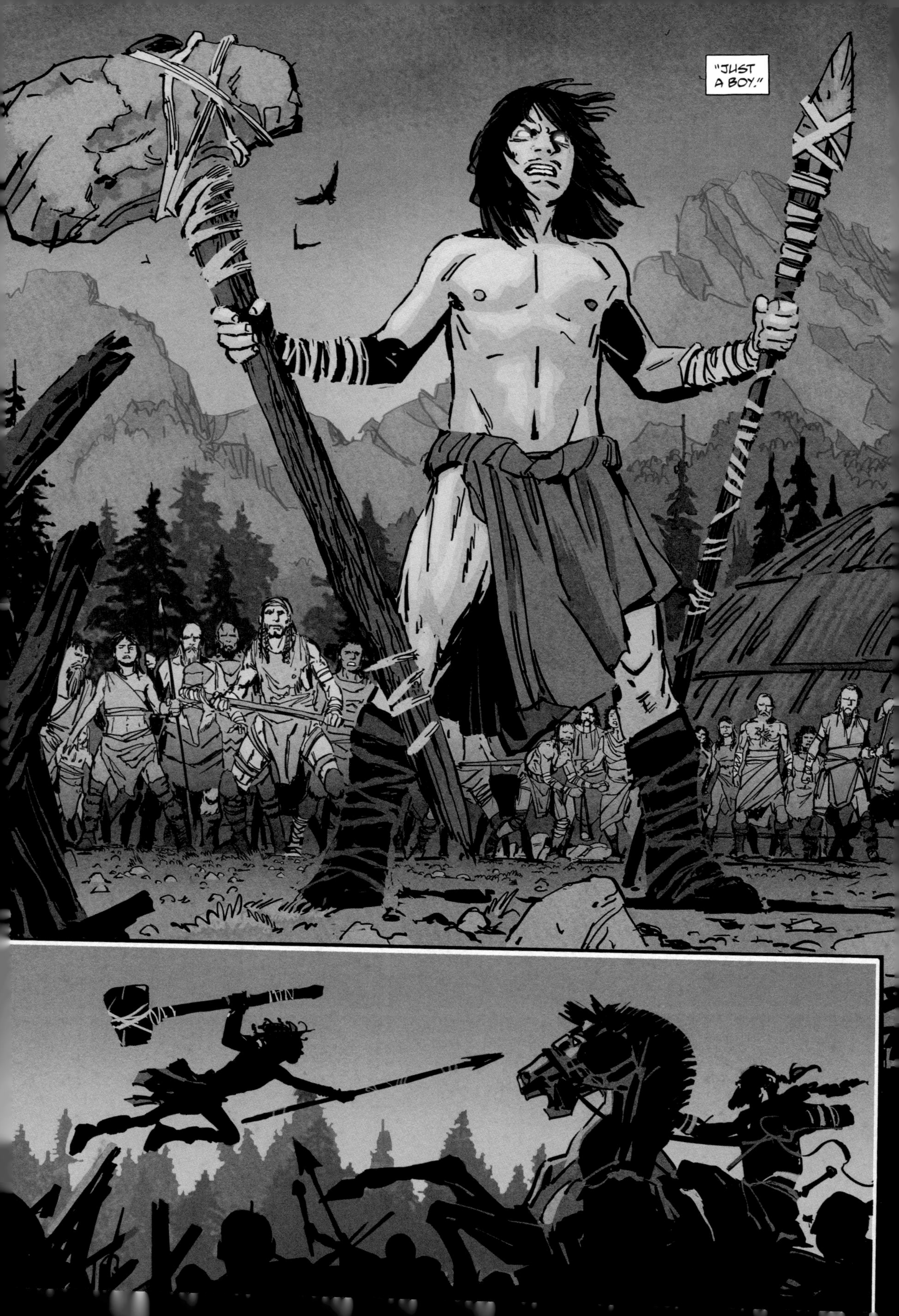
"JUST A BOY."

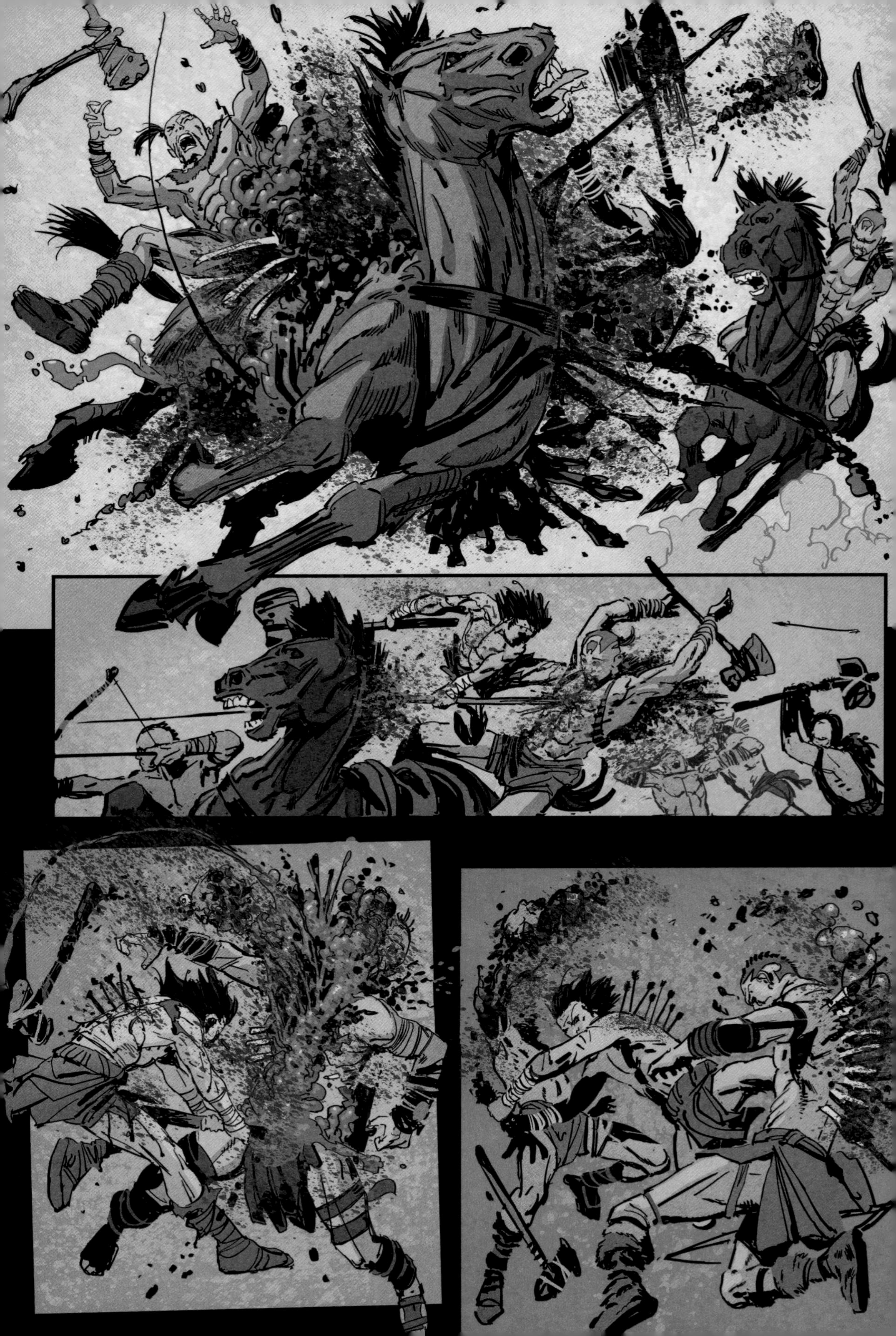

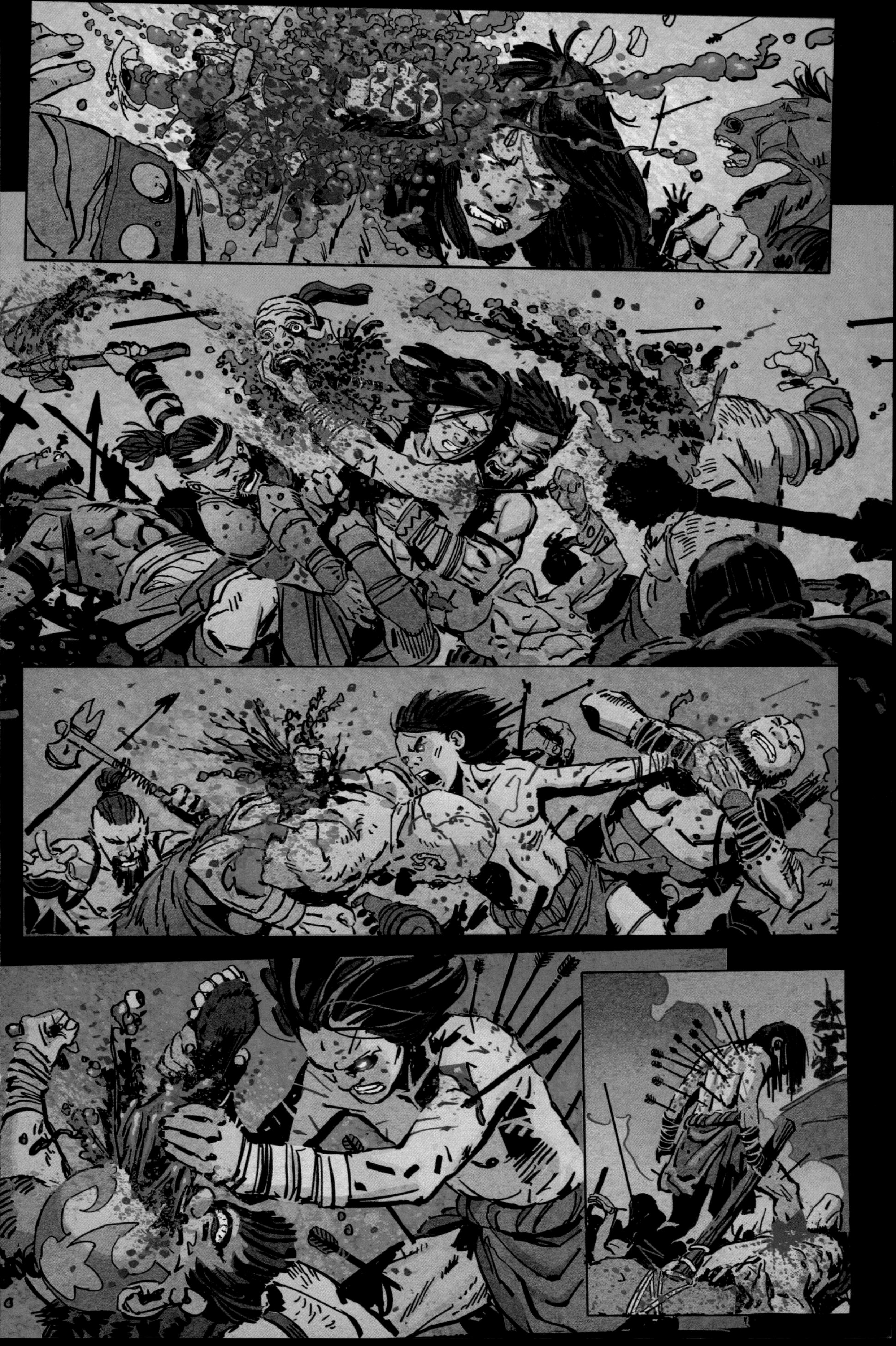

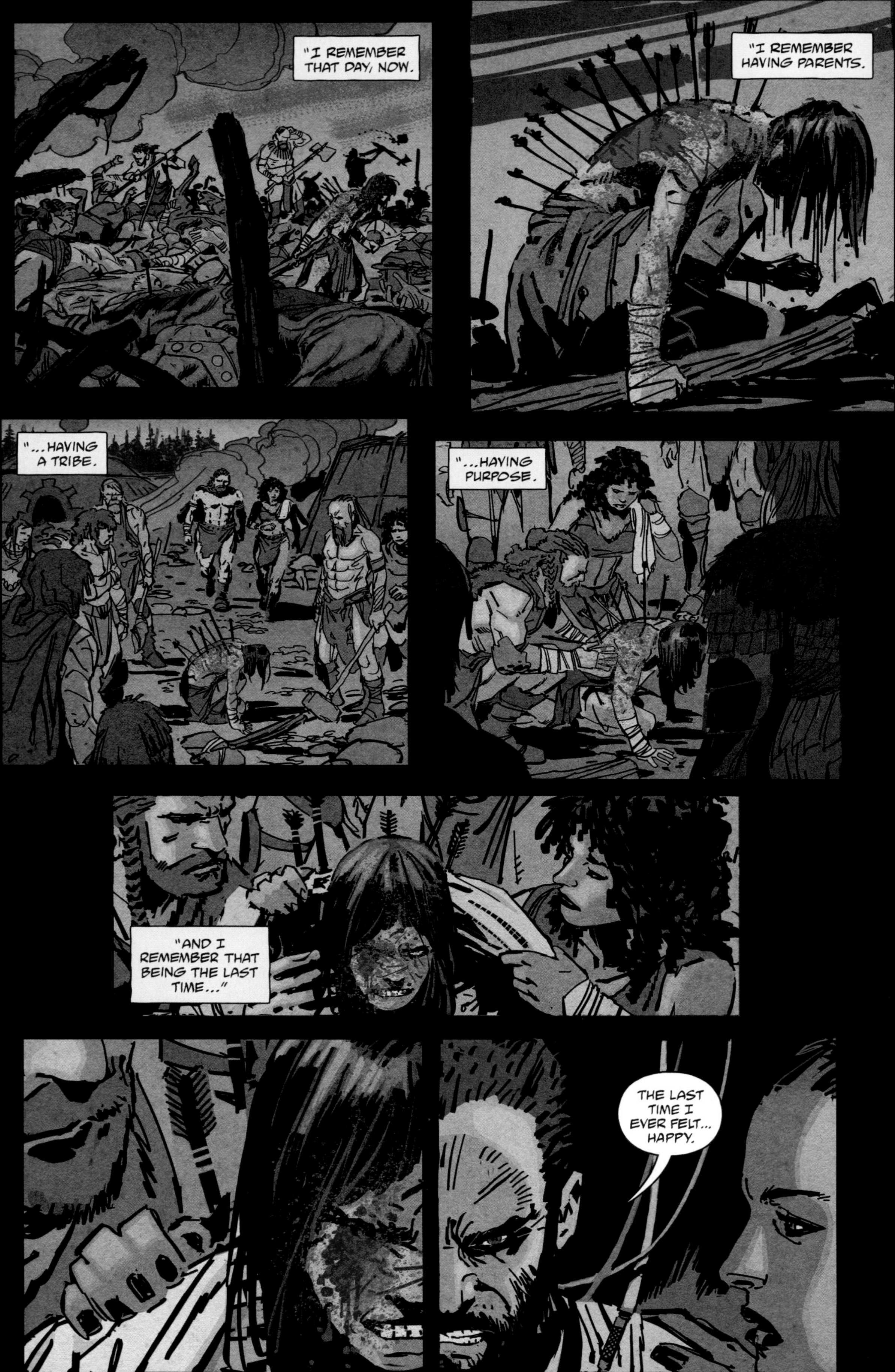
"I REMEMBER THAT DAY, NOW.
"I REMEMBER HAVING PARENTS.
"...HAVING A TRIBE.
"...HAVING PURPOSE.
"AND I REMEMBER THAT BEING THE LAST TIME..."
THE LAST TIME I EVER FELT... HAPPY.

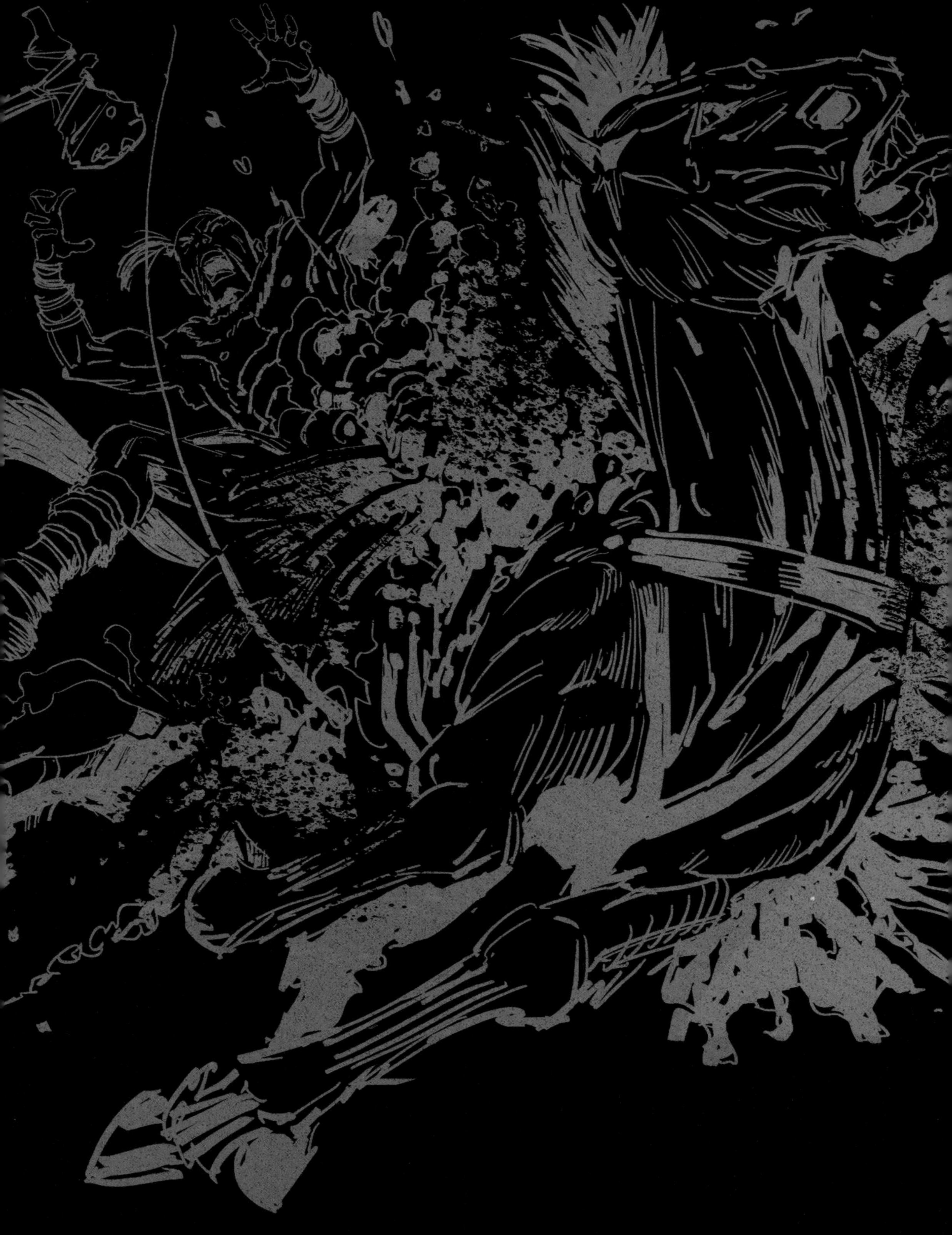

CHAPTER
THREE

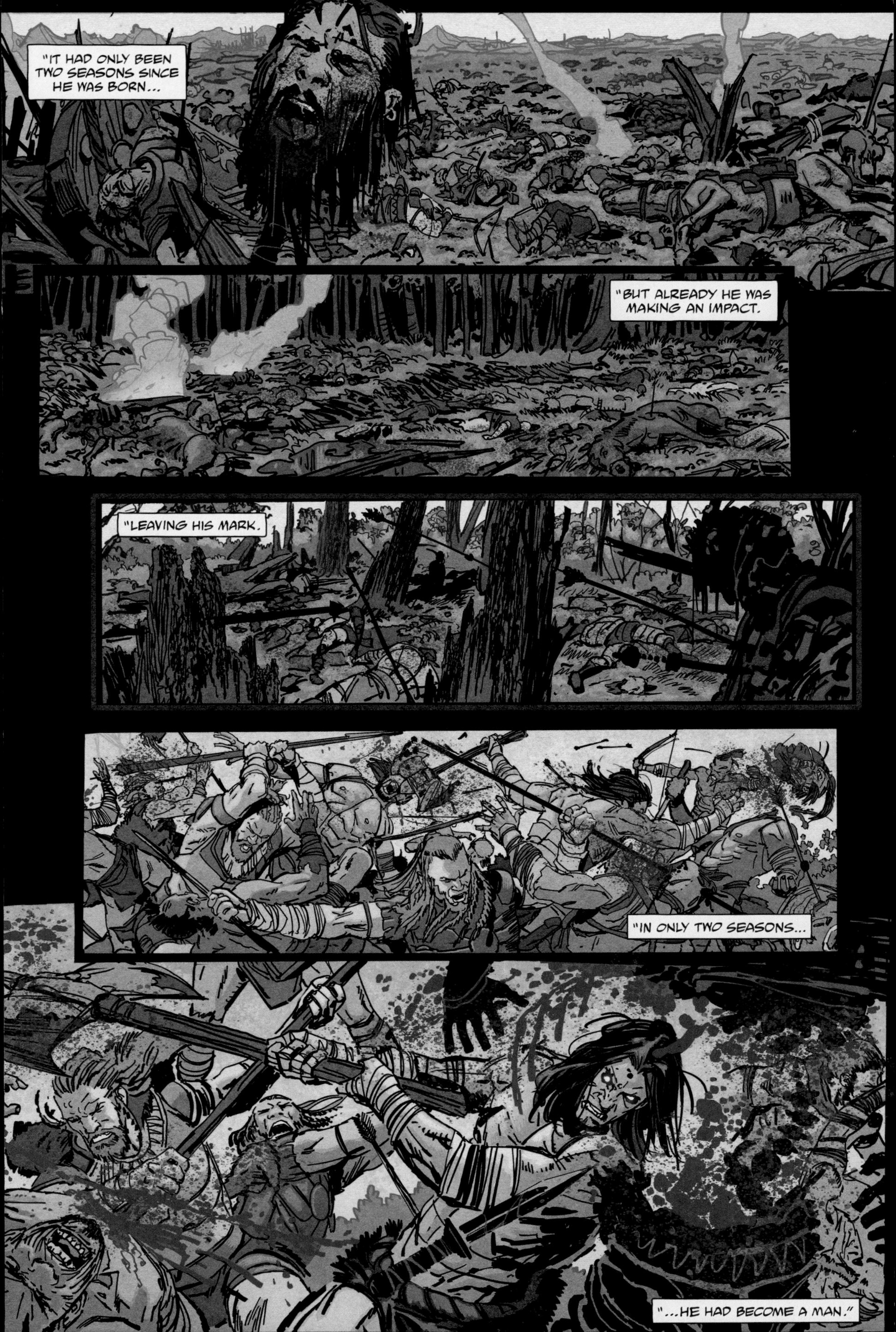
"IT HAD ONLY BEEN TWO SEASONS SINCE HE WAS BORN...
"BUT ALREADY HE WAS MAKING AN IMPACT.
"LEAVING HIS MARK.
"IN ONLY TWO SEASONS...
"...HE HAD BECOME A MAN."

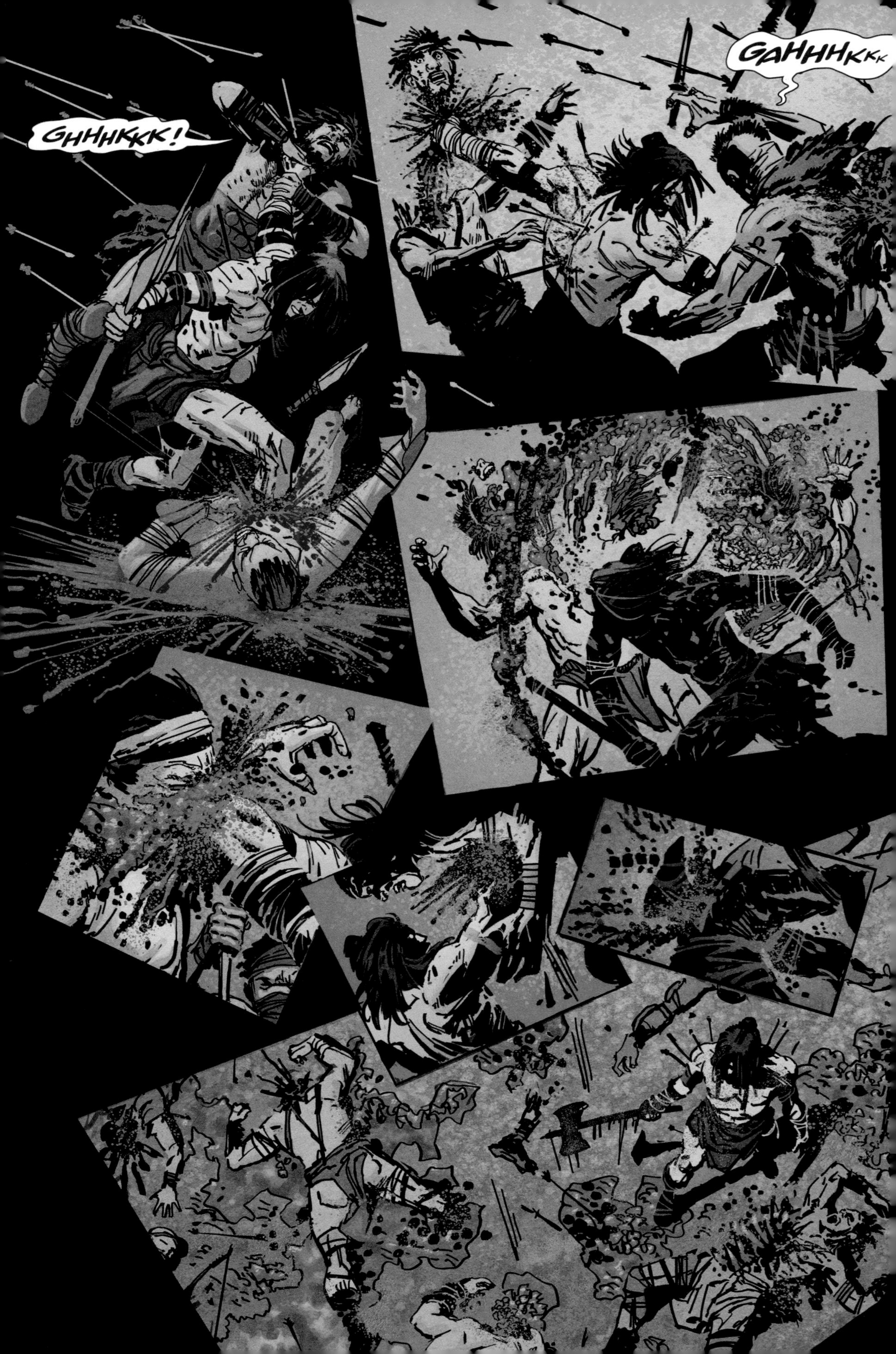
GHHHKKK!
GAHHHKKK

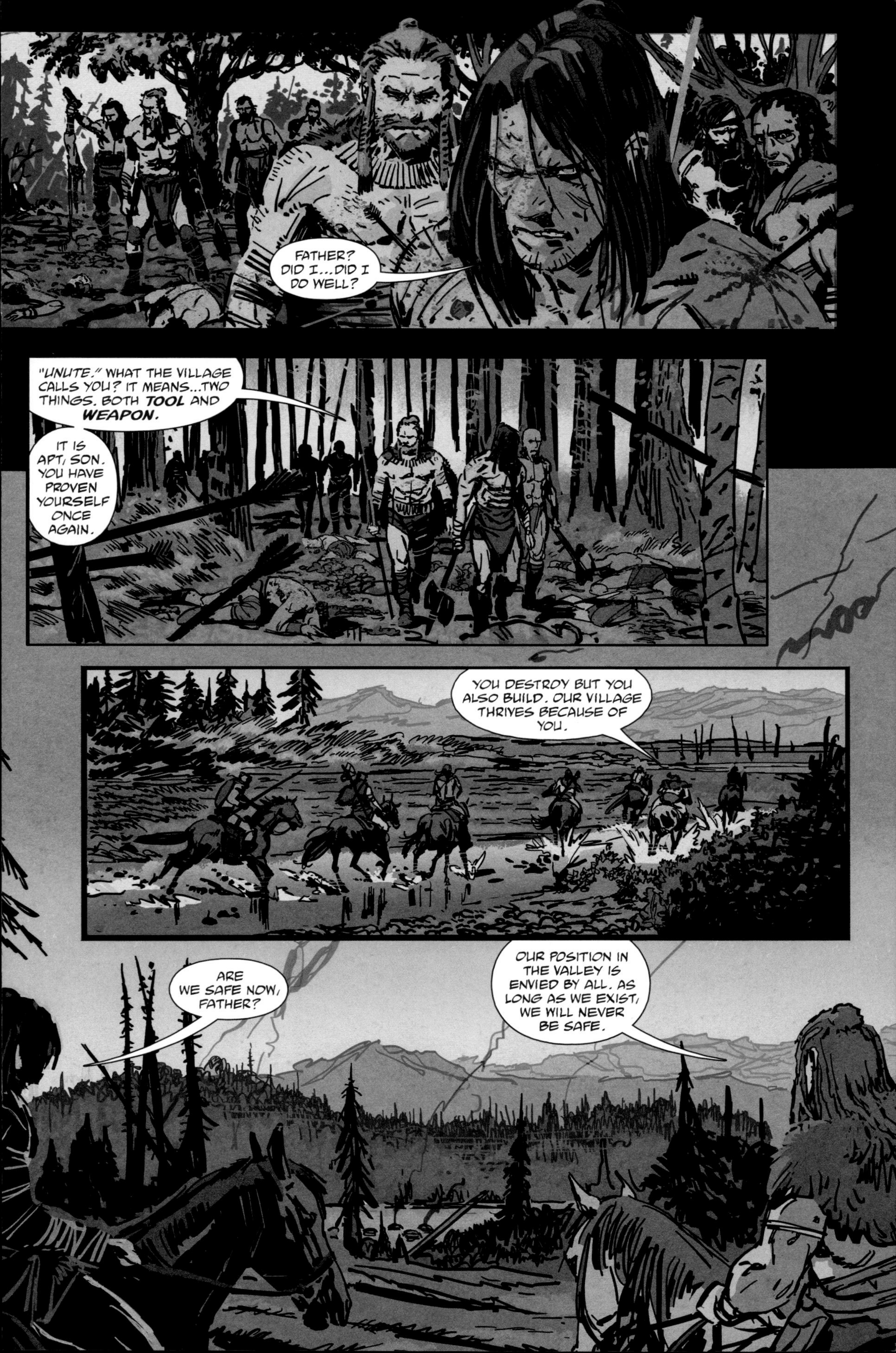
FATHER? DID I...DID I DO WELL?
"UNUTE." WHAT THE VILLAGE CALLS YOU? IT MEANS...TWO THINGS. BOTH **TOOL** AND **WEAPON.**
IT IS APT, SON. YOU HAVE PROVEN YOURSELF ONCE AGAIN.
YOU DESTROY BUT YOU ALSO BUILD. OUR VILLAGE THRIVES BECAUSE OF YOU.
ARE WE SAFE NOW, FATHER?
OUR POSITION IN THE VALLEY IS ENVIED BY ALL. AS LONG AS WE EXIST, WE WILL NEVER BE SAFE.

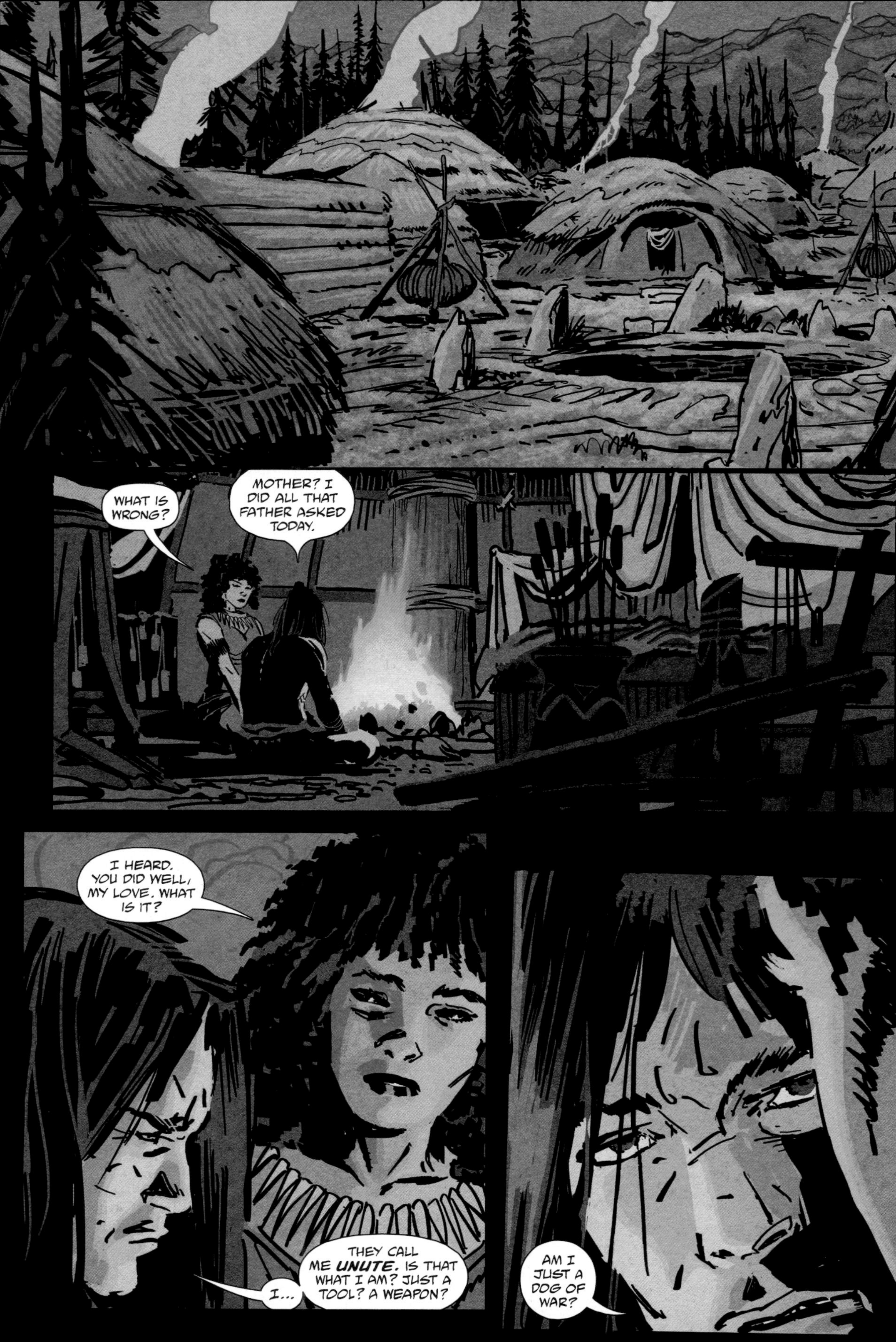
MOTHER? I DID ALL THAT FATHER ASKED TODAY.
WHAT IS WRONG?
I HEARD. YOU DID WELL, MY LOVE. WHAT IS IT?
I...
THEY CALL ME UNUTE. IS THAT WHAT I AM? JUST A TOOL? A WEAPON?
AM I JUST A DOG OF WAR?

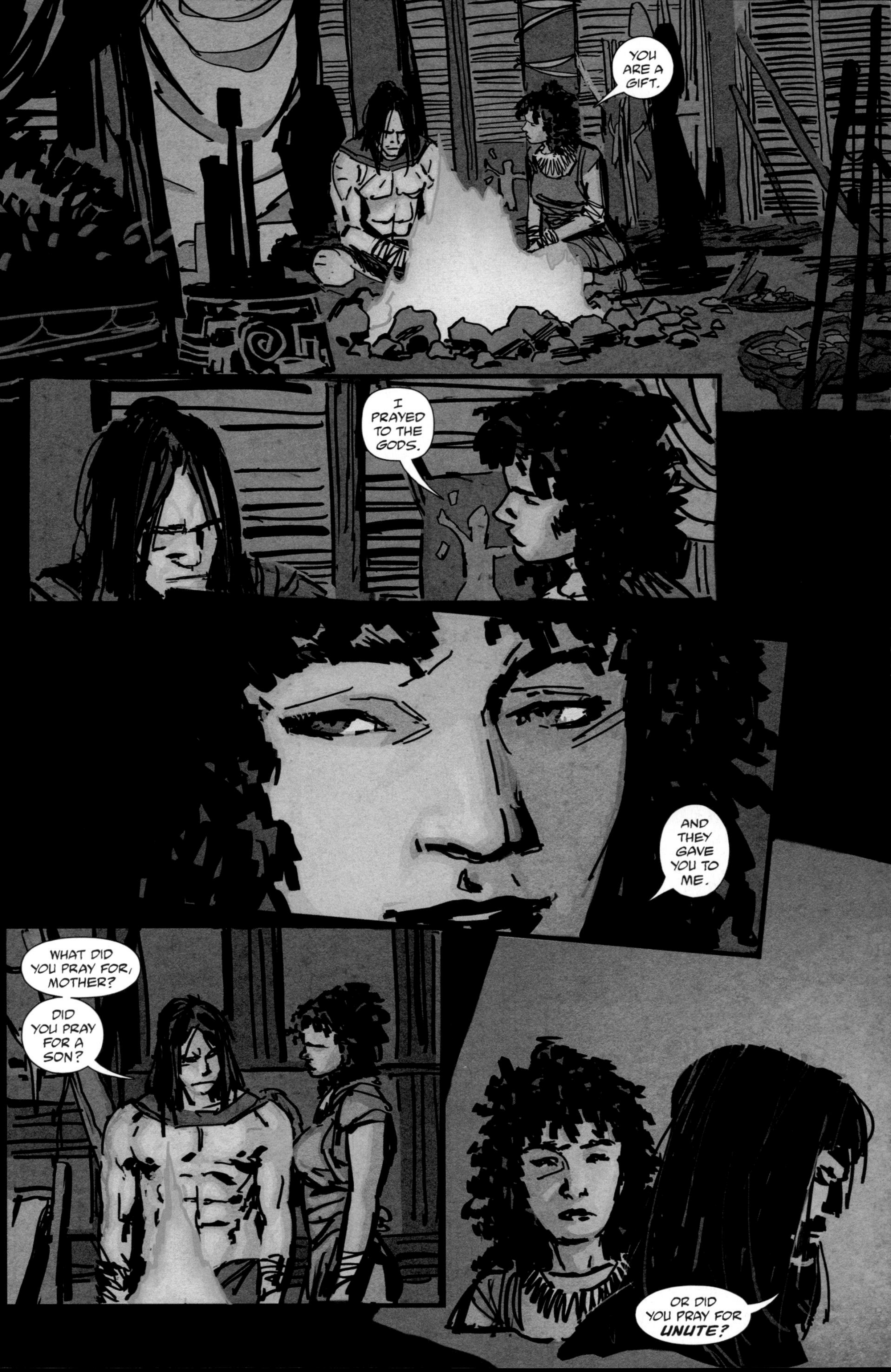
YOU ARE A GIFT.
I PRAYED TO THE GODS.
AND THEY GAVE YOU TO ME.
WHAT DID YOU PRAY FOR, MOTHER?
DID YOU PRAY FOR A SON?
OR DID YOU PRAY FOR UNUTE?

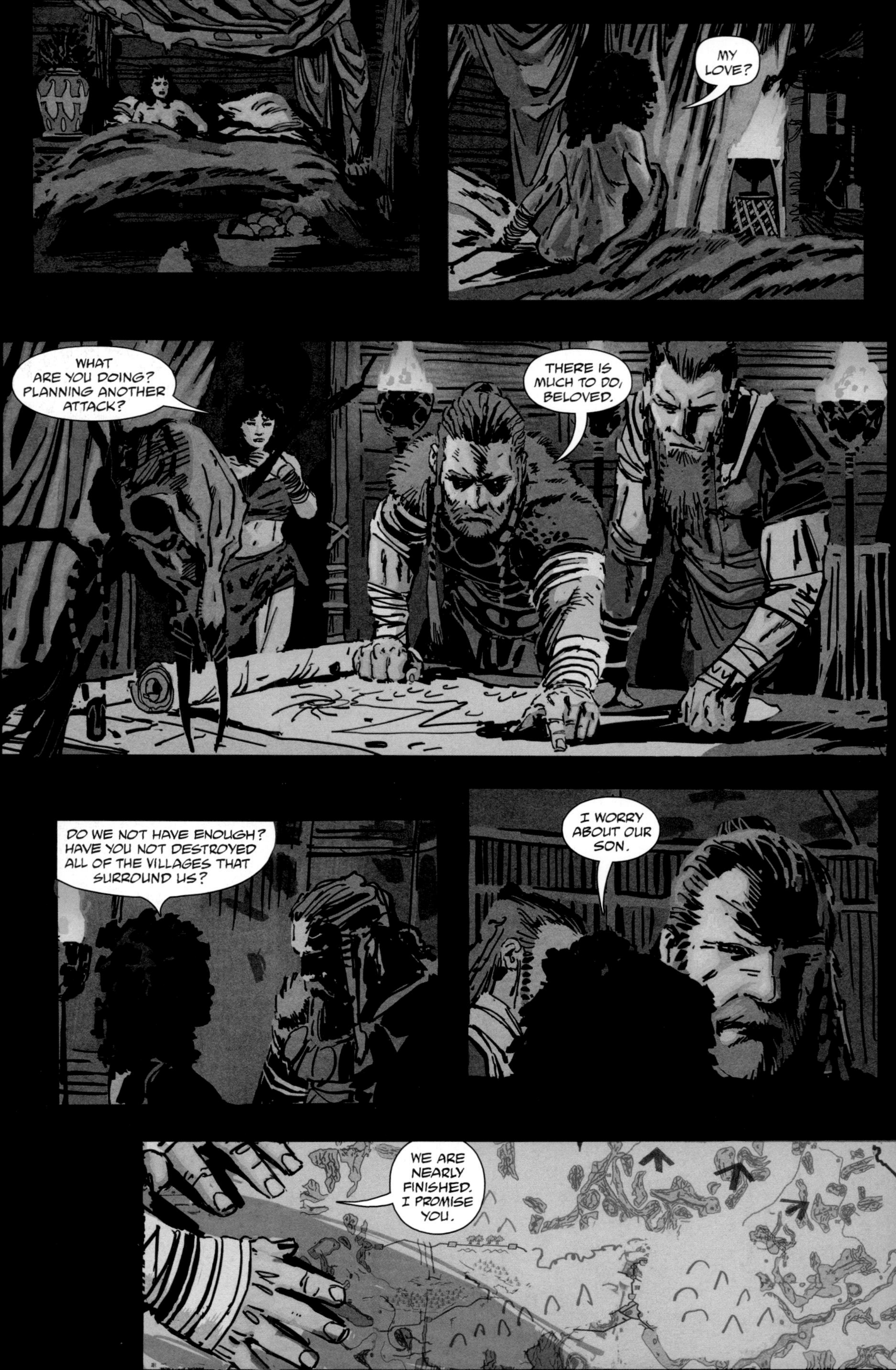
MY LOVE?
WHAT ARE YOU DOING? PLANNING ANOTHER ATTACK?
THERE IS MUCH TO DO, BELOVED.
DO WE NOT HAVE ENOUGH? HAVE YOU NOT DESTROYED ALL OF THE VILLAGES THAT SURROUND US?
I WORRY ABOUT OUR SON.
WE ARE NEARLY FINISHED. I PROMISE YOU.

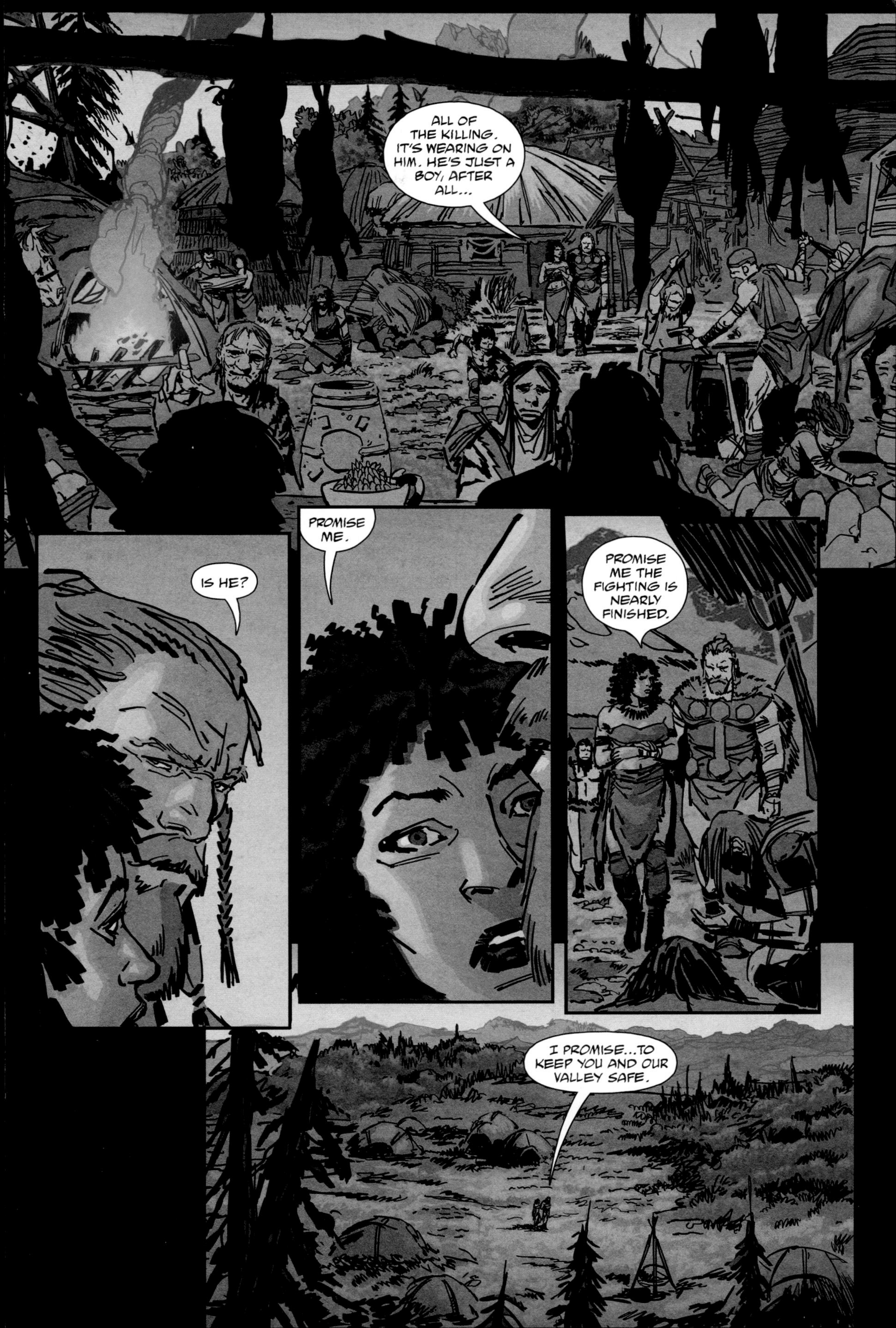
ALL OF THE KILLING. IT'S WEARING ON HIM. HE'S JUST A BOY, AFTER ALL...
IS HE?
PROMISE ME.
PROMISE ME THE FIGHTING IS NEARLY FINISHED.
I PROMISE...TO KEEP YOU AND OUR VALLEY SAFE.

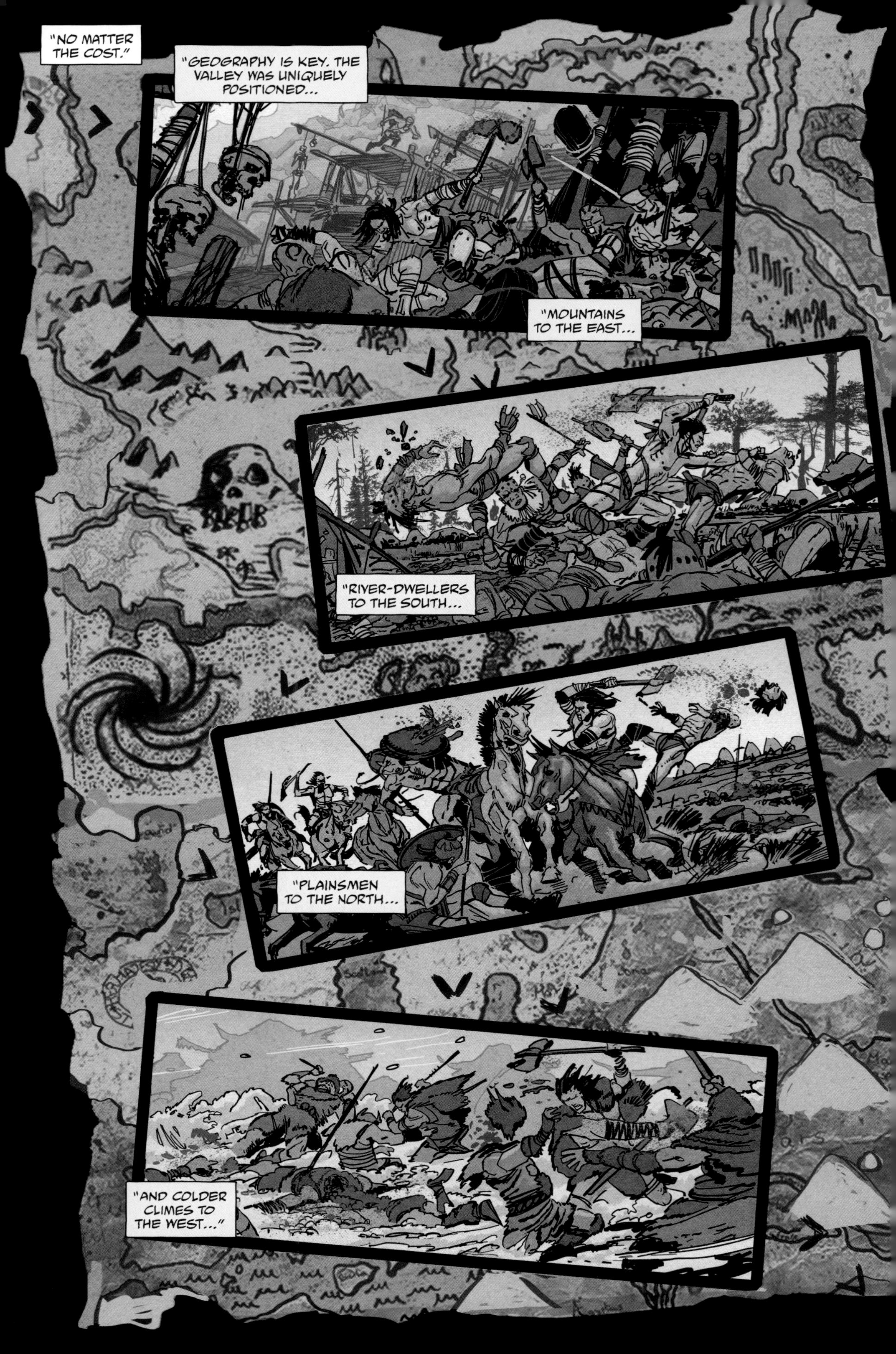
"NO MATTER THE COST."
"GEOGRAPHY IS KEY. THE VALLEY WAS UNIQUELY POSITIONED...
"MOUNTAINS TO THE EAST...
"RIVER-DWELLERS TO THE SOUTH...
"PLAINSMEN TO THE NORTH...
"AND COLDER CLIMES TO THE WEST..."

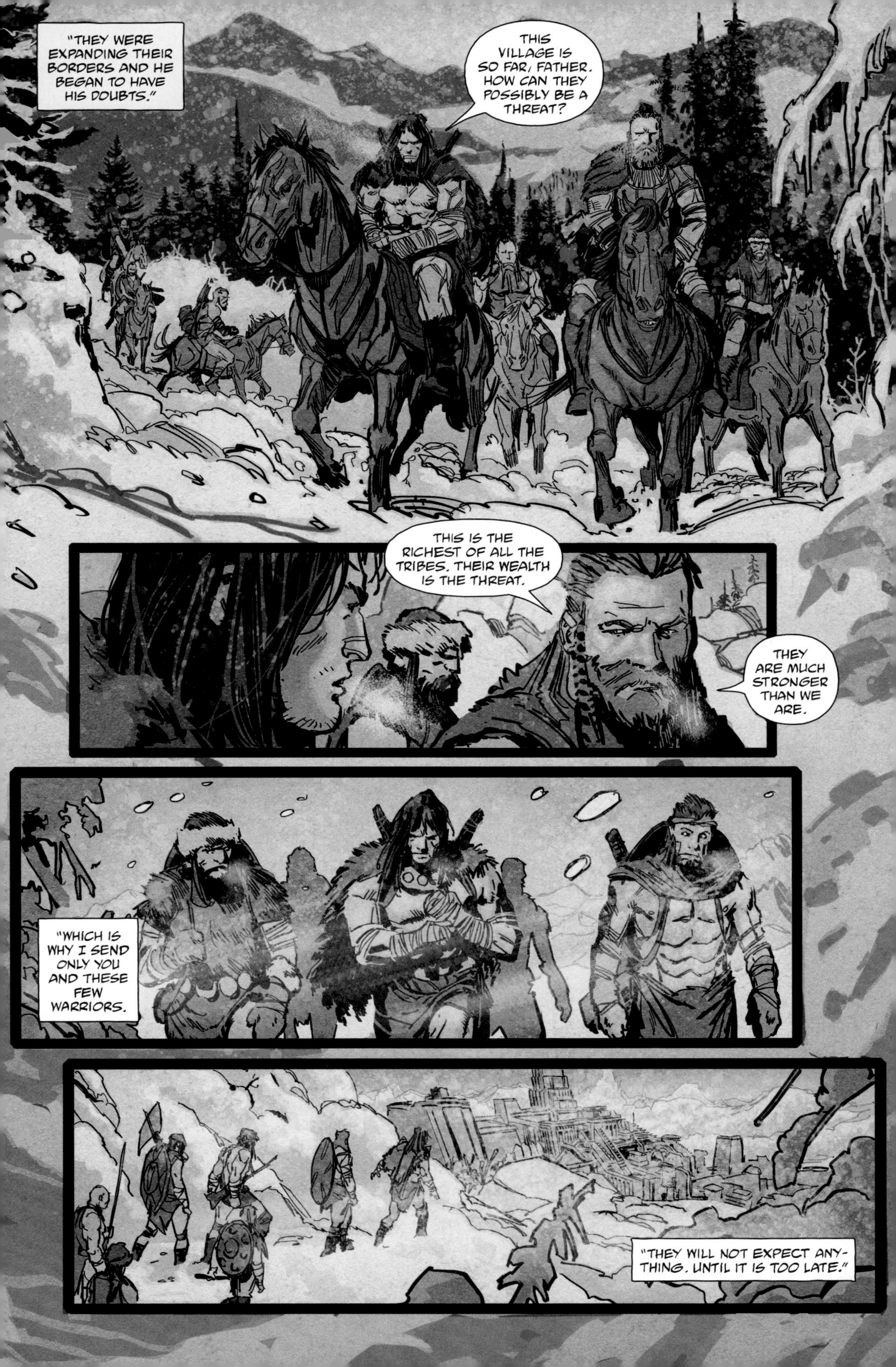
"THEY WERE EXPANDING THEIR BORDERS AND HE BEGAN TO HAVE HIS DOUBTS."
THIS VILLAGE IS SO FAR, FATHER. HOW CAN THEY POSSIBLY BE A THREAT?
THIS IS THE RICHEST OF ALL THE TRIBES. THEIR WEALTH IS THE THREAT.
THEY ARE MUCH STRONGER THAN WE ARE.
"WHICH IS WHY I SEND ONLY YOU AND THESE FEW WARRIORS.
"THEY WILL NOT EXPECT ANYTHING. UNTIL IT IS TOO LATE."

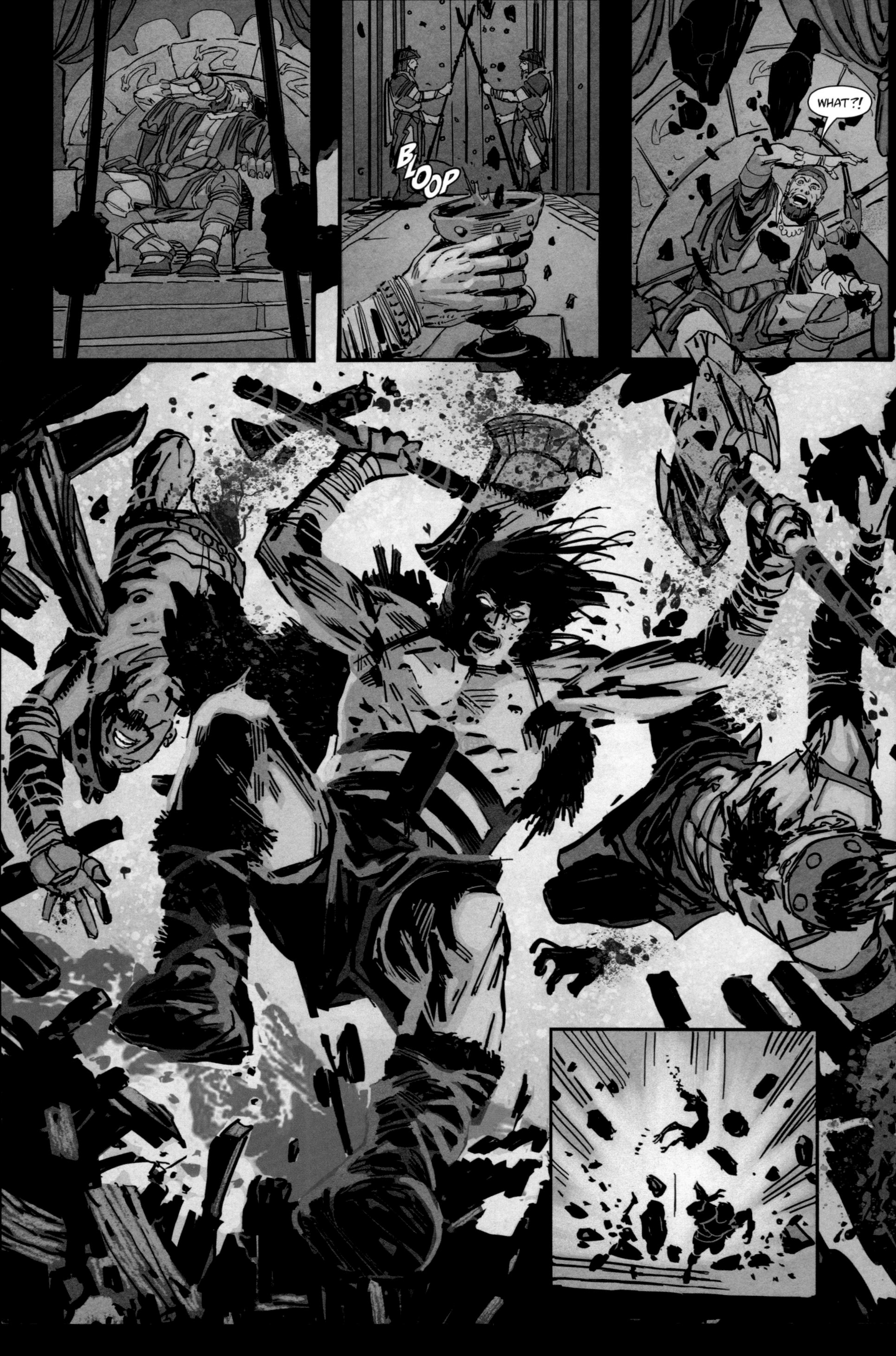
BLOOP
WHAT?!

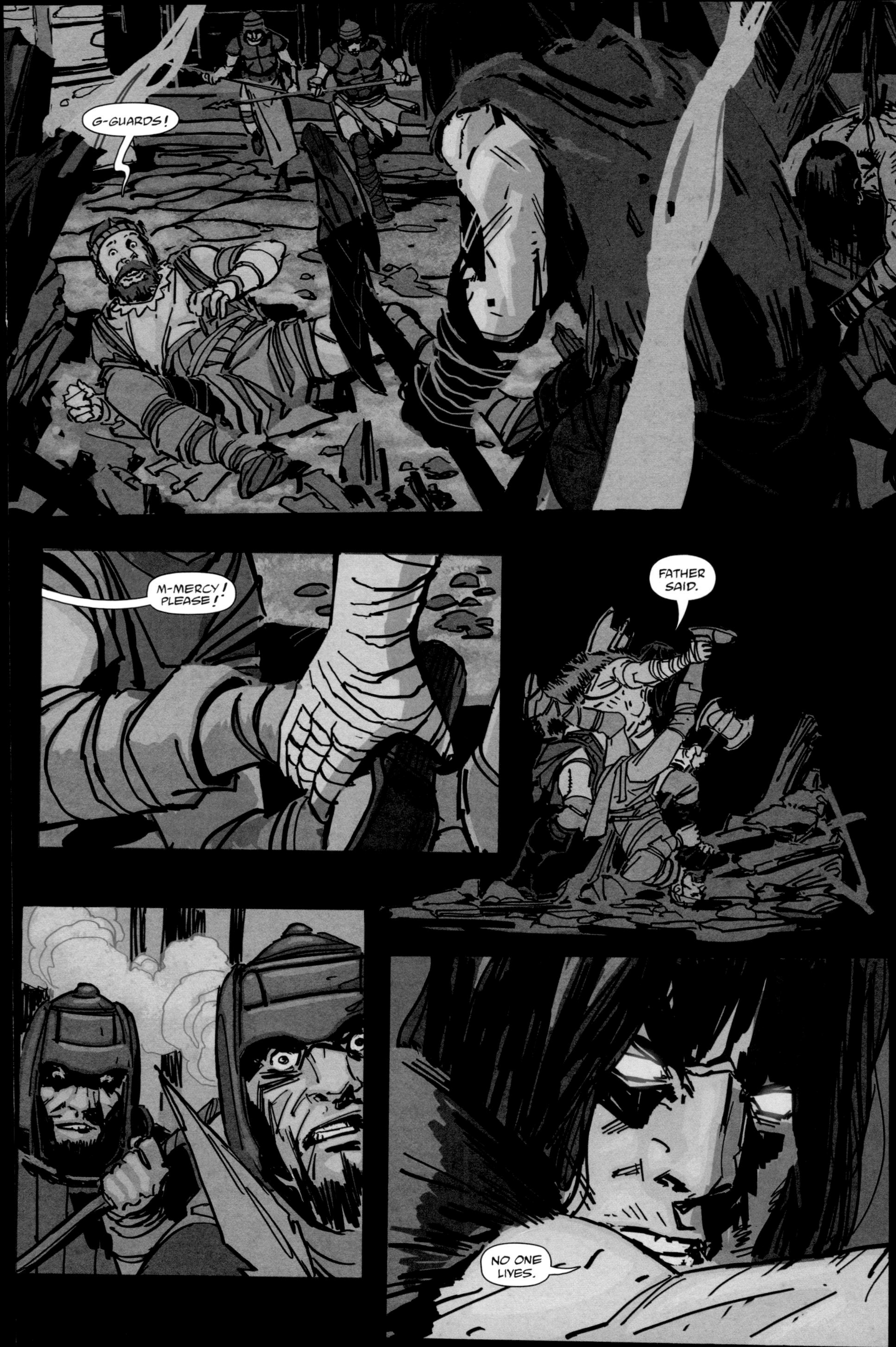
G-GUARDS!
M-MERCY! PLEASE!
FATHER SAID.
NO ONE LIVES.

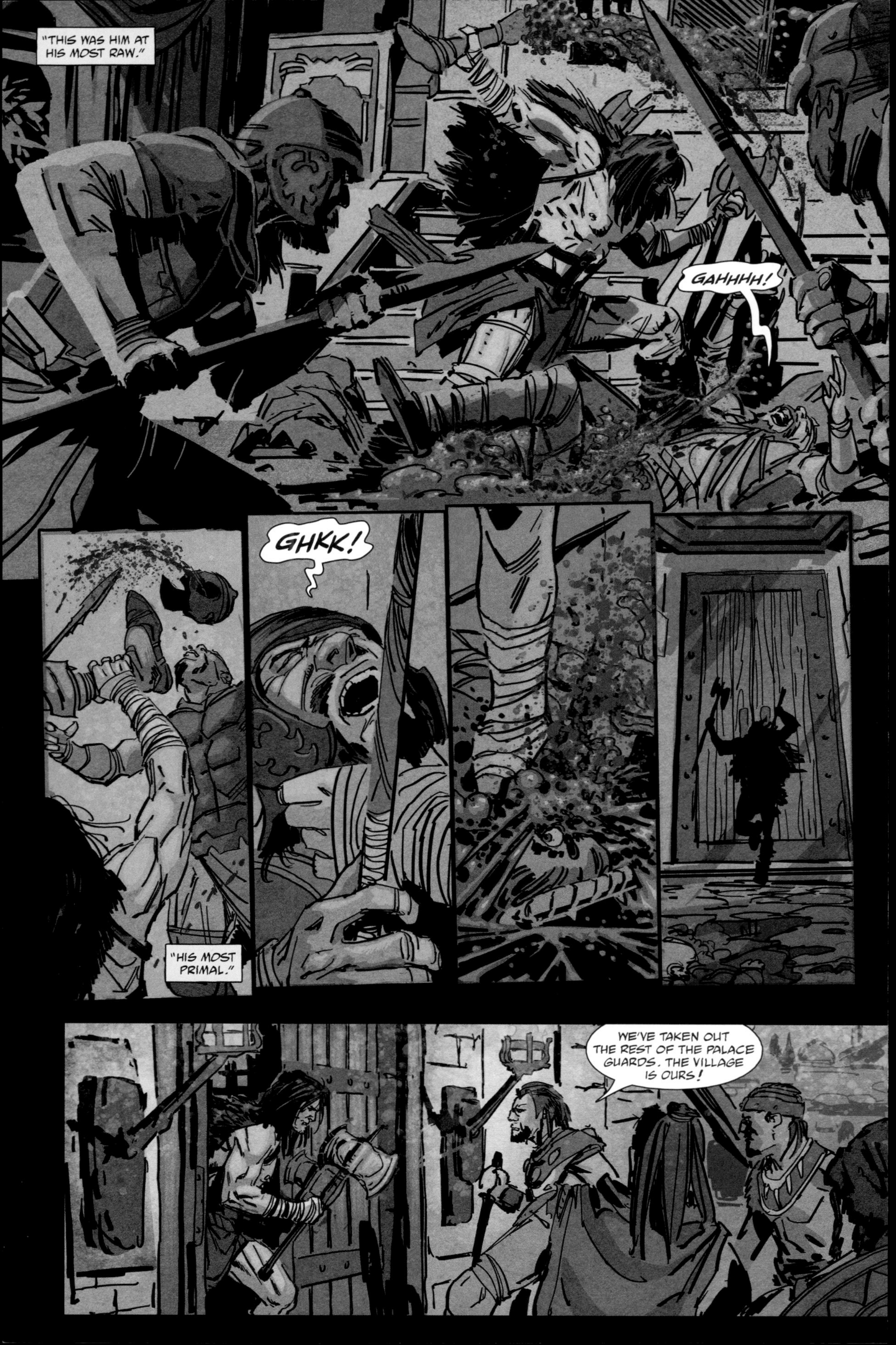
"THIS WAS HIM AT HIS MOST RAW."
GAHHHH!
GHKK!
"HIS MOST PRIMAL."
WE'VE TAKEN OUT THE REST OF THE PALACE GUARDS. THE VILLAGE IS OURS!

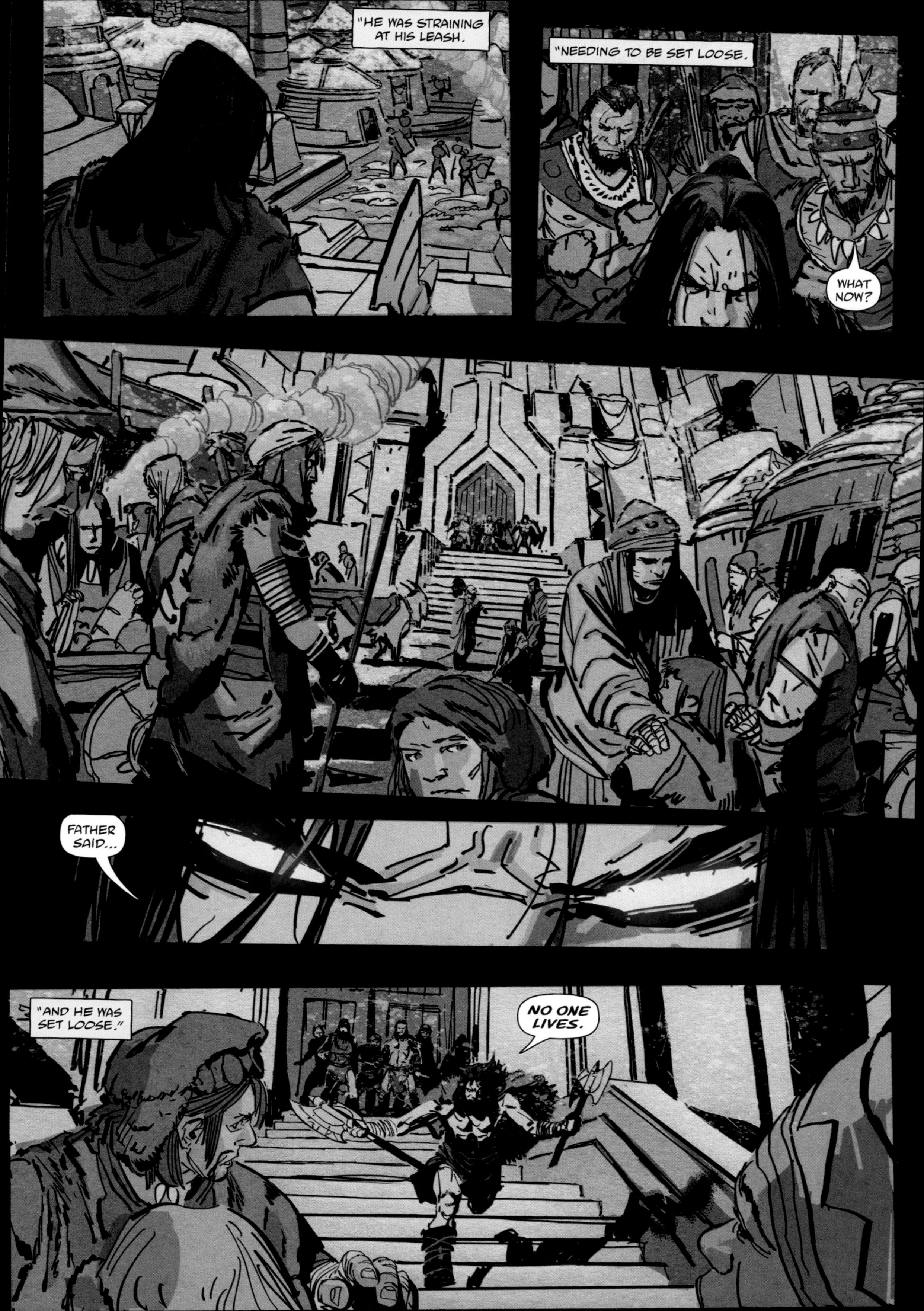
"HE WAS STRAINING AT HIS LEASH.
"NEEDING TO BE SET LOOSE.
WHAT NOW?
FATHER SAID...
"AND HE WAS SET LOOSE."
NO ONE LIVES.

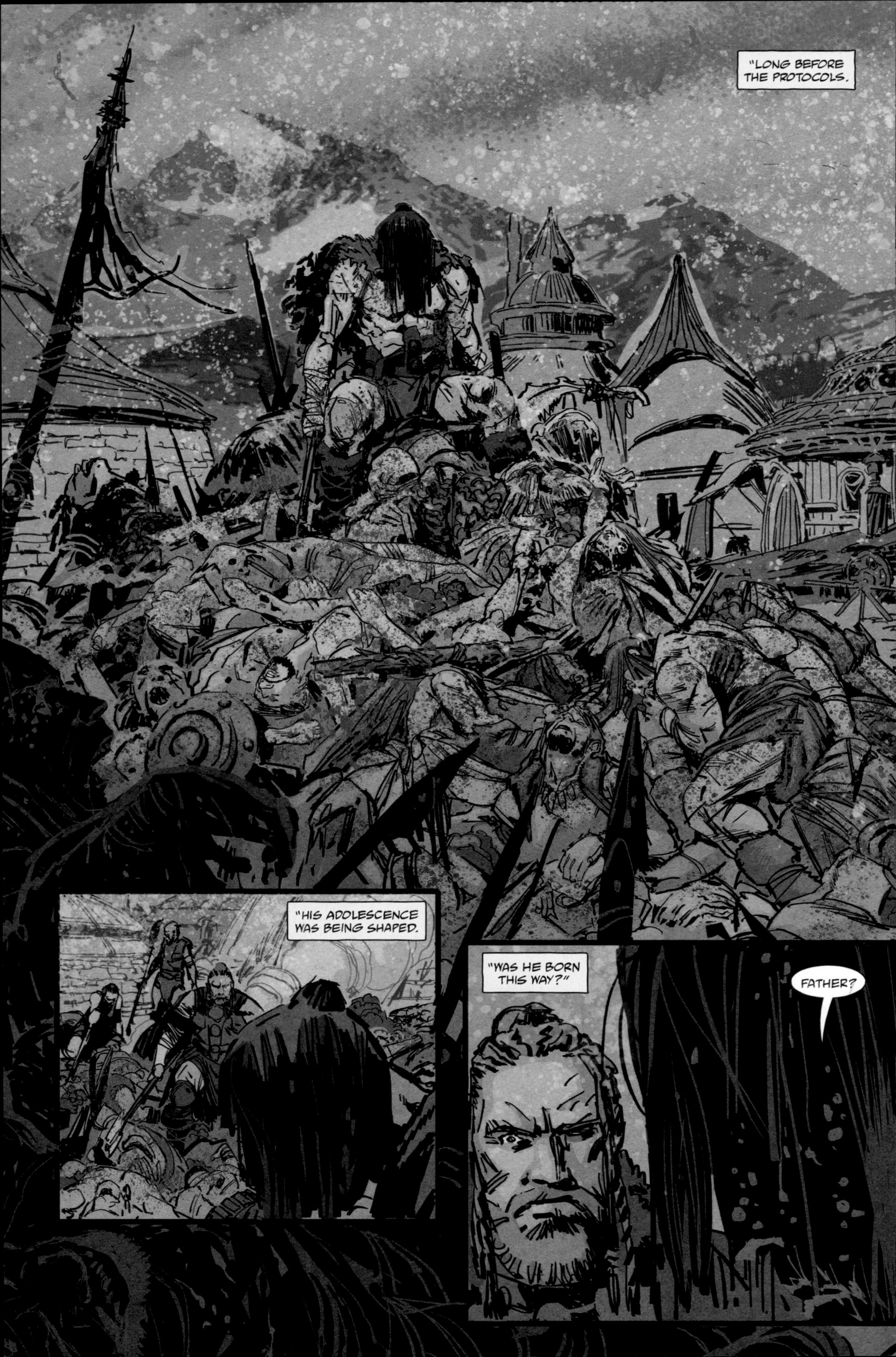
"LONG BEFORE THE PROTOCOLS.
"HIS ADOLESCENCE WAS BEING SHAPED.
"WAS HE BORN THIS WAY?"
FATHER?

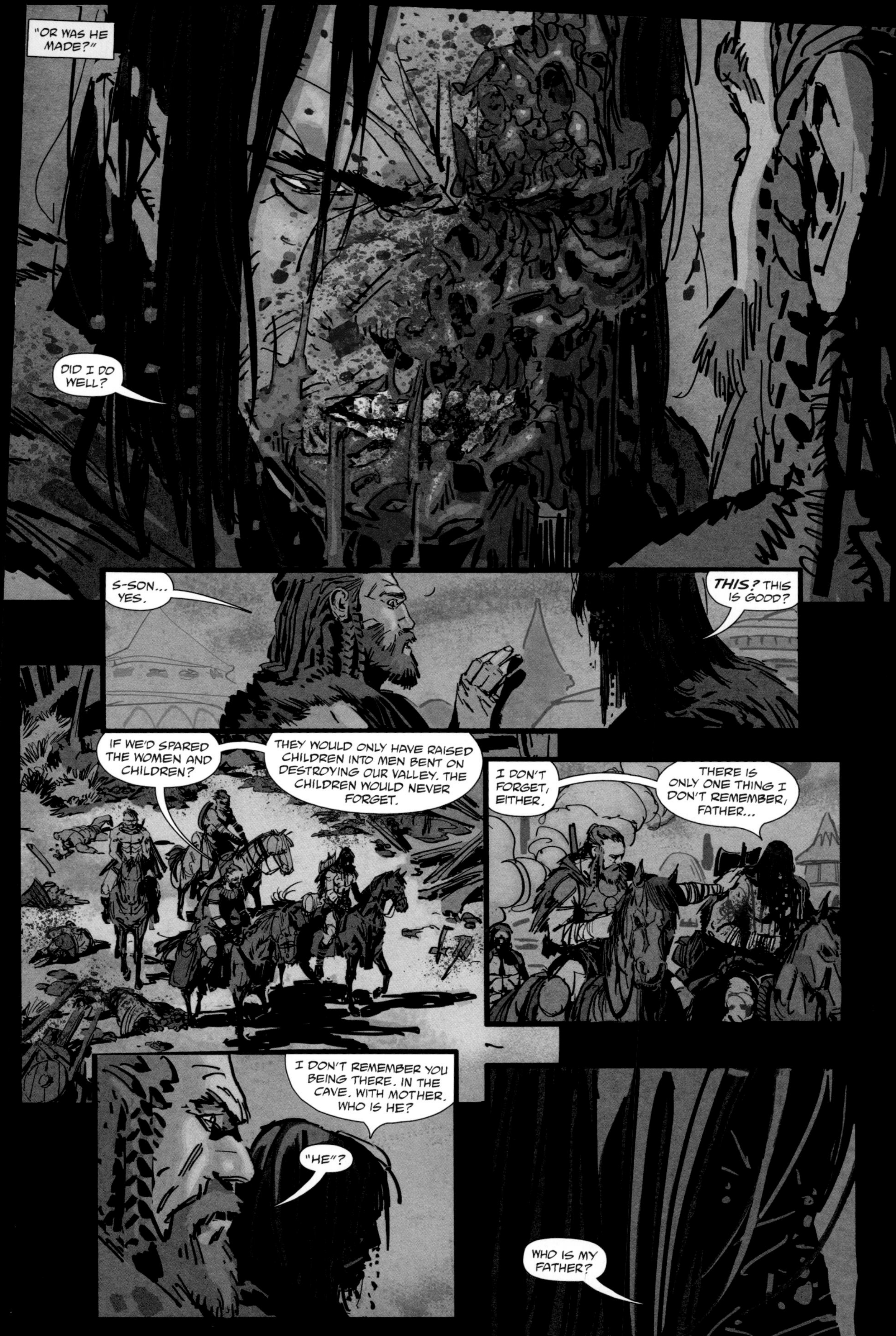
"OR WAS HE MADE?"
DID I DO WELL?
S-SON... YES.
THIS? THIS IS GOOD?
IF WE'D SPARED THE WOMEN AND CHILDREN?
THEY WOULD ONLY HAVE RAISED CHILDREN INTO MEN BENT ON DESTROYING OUR VALLEY. THE CHILDREN WOULD NEVER FORGET.
I DON'T FORGET, EITHER.
THERE IS ONLY ONE THING I DON'T REMEMBER, FATHER...
I DON'T REMEMBER YOU BEING THERE. IN THE CAVE. WITH MOTHER. WHO IS HE?
"HE"?
WHO IS MY FATHER?

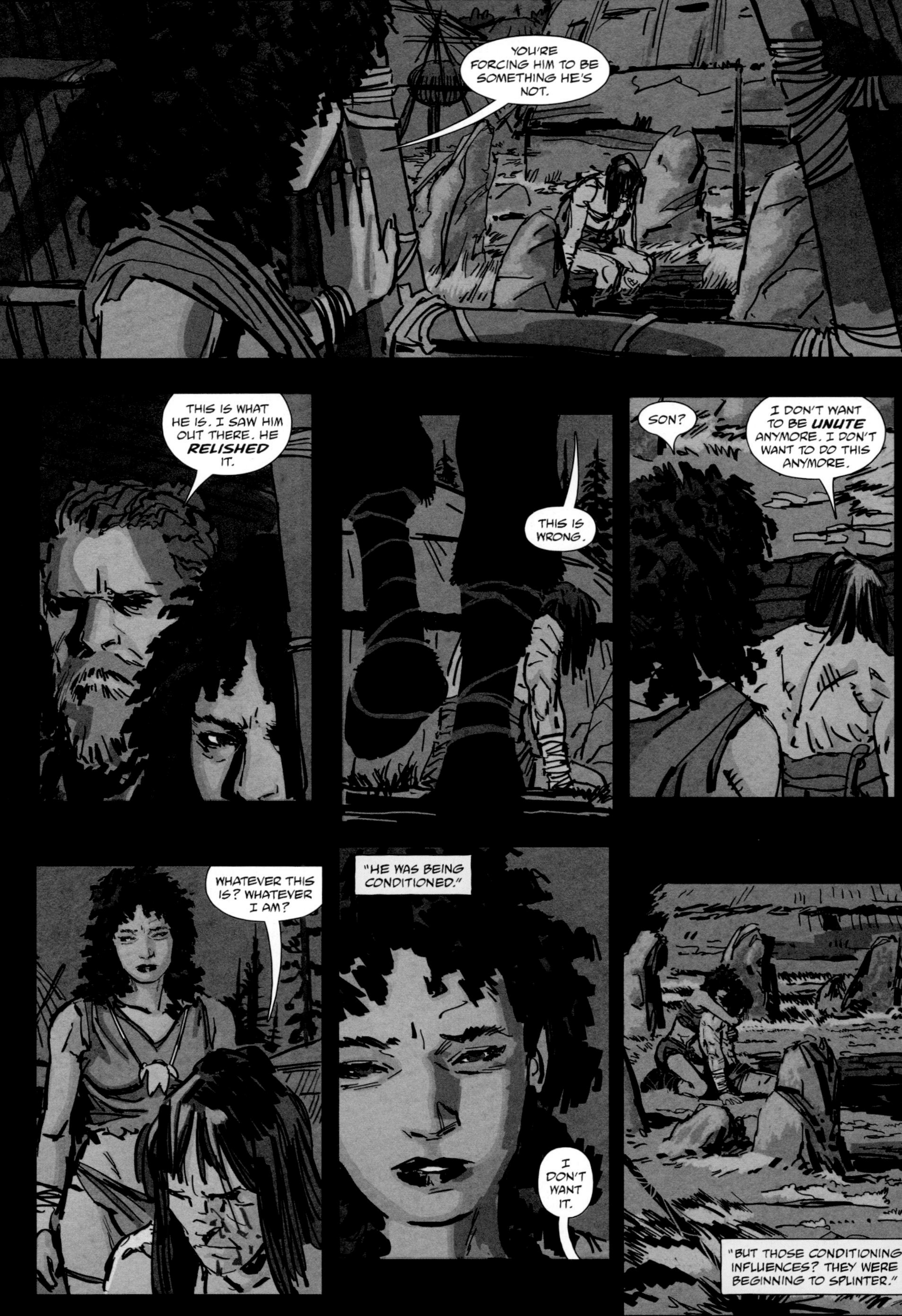
YOU'RE FORCING HIM TO BE SOMETHING HE'S NOT.
THIS IS WHAT HE IS. I SAW HIM OUT THERE. HE RELISHED IT.
THIS IS WRONG.
SON?
I DON'T WANT TO BE UNUTE ANYMORE. I DON'T WANT TO DO THIS ANYMORE.
WHATEVER THIS IS? WHATEVER I AM?
"HE WAS BEING CONDITIONED."
I DON'T WANT IT.
"BUT THOSE CONDITIONING INFLUENCES? THEY WERE BEGINNING TO SPLINTER."

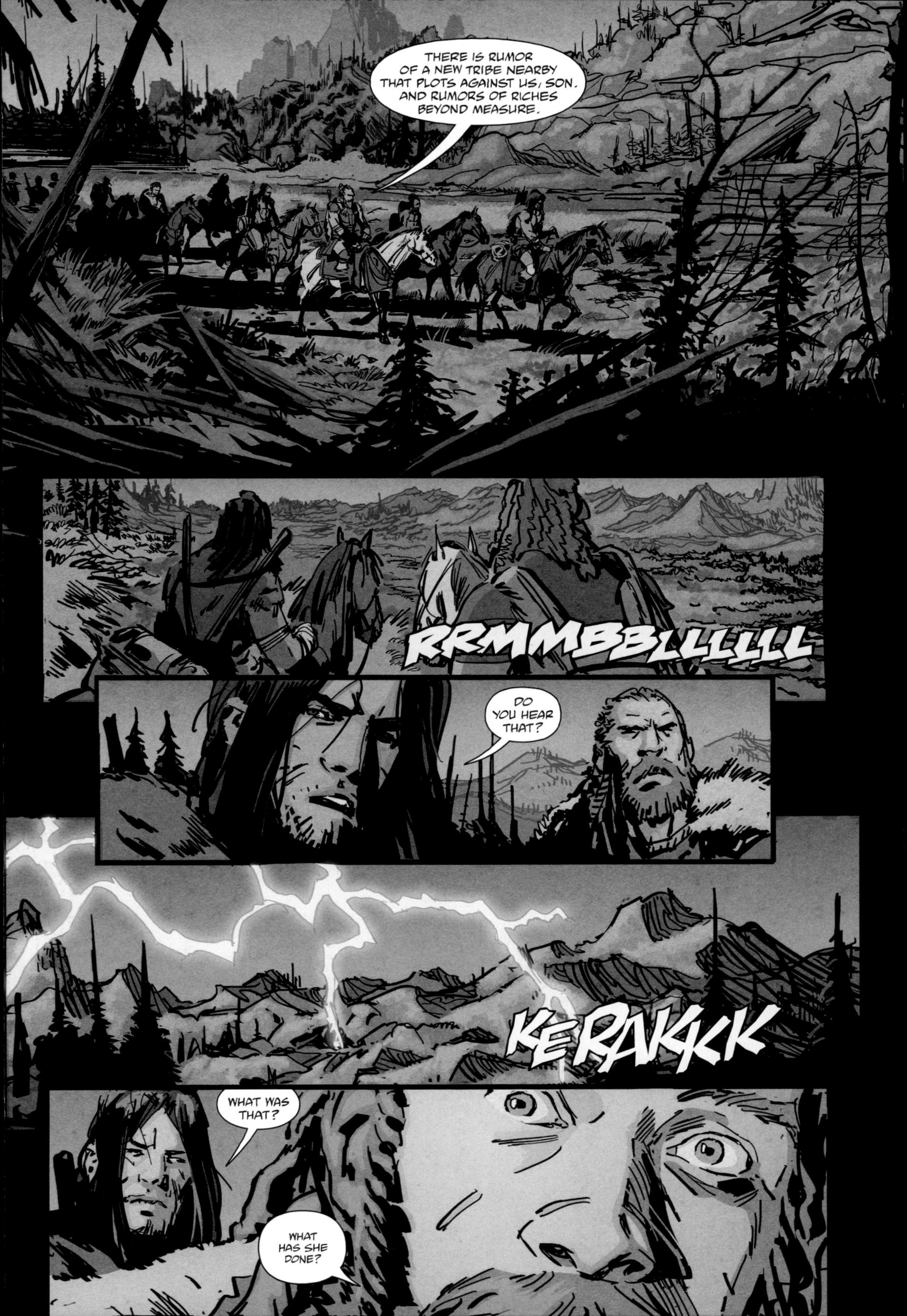

THERE IS RUMOR OF A NEW TRIBE NEARBY THAT PLOTS AGAINST US, SON. AND RUMORS OF RICHES BEYOND MEASURE.
RRMMBBLLLLLL
DO YOU HEAR THAT?
KERAKKK
WHAT WAS THAT?
WHAT HAS SHE DONE?

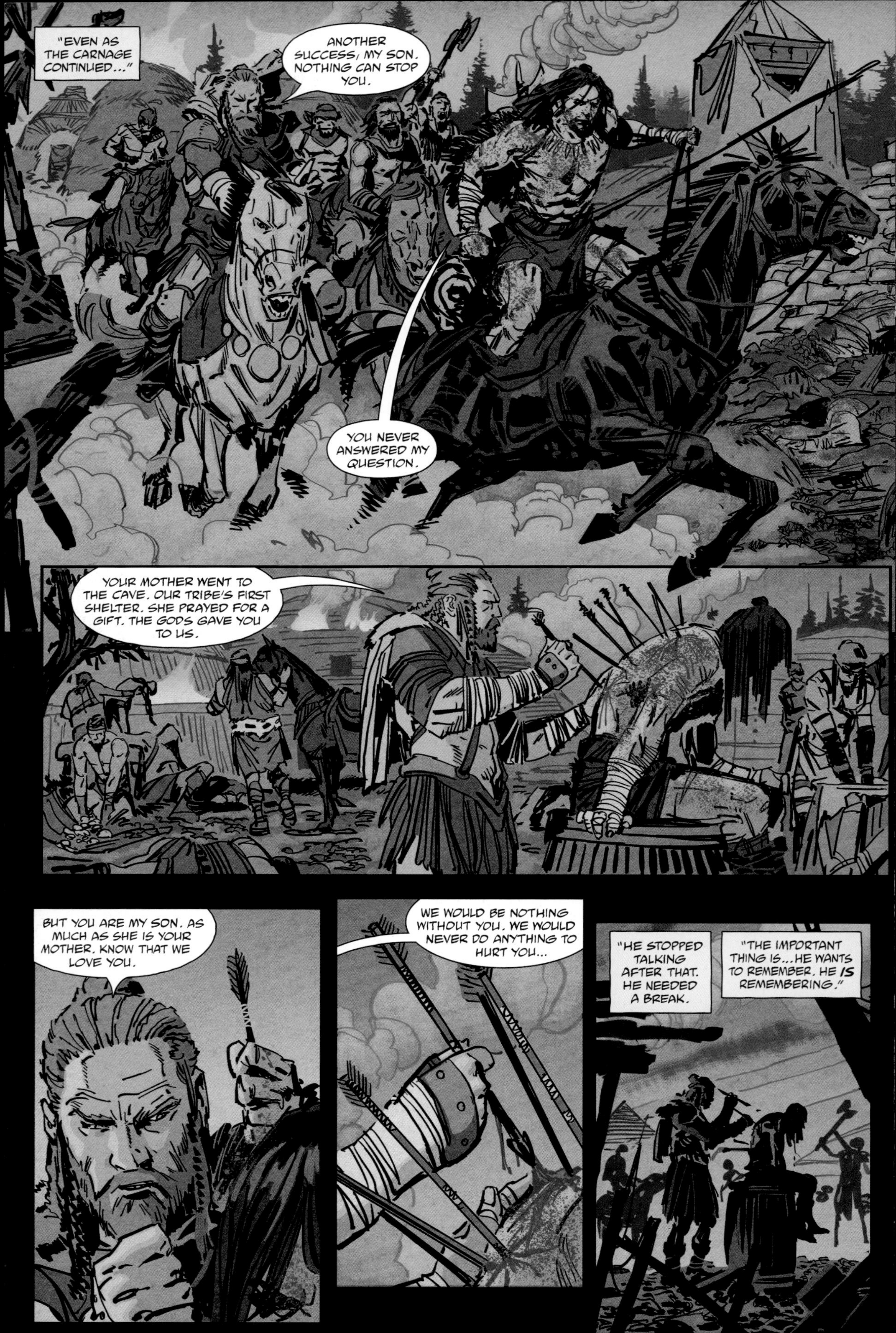
"EVEN AS THE CARNAGE CONTINUED..."
ANOTHER SUCCESS, MY SON. NOTHING CAN STOP YOU.
YOU NEVER ANSWERED MY QUESTION.
YOUR MOTHER WENT TO THE CAVE. OUR TRIBE'S FIRST SHELTER. SHE PRAYED FOR A GIFT. THE GODS GAVE YOU TO US.
BUT YOU ARE MY SON. AS MUCH AS SHE IS YOUR MOTHER. KNOW THAT WE LOVE YOU.
WE WOULD BE NOTHING WITHOUT YOU. WE WOULD NEVER DO ANYTHING TO HURT YOU...
"HE STOPPED TALKING AFTER THAT. HE NEEDED A BREAK.
"THE IMPORTANT THING IS... HE WANTS TO REMEMBER. HE *IS* REMEMBERING."

BUT WE STILL DON'T KNOW **ANYTHING**.

WE HAVEN'T UNLOCKED HIS **DNA**. OR SOLVED THE MYSTERY OF HIS **INCONGRUOUS** AMINO ACIDS. HIS **QUANTUM MOLECULES**?

I MEAN...HIS FATHER A "**GOD**"? ARRIVING VIA A **LIGHTNING STRIKE**? WHAT THE HELL AM I SUPPOSED TO DO WITH THAT?

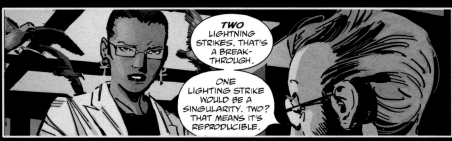

TWO LIGHTNING STRIKES. THAT'S A BREAK-THROUGH.

ONE LIGHTING STRIKE WOULD BE A SINGULARITY. TWO? THAT MEANS IT'S REPRODUCIBLE.

KEEP HIM TALKING. KEEP HIM REMEMBERING...

ALL OF THESE NEW TRIBAL AND GEOGRAPHICAL DETAILS SHOULD HELP US FIND HIS PLACE OF ORIGIN.

AND JUST AS IMPORTANT... HE TRUSTS YOU...

YEAH. HE TRUSTS ME. IN THE MEANTIME? I'M GOING TO KEEP CALIBRATING HIS PROTOCOLS.

WHERE IS HE NOW?

RIGHT NOW...?

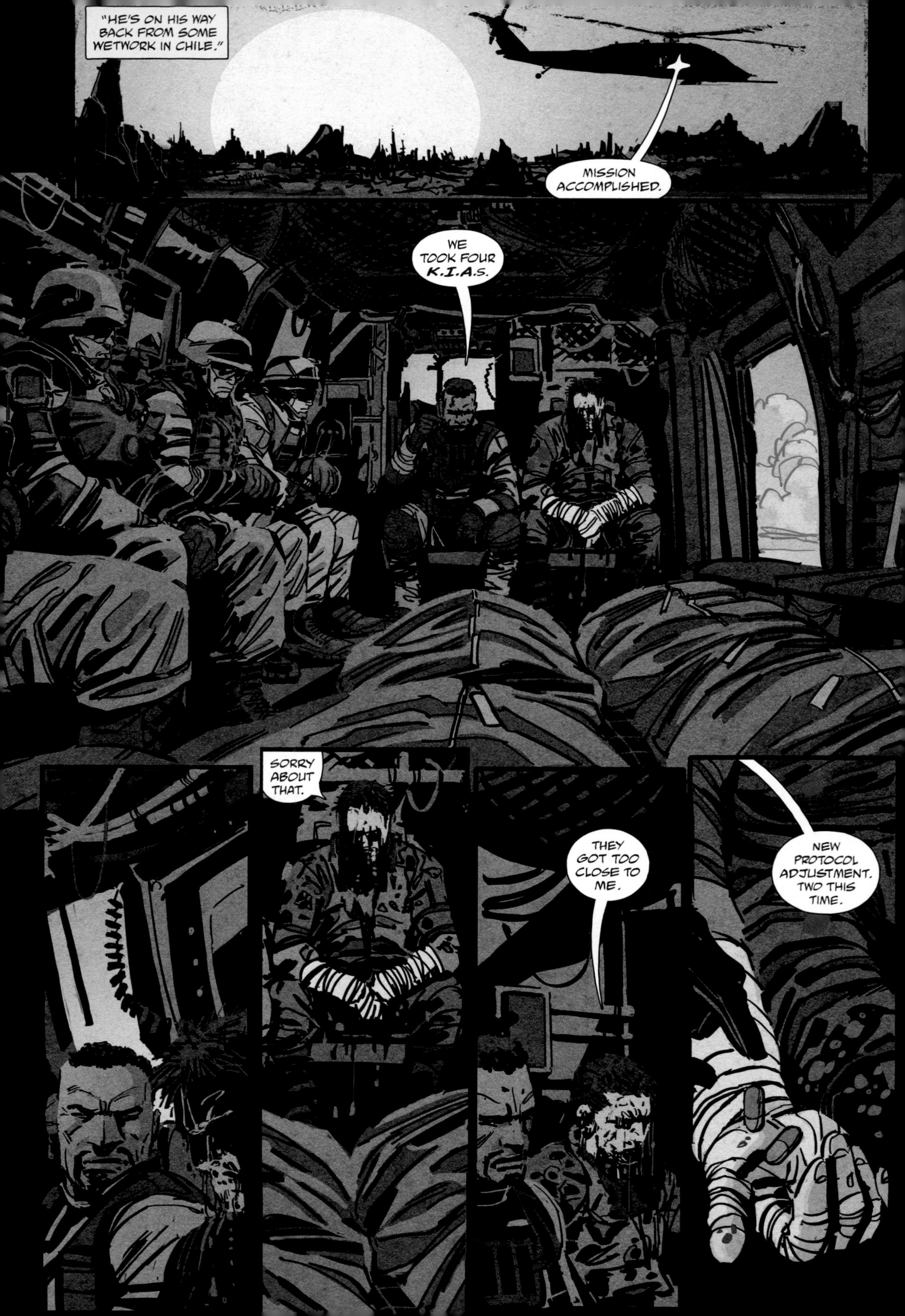
"HE'S ON HIS WAY BACK FROM SOME WETWORK IN CHILE."
MISSION ACCOMPLISHED.
WE TOOK FOUR K.I.A.S.
SORRY ABOUT THAT.
THEY GOT TOO CLOSE TO ME.
NEW PROTOCOL ADJUSTMENT. TWO THIS TIME.

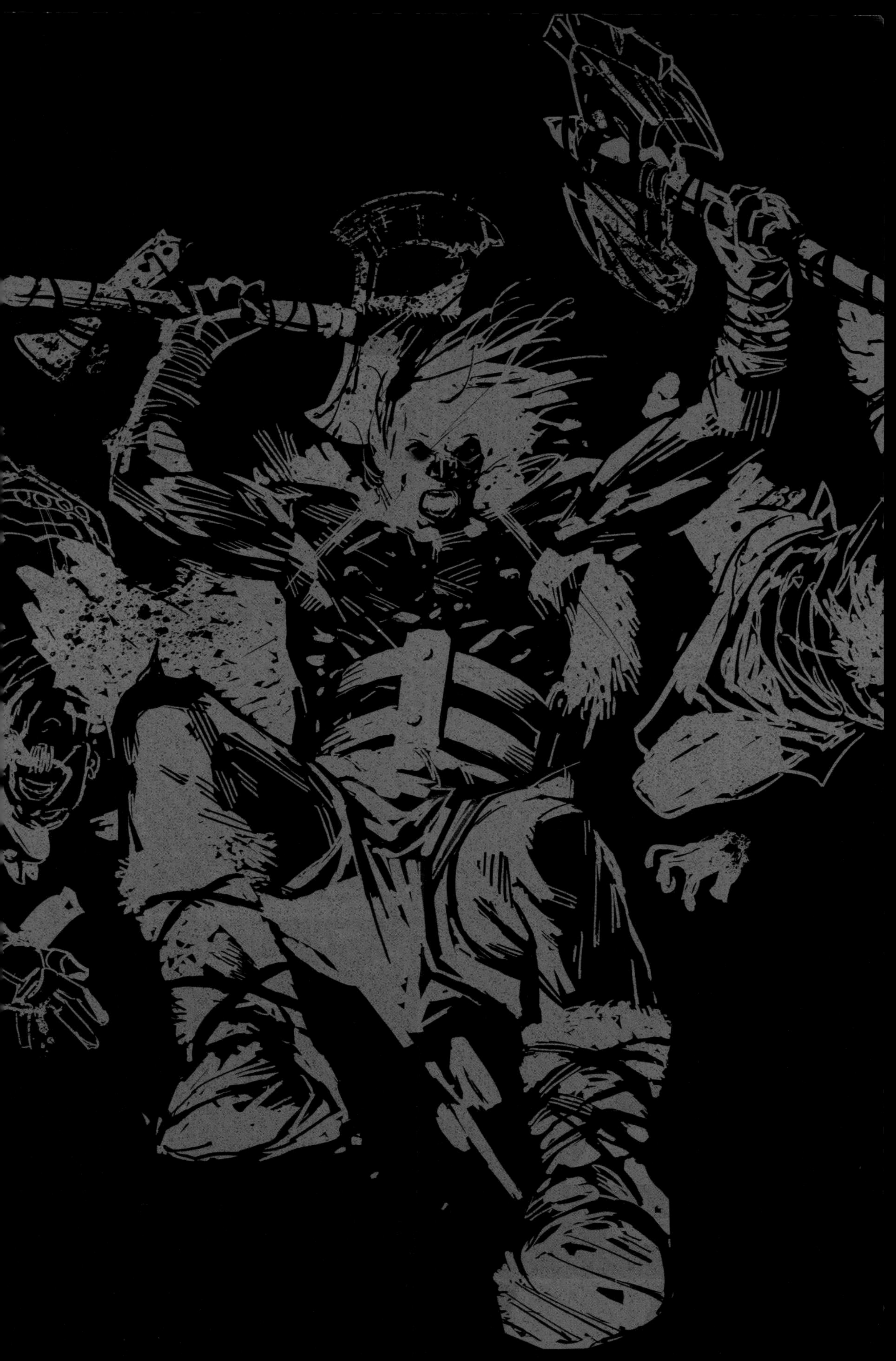

CHAPTER
FOUR

THIS IS REAL PROGRESS. THE SCIENCE CAN UNLOCK YOUR DNA, BUT YOUR STORY? IT'S JUST AS ESSENTIAL.

IT'S WORKING. I PROMISE.

THAT'S IT. I'M DONE FOR TODAY.

I DON'T KNOW WHAT ELSE CAN TELL YOU.

I GET IT. YOU'RE GIVING ME WHAT I WANT. HUMORING ME SO YOU CAN MAKE YOUR IMMORTAL SUPER SOLDIERS.

YOU KNOW YOUR ORIGINS ARE IMPORTANT. OUR SCIENCE, IT MIGHT HELP US...BUT IT CAN ALSO HELP YOU. CURE YOU.

SOMETHING TELLS ME I WON'T BE CURED UNTIL YOU HAVE AN ARMY OF ME.

IT'S OKAY. LET ME KNOW WHEN YOU HAVE IT FIGURED OUT. I'M DONE FOR TODAY.

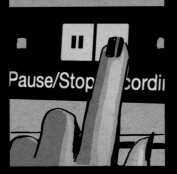

Pause/Stop Recordi

PLAY BACK SESSION 392.

INTERVIEWING SUBJECT B.

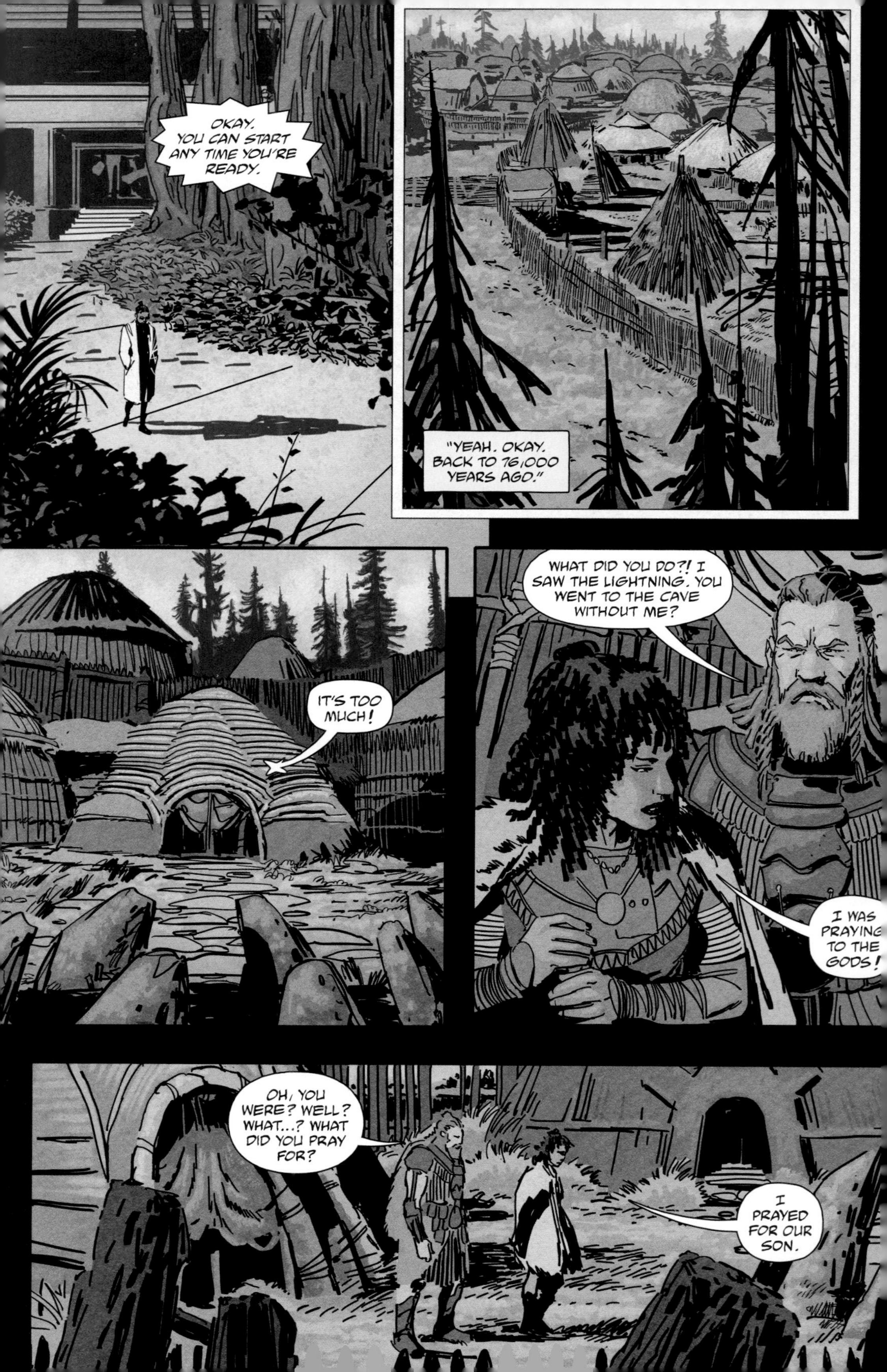
OKAY. YOU CAN START ANY TIME YOU'RE READY.
"YEAH. OKAY. BACK TO 76,000 YEARS AGO."
IT'S TOO MUCH!
WHAT DID YOU DO?! I SAW THE LIGHTNING. YOU WENT TO THE CAVE WITHOUT ME?
I WAS PRAYING TO THE GODS!
OH, YOU WERE? WELL? WHAT...? WHAT DID YOU PRAY FOR?
I PRAYED FOR OUR SON.

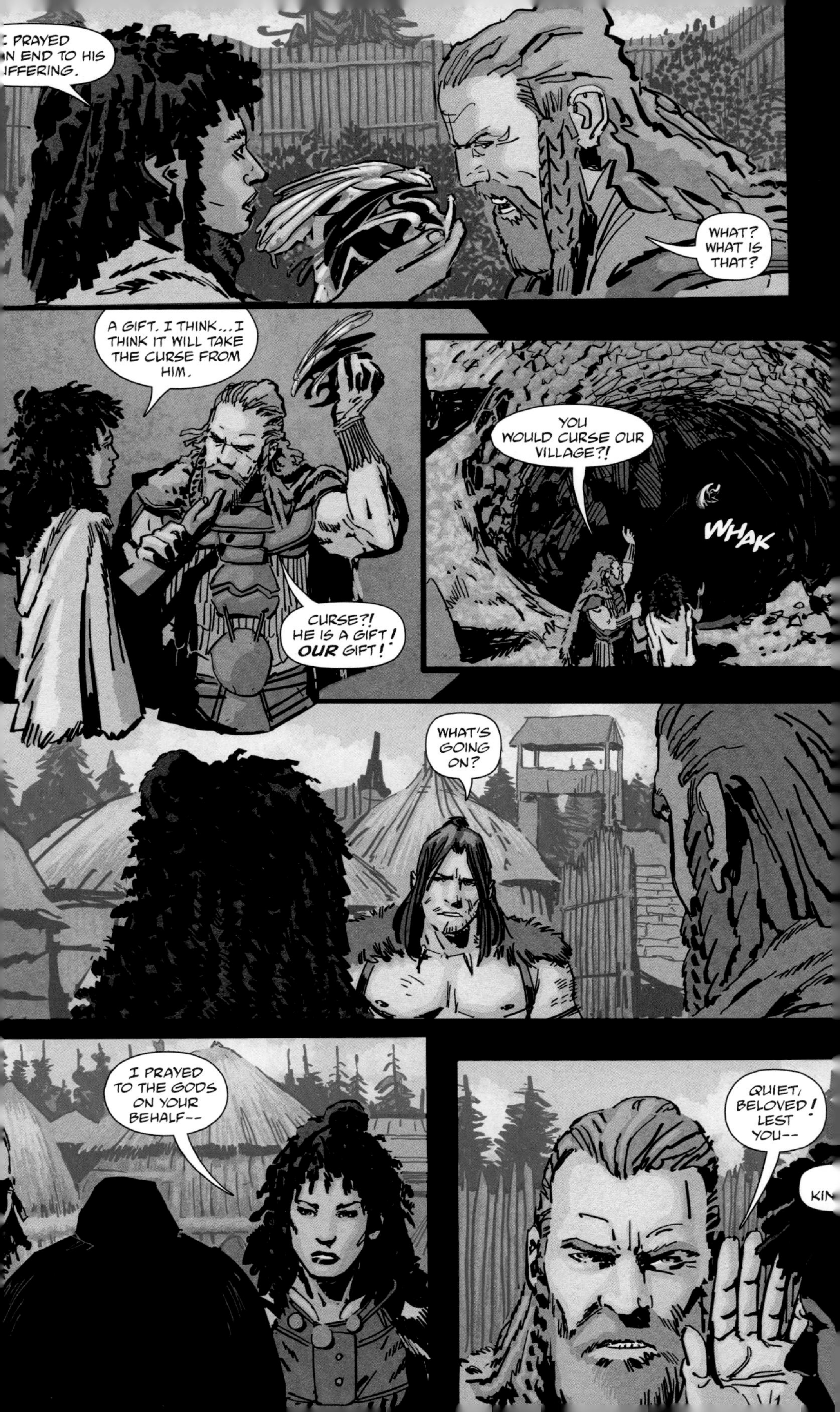

PRAYED
N END TO HIS
IFFERING.
WHAT? WHAT IS THAT?
A GIFT. I THINK... I THINK IT WILL TAKE THE CURSE FROM HIM.
CURSE?! HE IS A GIFT! OUR GIFT!
YOU WOULD CURSE OUR VILLAGE?!
WHAK
WHAT'S GOING ON?
I PRAYED TO THE GODS ON YOUR BEHALF--
QUIET, BELOVED! LEST YOU--
KI

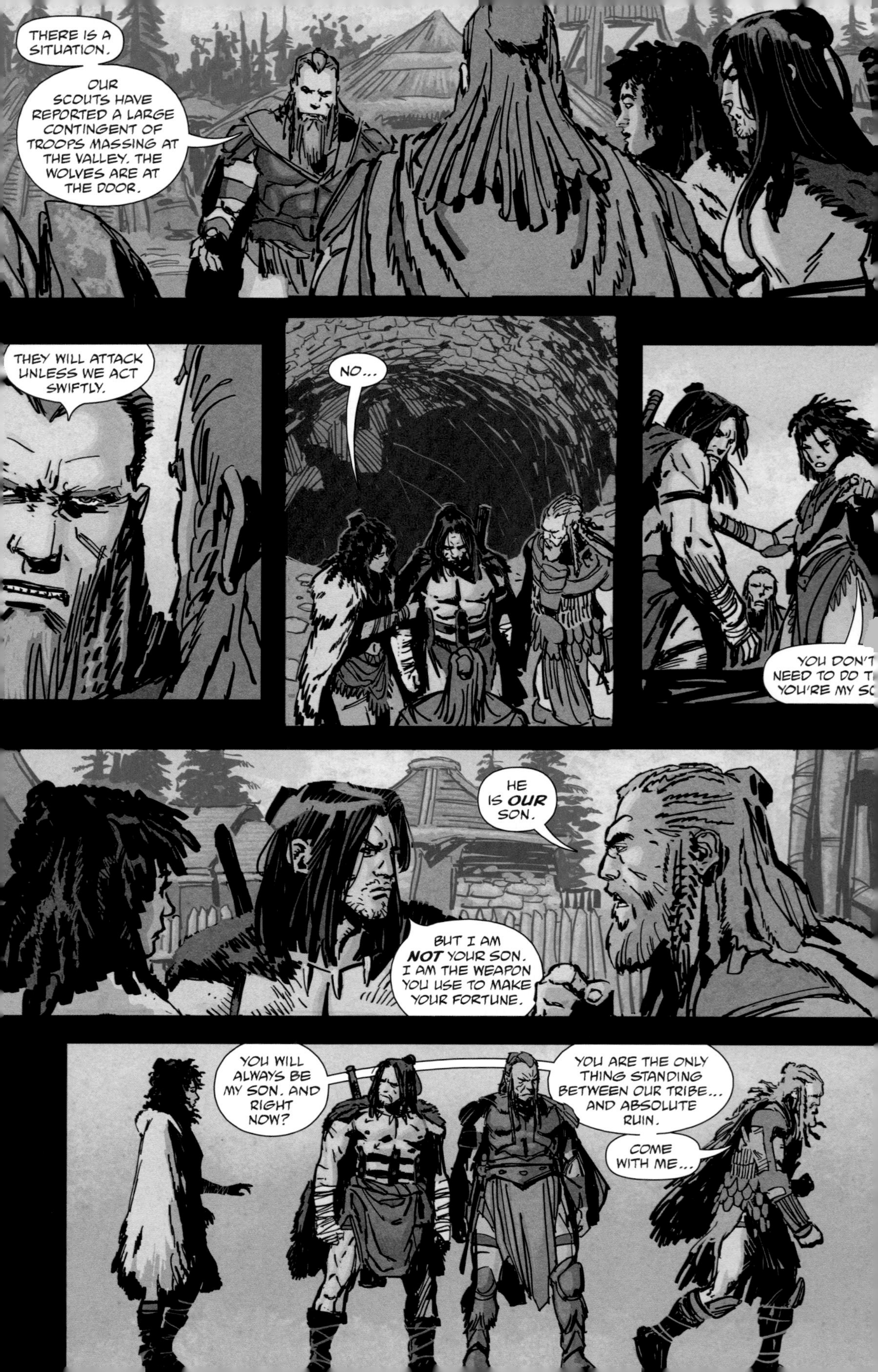
THERE IS A SITUATION.
OUR SCOUTS HAVE REPORTED A LARGE CONTINGENT OF TROOPS MASSING AT THE VALLEY. THE WOLVES ARE AT THE DOOR.
THEY WILL ATTACK UNLESS WE ACT SWIFTLY.
NO...
YOU DON'T NEED TO DO T YOU'RE MY S
HE IS **OUR** SON.
BUT I AM **NOT** YOUR SON. I AM THE WEAPON YOU USE TO MAKE YOUR FORTUNE.
YOU WILL ALWAYS BE MY SON. AND RIGHT NOW?
YOU ARE THE ONLY THING STANDING BETWEEN OUR TRIBE... AND ABSOLUTE RUIN.
COME WITH ME...

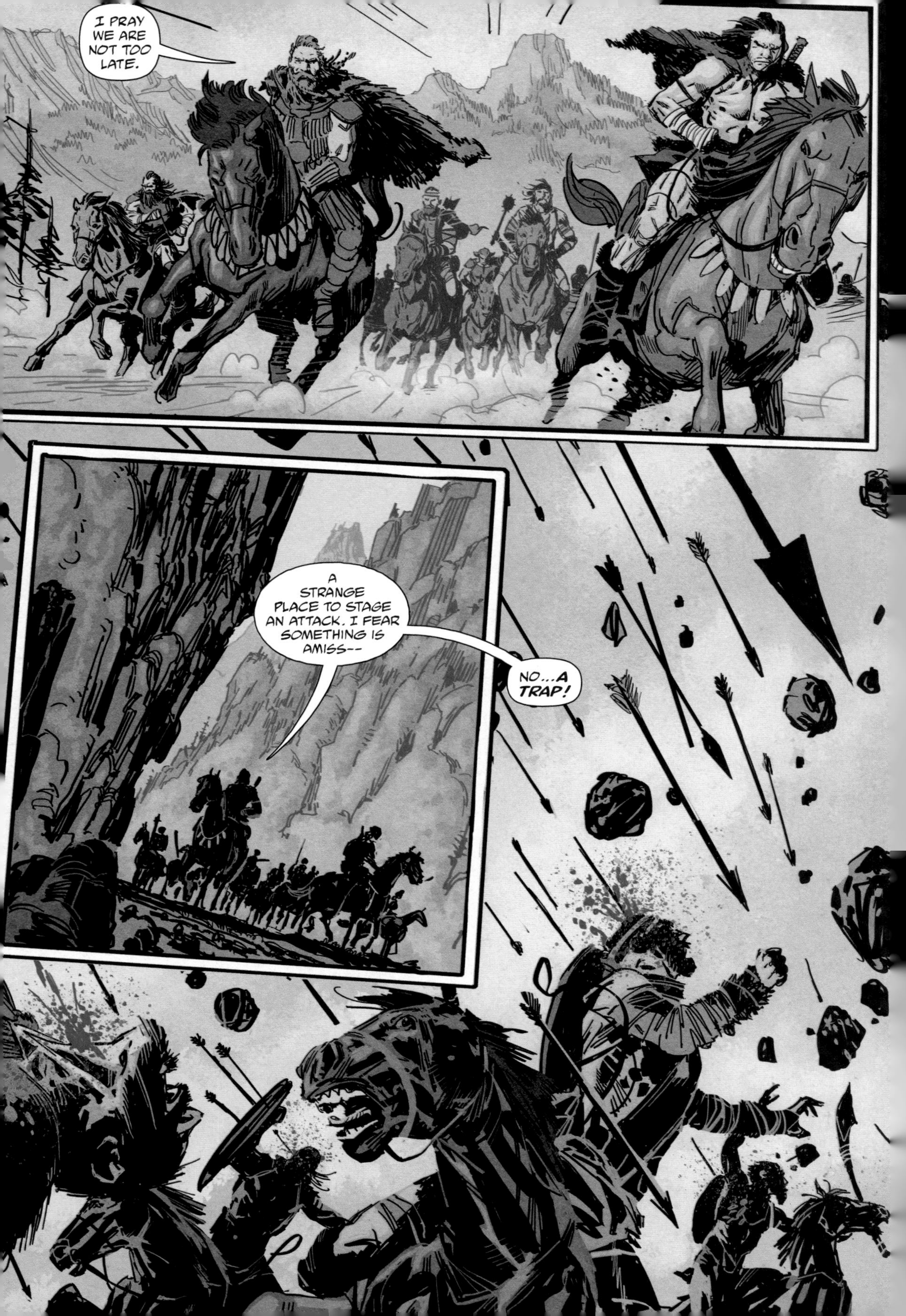

I PRAY WE ARE NOT TOO LATE.
A STRANGE PLACE TO STAGE AN ATTACK. I FEAR SOMETHING IS AMISS--
NO...A TRAP!

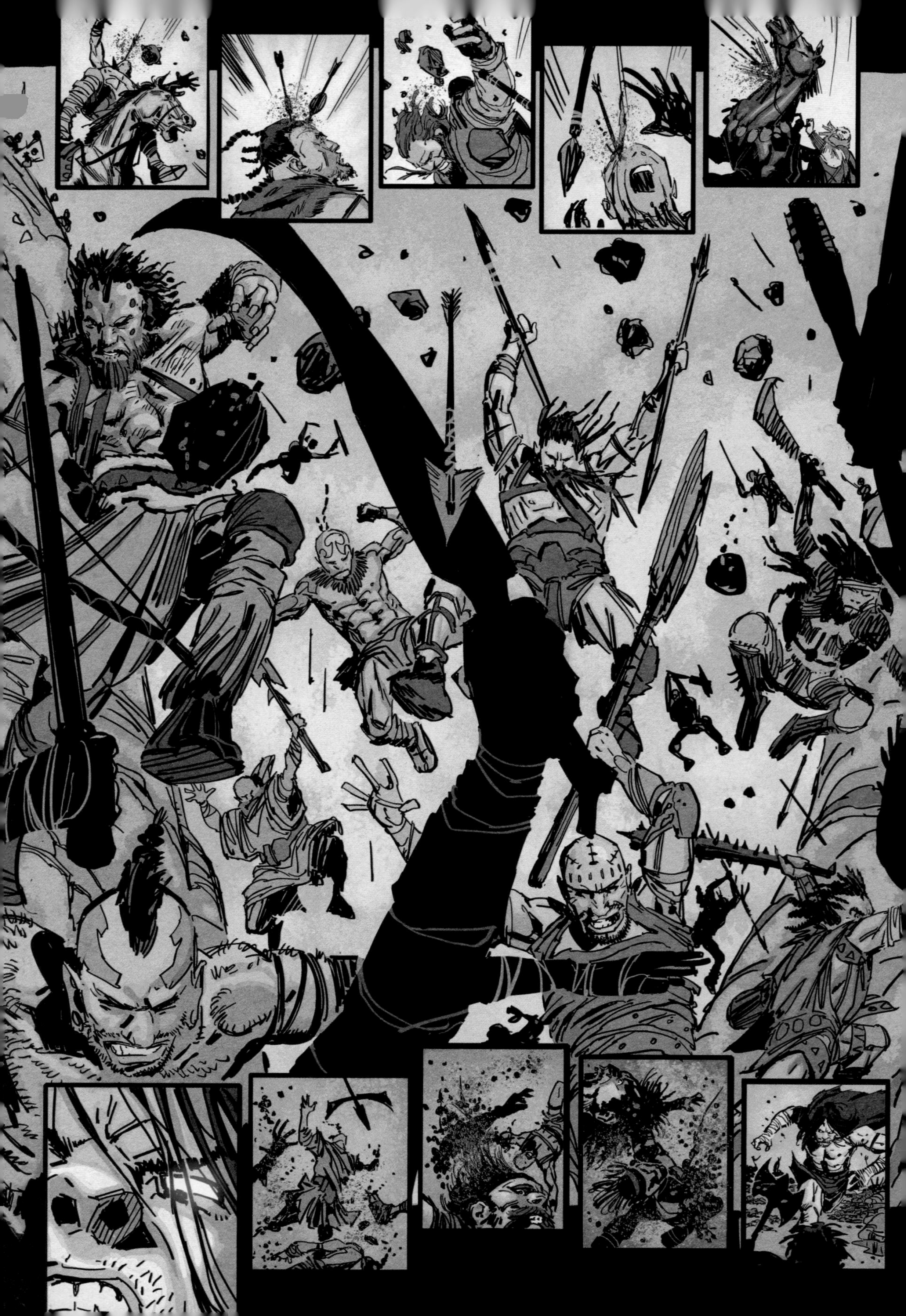

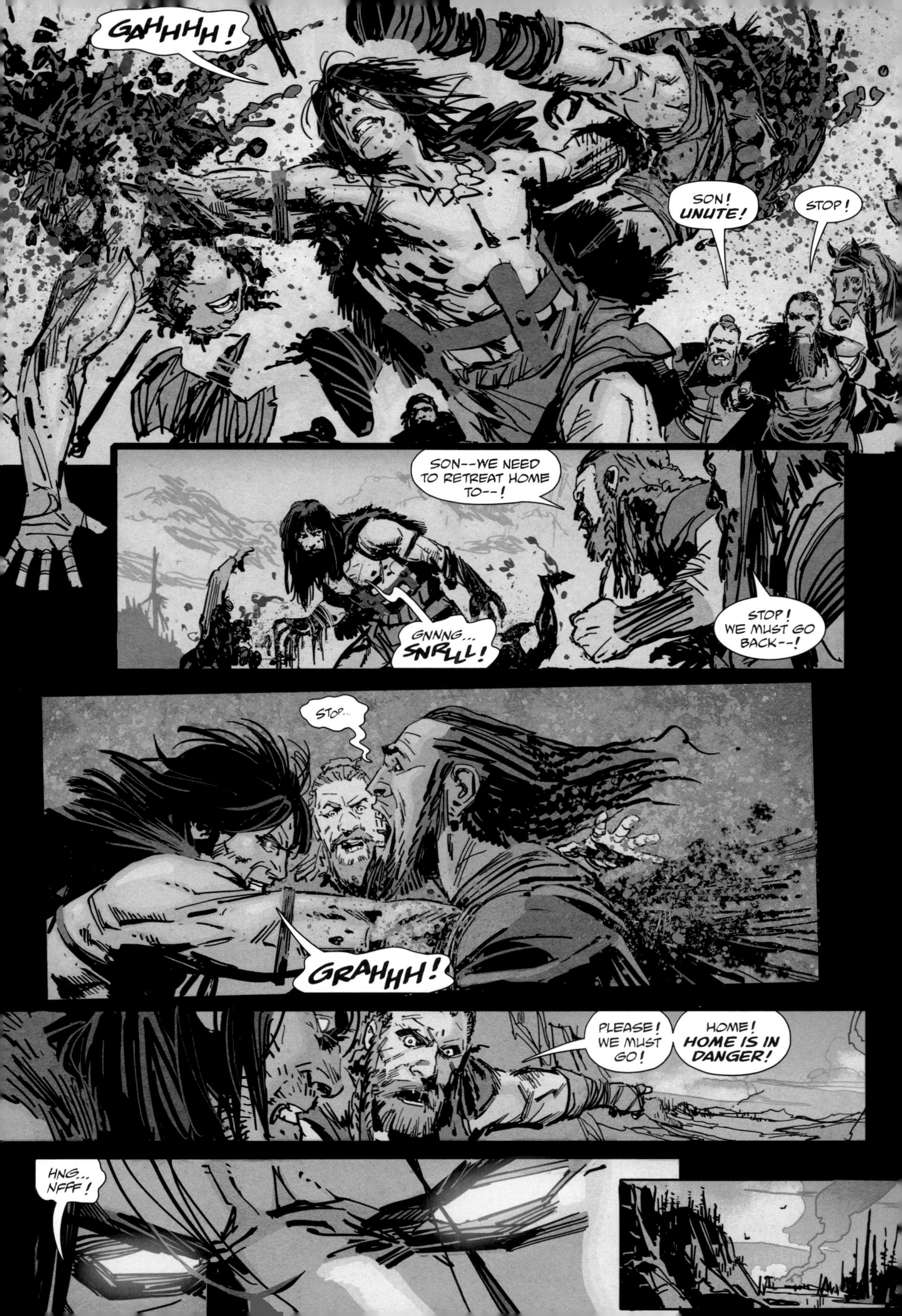
GAHHHH!
SON! UNUTE!
STOP!
SON--WE NEED TO RETREAT HOME TO--!
GNNNG... SNRLLL!
STOP! WE MUST GO BACK--!
STOP...
GRAHHH!
PLEASE! WE MUST GO!
HOME! HOME IS IN DANGER!
HNG... NFFF!

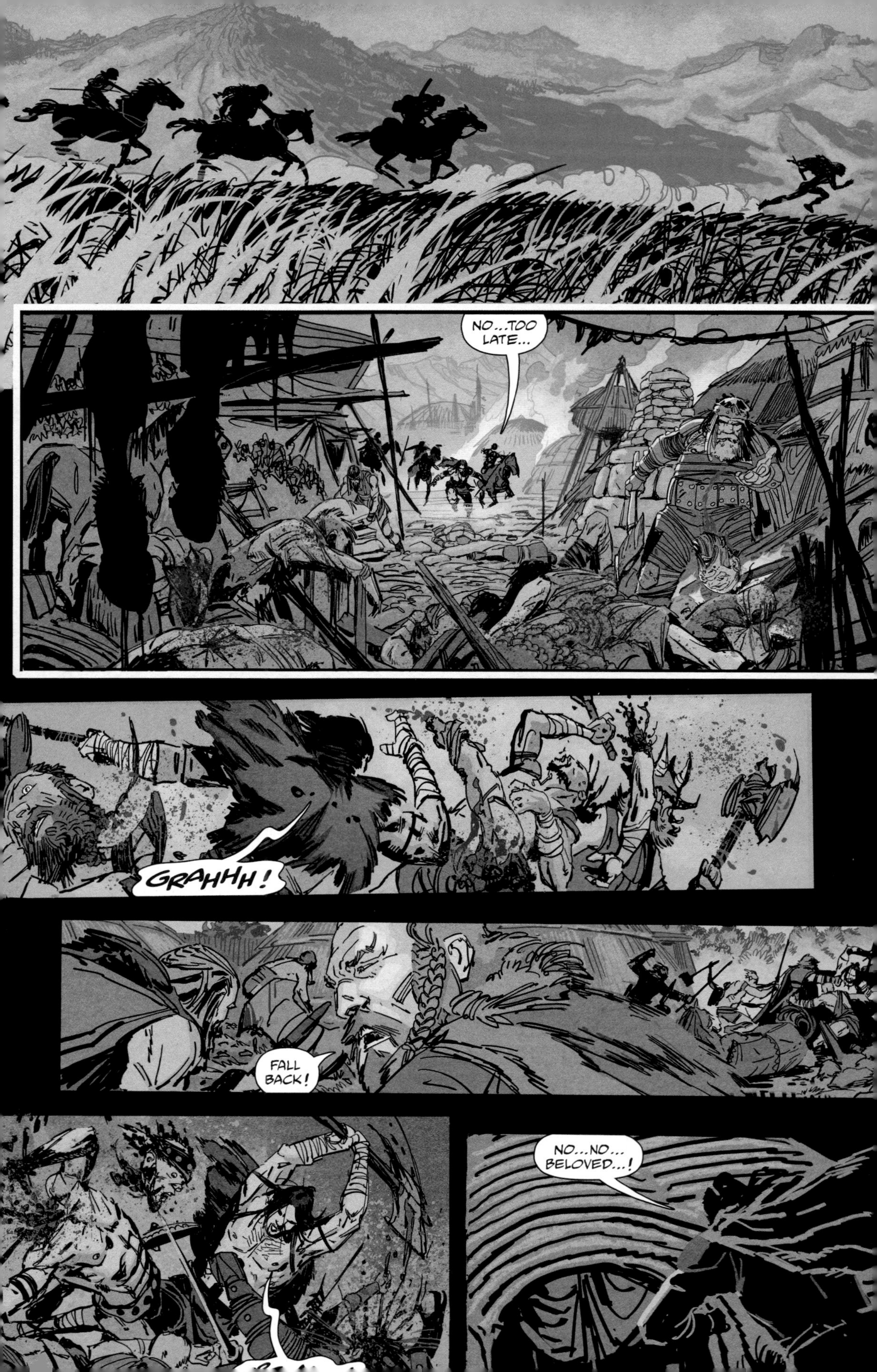
NO...TOO LATE...
GRAHHH!
FALL BACK!
NO...NO... BELOVED...!

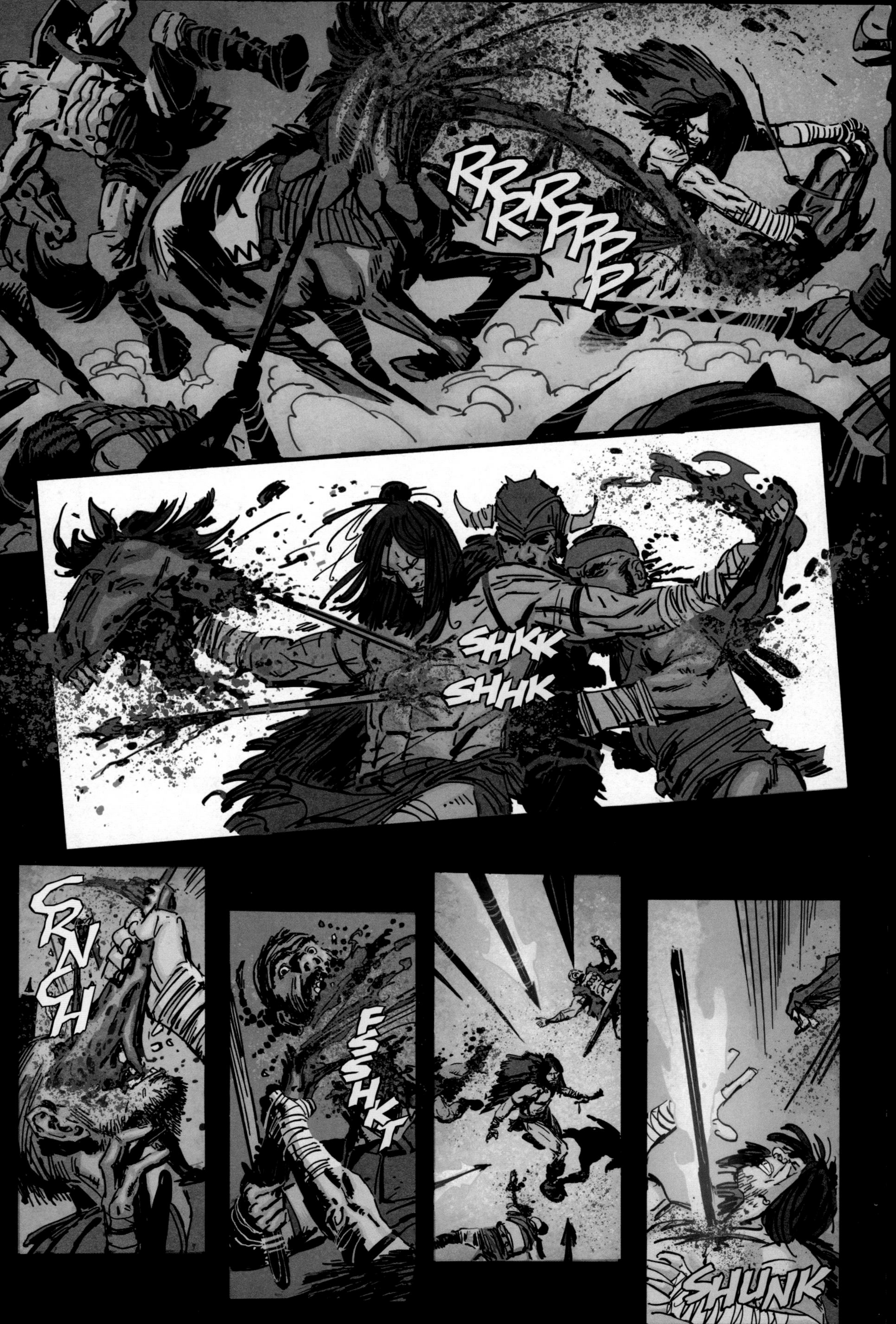
RRRRPPPP
SHKK
SHHK
CRNCH
FSSHKT
SHUNK

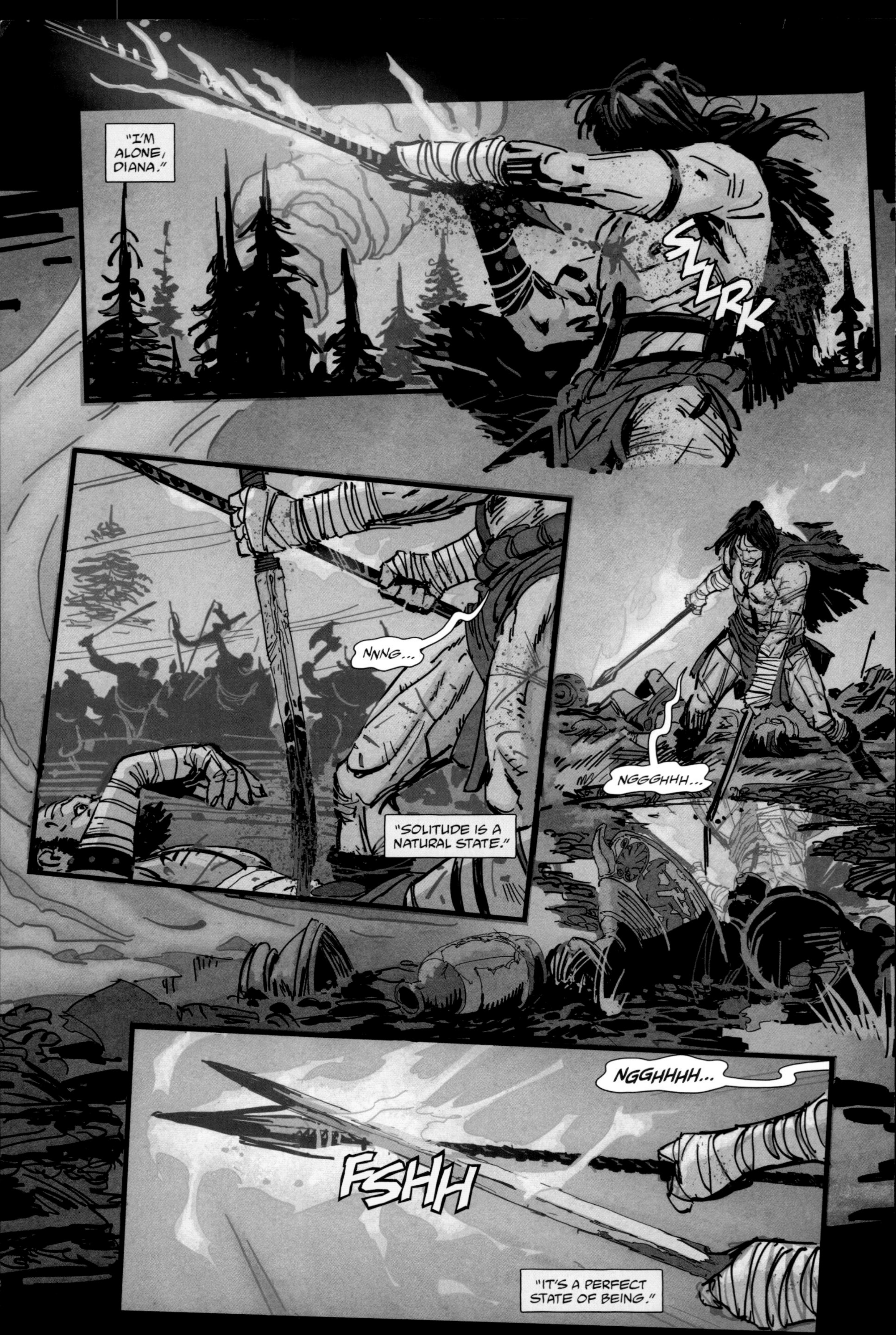
"I'M ALONE, DIANA."
SHRK
NNNG...
"SOLITUDE IS A NATURAL STATE."
NGGGHHH...
NGGHHHH...
FSHH
"IT'S A PERFECT STATE OF BEING."

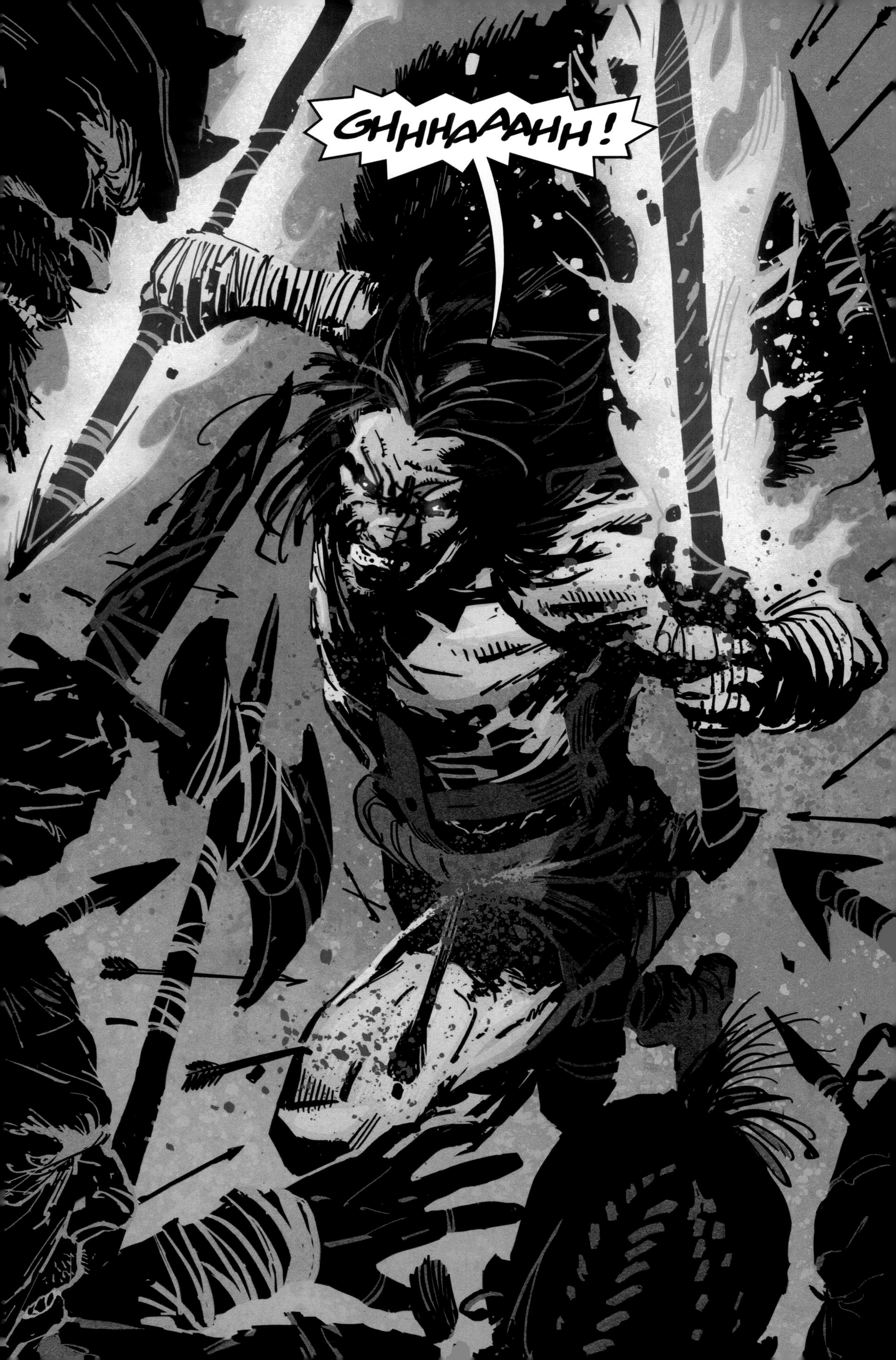
GHHHAAAHH!

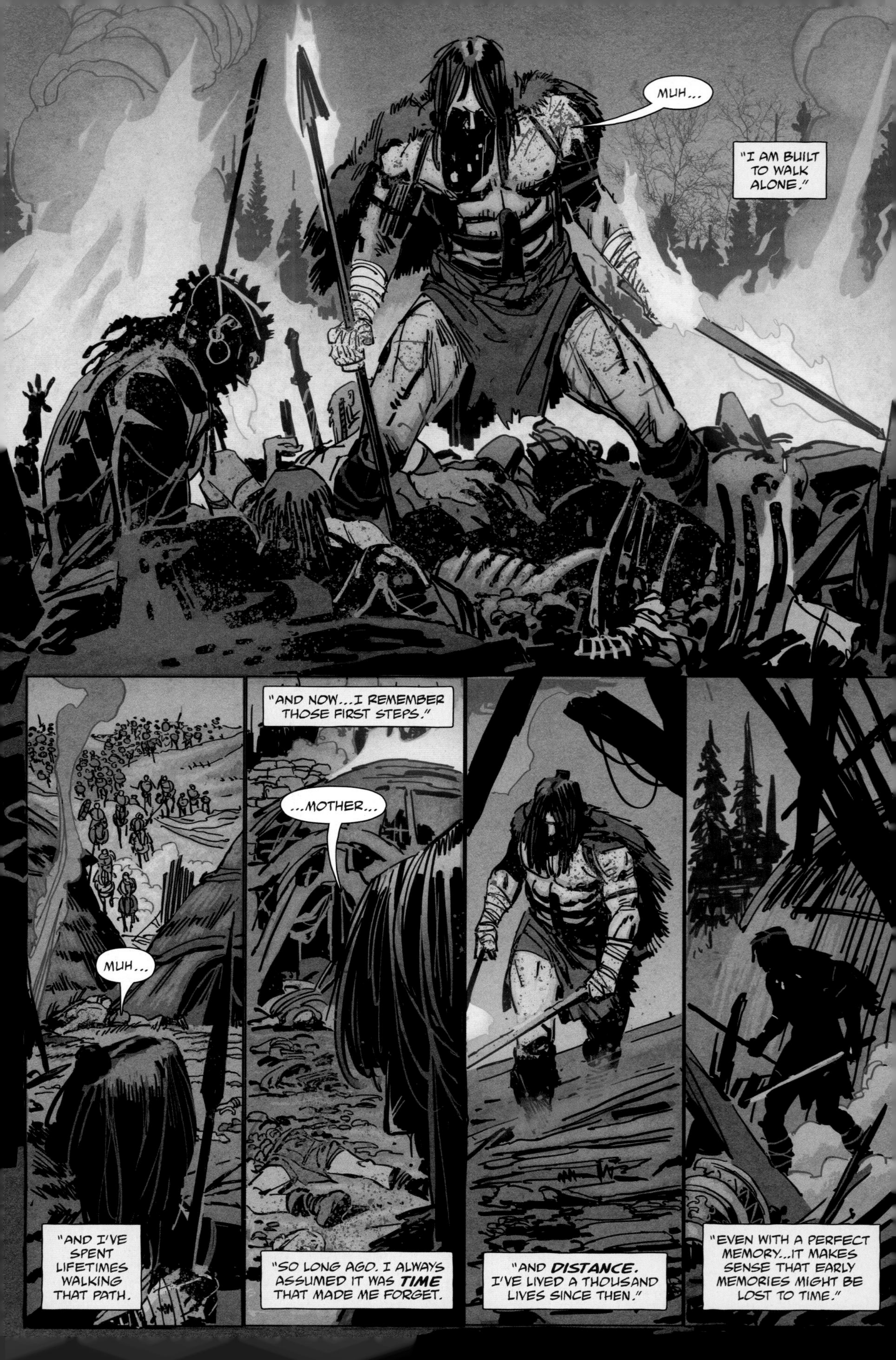
MUH...
"I AM BUILT TO WALK ALONE."
MUH...
"AND I'VE SPENT LIFETIMES WALKING THAT PATH.
"AND NOW...I REMEMBER THOSE FIRST STEPS."
...MOTHER...
"SO LONG AGO. I ALWAYS ASSUMED IT WAS TIME THAT MADE ME FORGET.
"AND DISTANCE. I'VE LIVED A THOUSAND LIVES SINCE THEN."
"EVEN WITH A PERFECT MEMORY...IT MAKES SENSE THAT EARLY MEMORIES MIGHT BE LOST TO TIME."

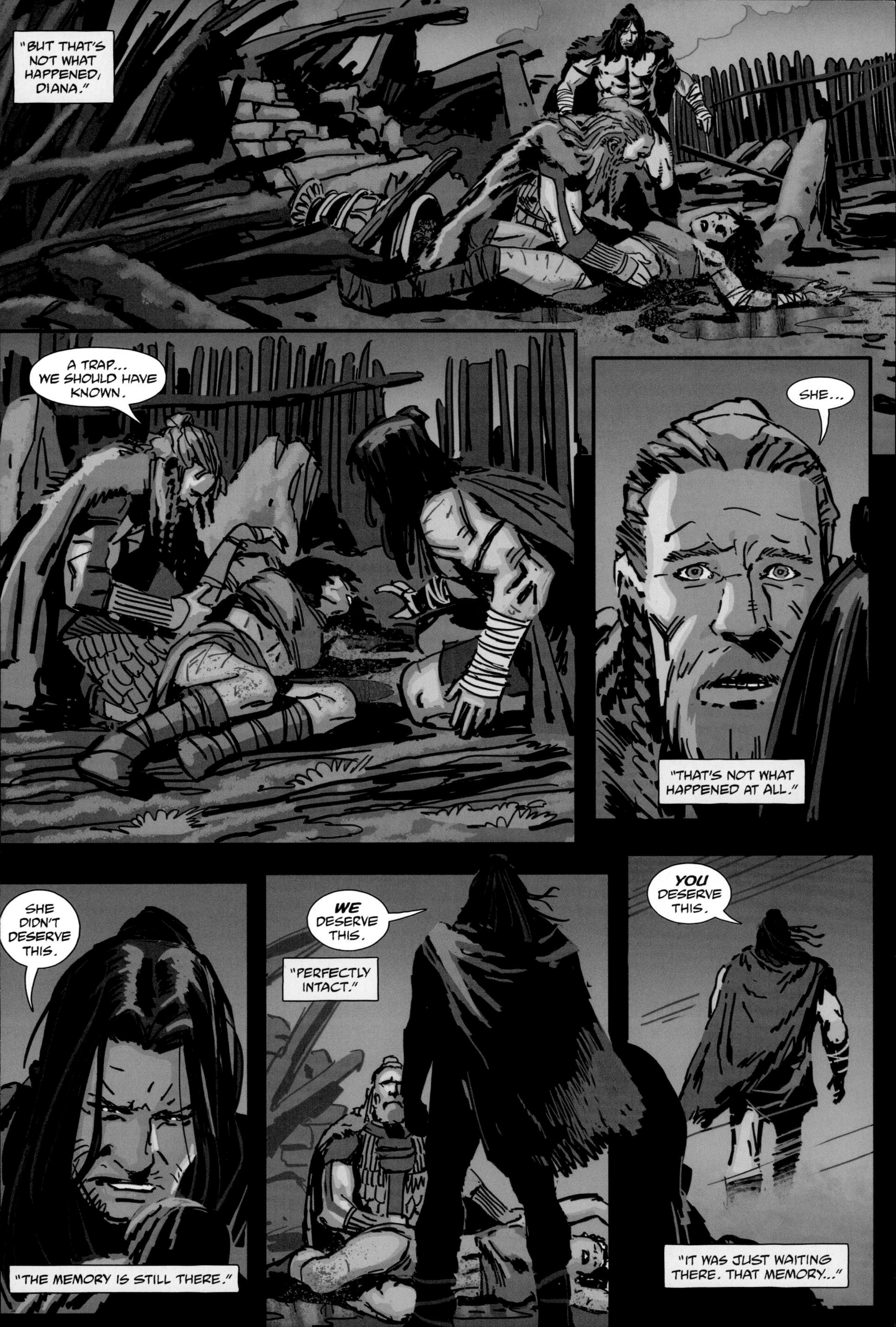
"BUT THAT'S NOT WHAT HAPPENED, DIANA."
A TRAP... WE SHOULD HAVE KNOWN.
SHE...
"THAT'S NOT WHAT HAPPENED AT ALL."
SHE DIDN'T DESERVE THIS.
"THE MEMORY IS STILL THERE."
WE DESERVE THIS.
"PERFECTLY INTACT."
YOU DESERVE THIS.
"IT WAS JUST WAITING THERE. THAT MEMORY..."

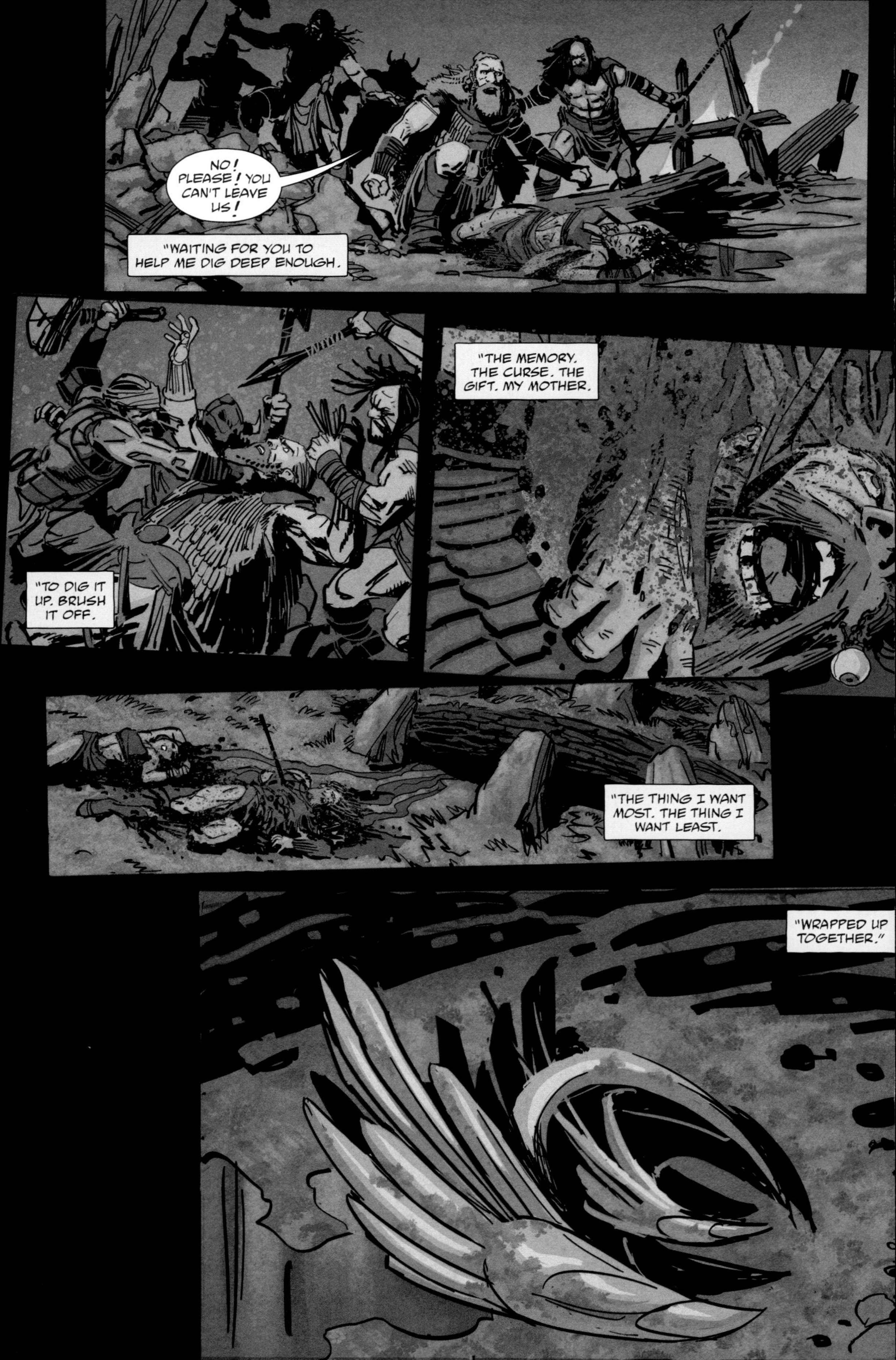
NO! PLEASE! YOU CAN'T LEAVE US!
"WAITING FOR YOU TO HELP ME DIG DEEP ENOUGH.
"TO DIG IT UP. BRUSH IT OFF.
"THE MEMORY. THE CURSE. THE GIFT. MY MOTHER.
"THE THING I WANT MOST. THE THING I WANT LEAST.
"WRAPPED UP TOGETHER."

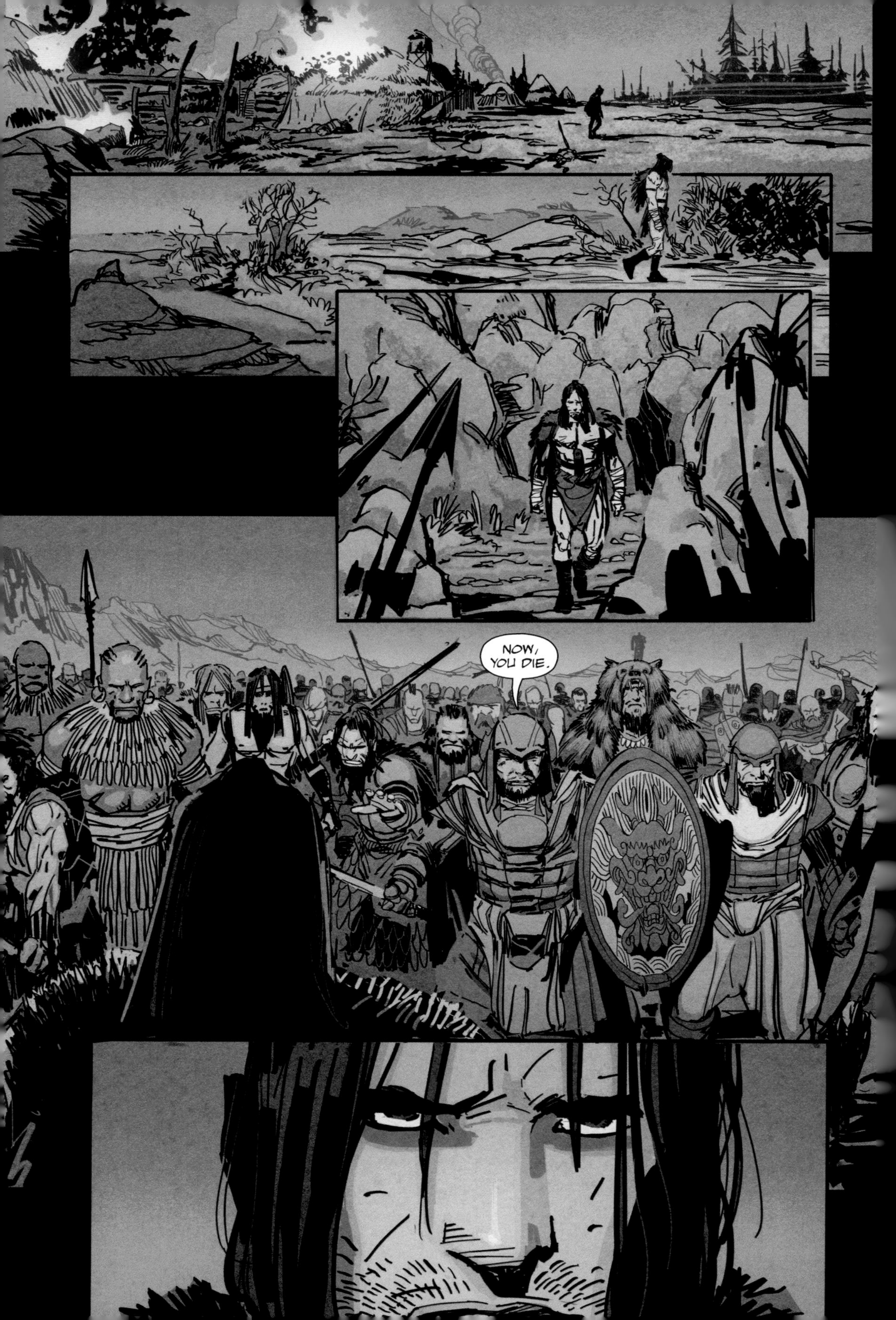
NOW, YOU DIE.

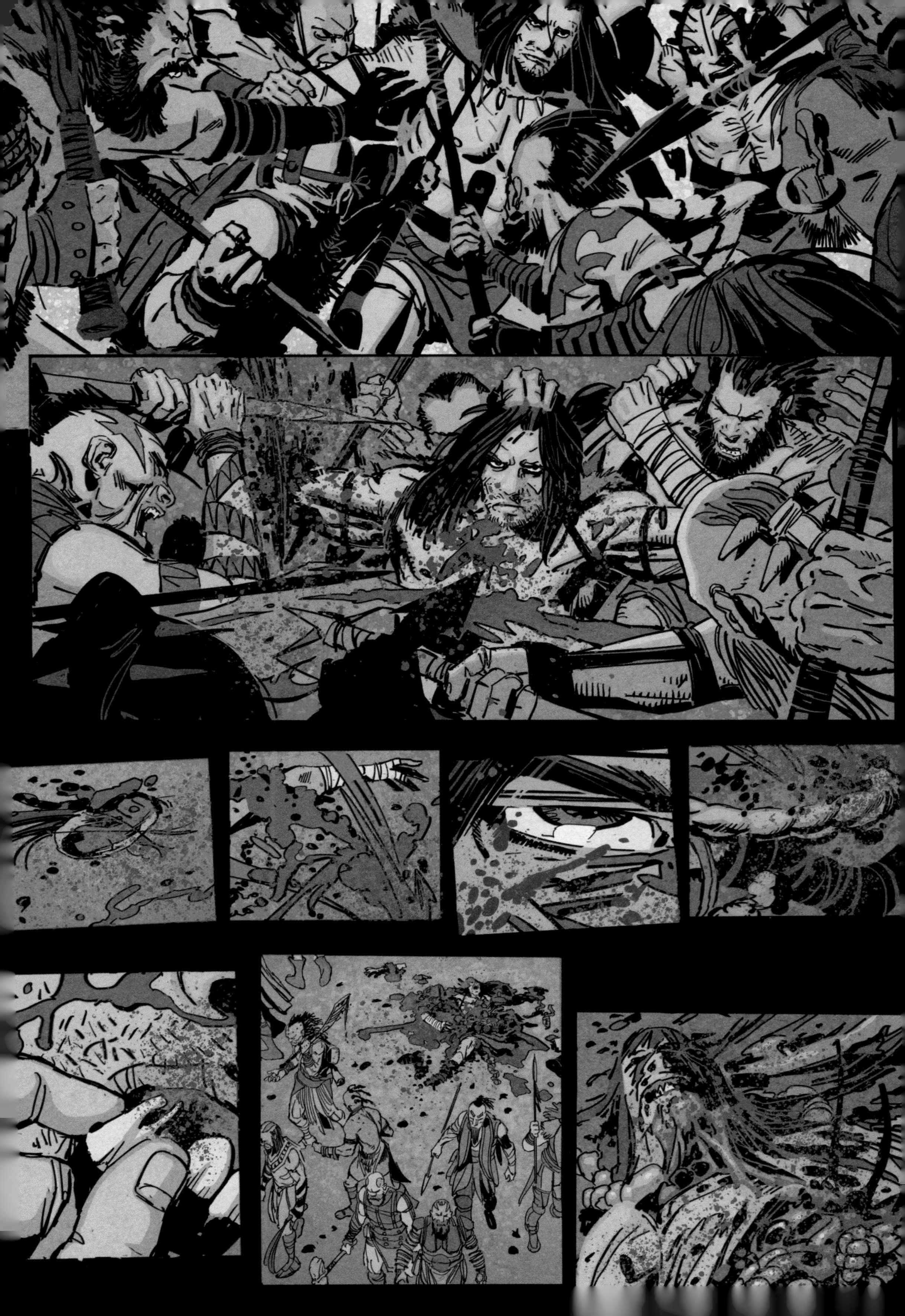

"YOU REMEMBER... DYING?"

"I REMEMBER EVERYTHING. NOW."

"YOU'RE SURE...?"

"I'M SURE. THOSE EARLIEST DAYS.

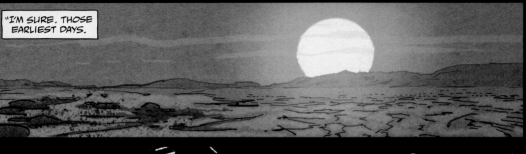

"MY EARLIE
LESSONS

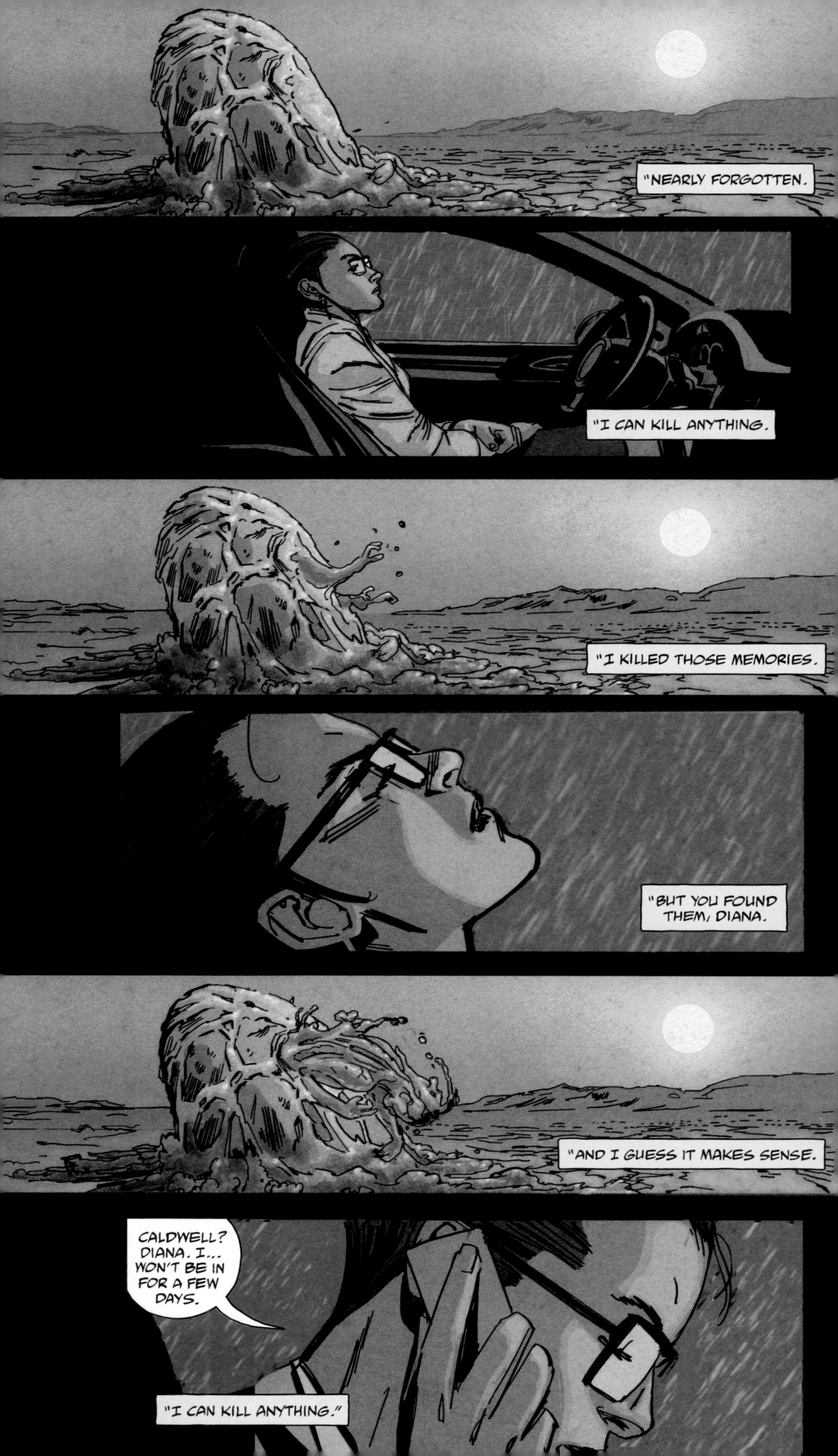
"NEARLY FORGOTTEN.
"I CAN KILL ANYTHING.
"I KILLED THOSE MEMORIES.
"BUT YOU FOUND THEM, DIANA.
"AND I GUESS IT MAKES SENSE.
CALDWELL? DIANA. I... WON'T BE IN FOR A FEW DAYS.
"I CAN KILL ANYTHING."

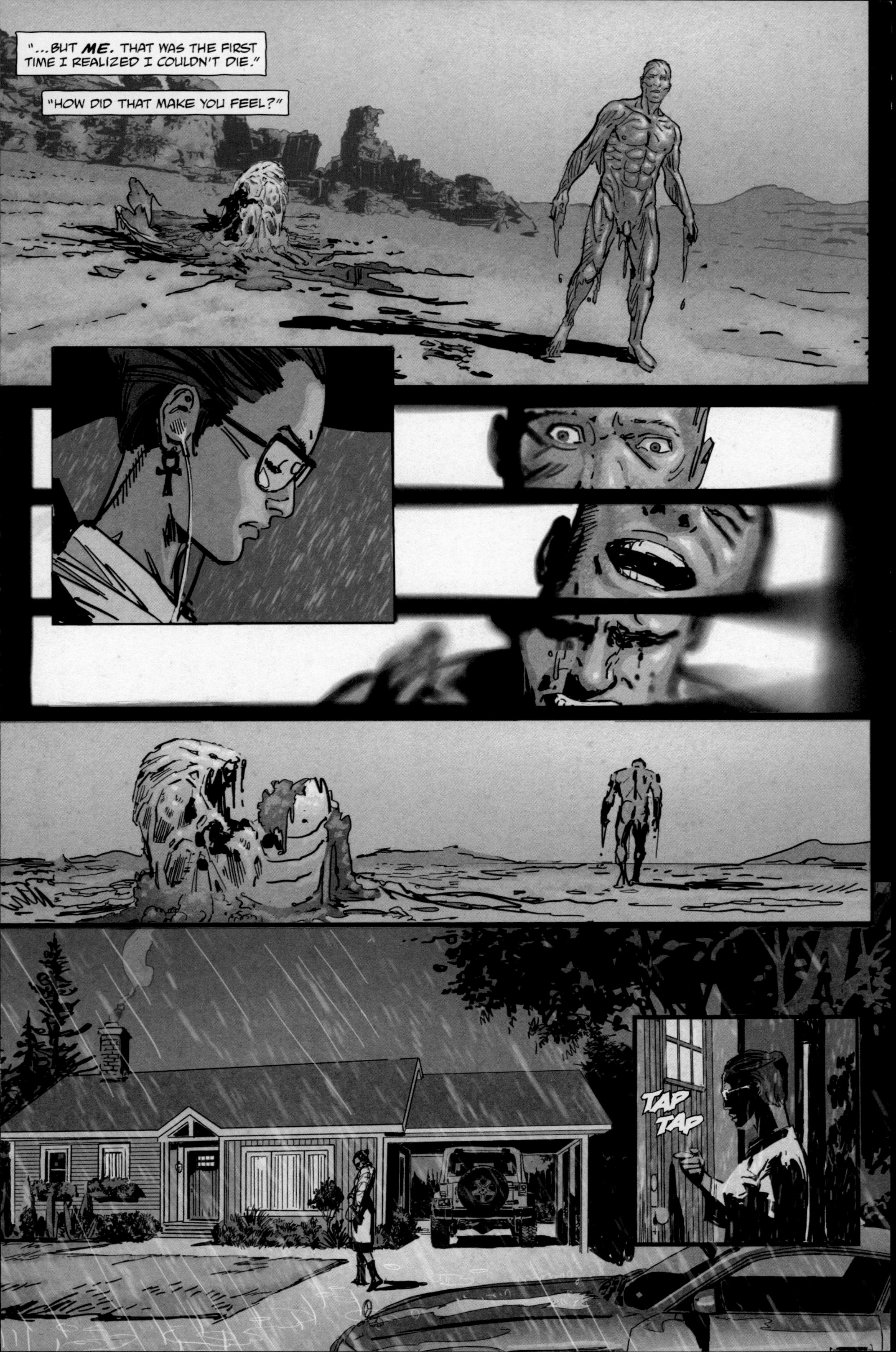
"...BUT ME. THAT WAS THE FIRST TIME I REALIZED I COULDN'T DIE."
"HOW DID THAT MAKE YOU FEEL?"
TAP
TAP

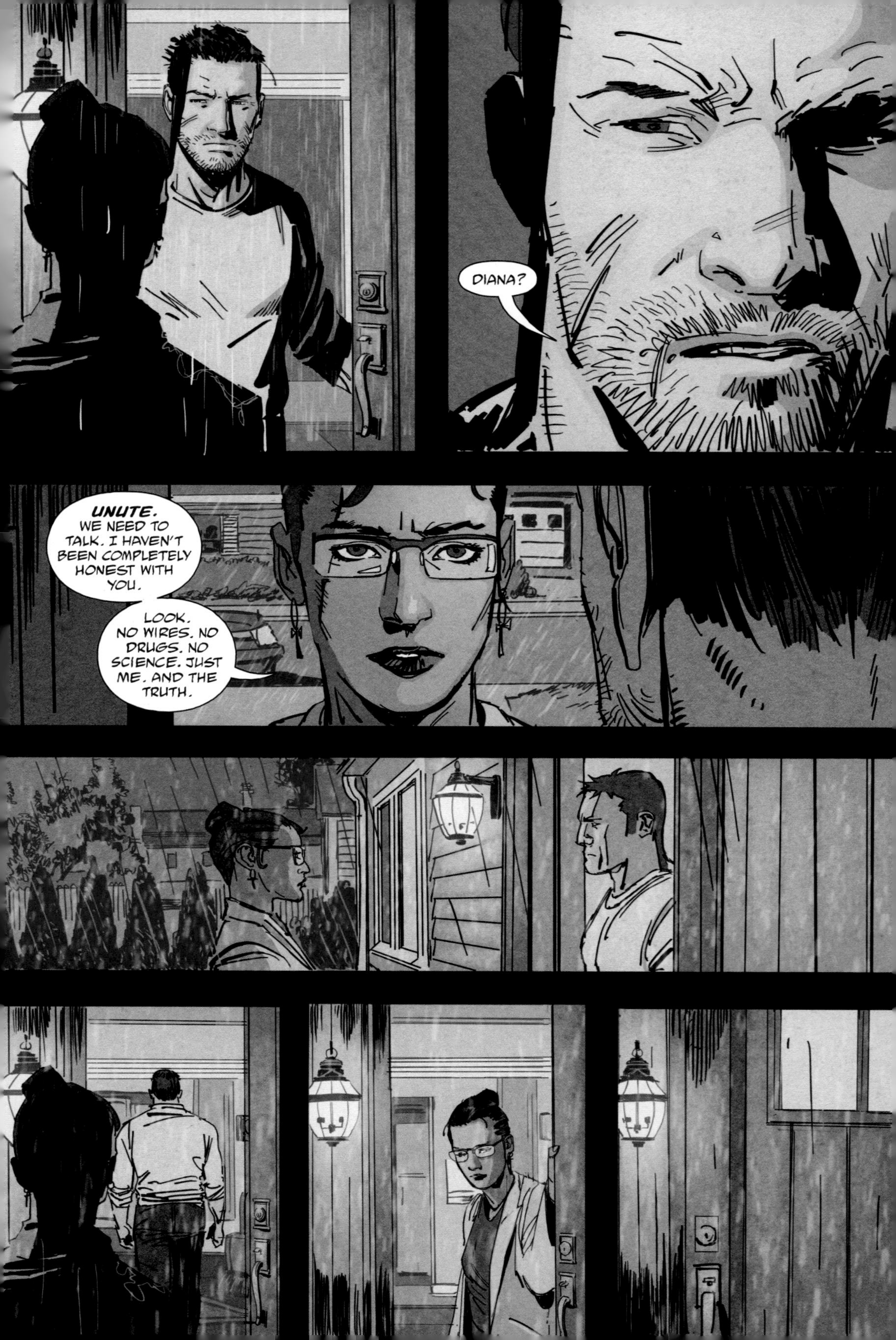
DIANA?
UNUTE. WE NEED TO TALK. I HAVEN'T BEEN COMPLETELY HONEST WITH YOU.
LOOK. NO WIRES. NO DRUGS. NO SCIENCE. JUST ME. AND THE TRUTH.

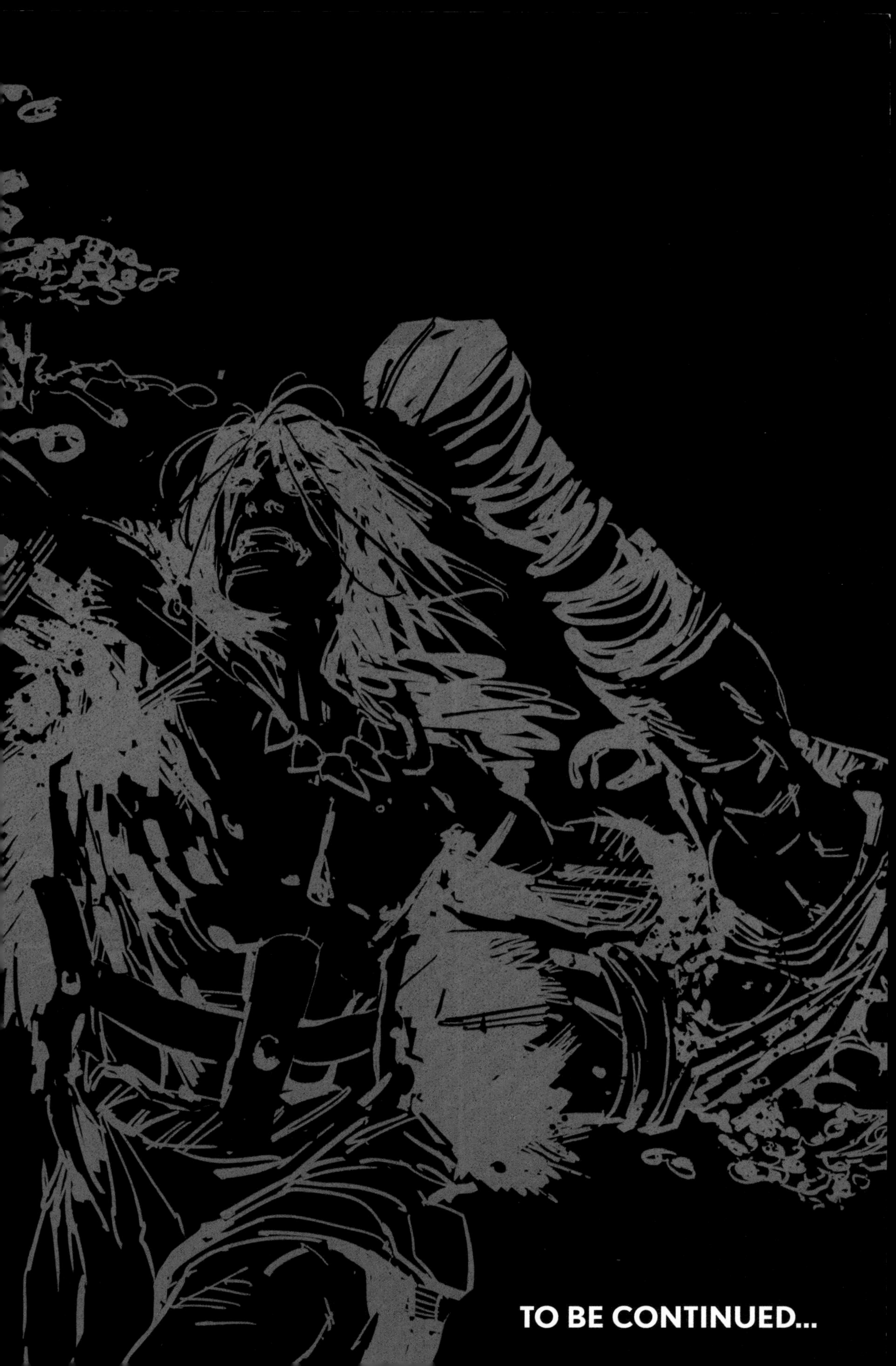
TO BE CONTINUED...

COVER GALLERY

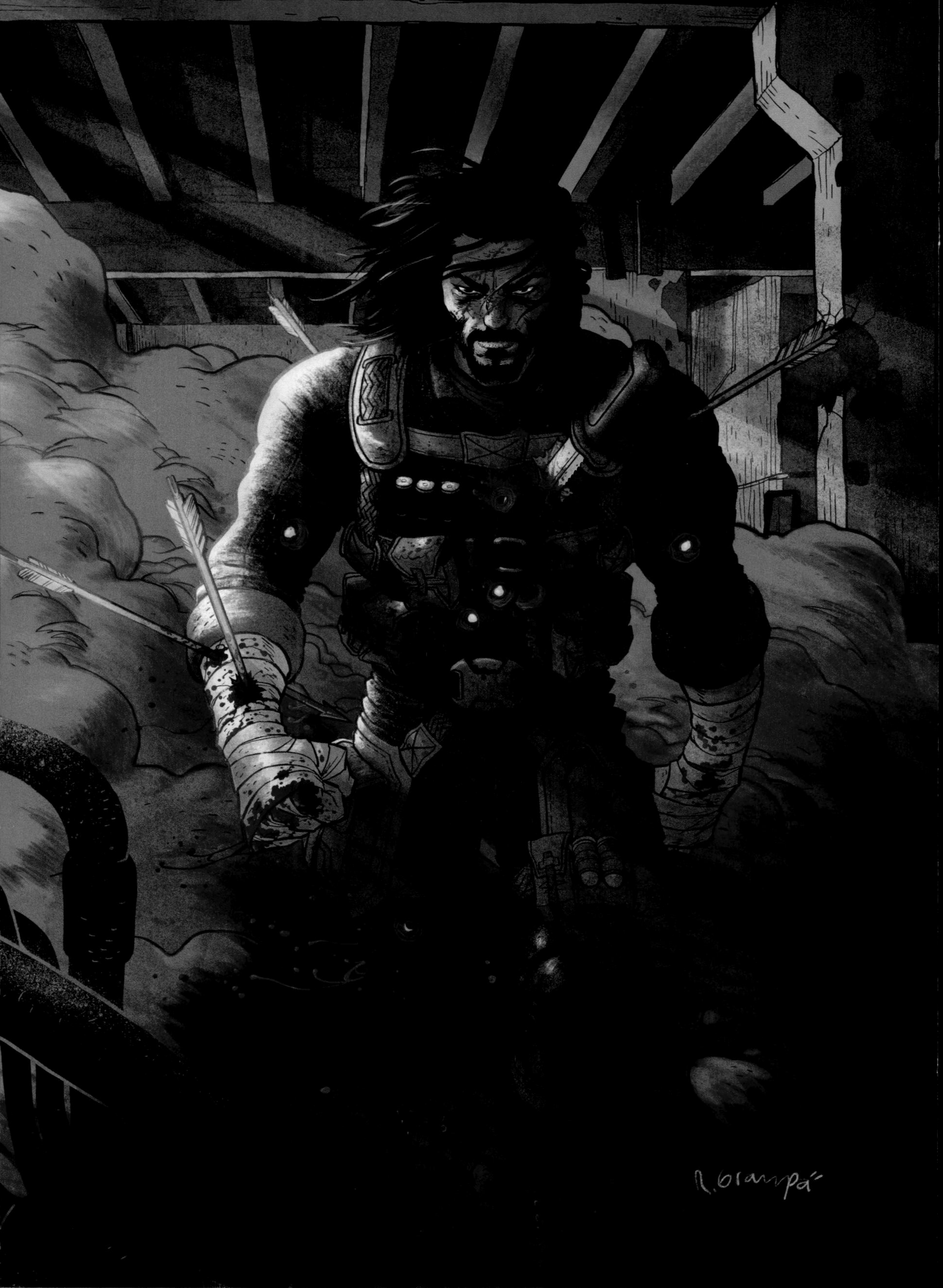

Issue #1 Cover by **RAFAEL GRAMPÁ**

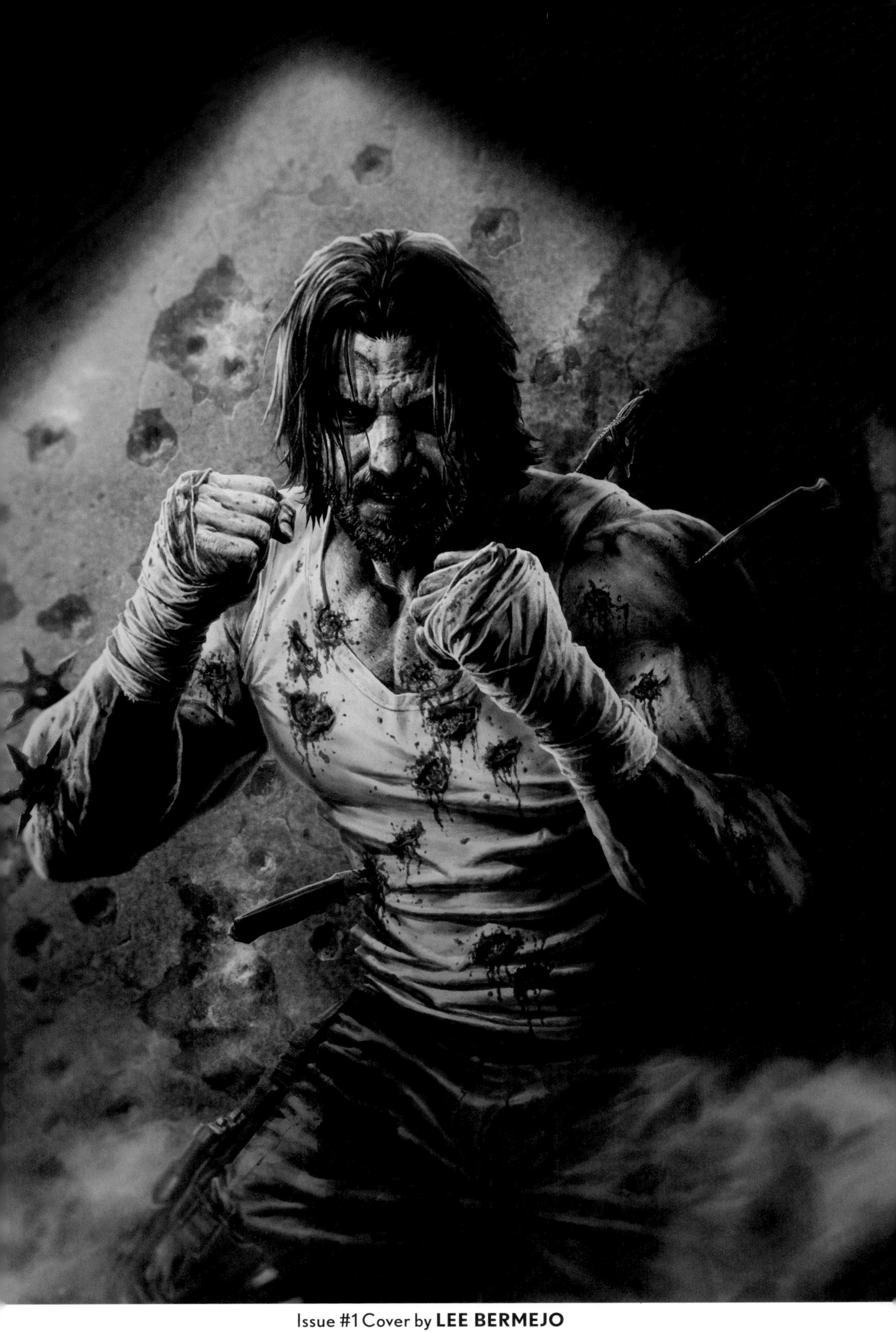

Issue #1 Cover by **LEE BERMEJO**

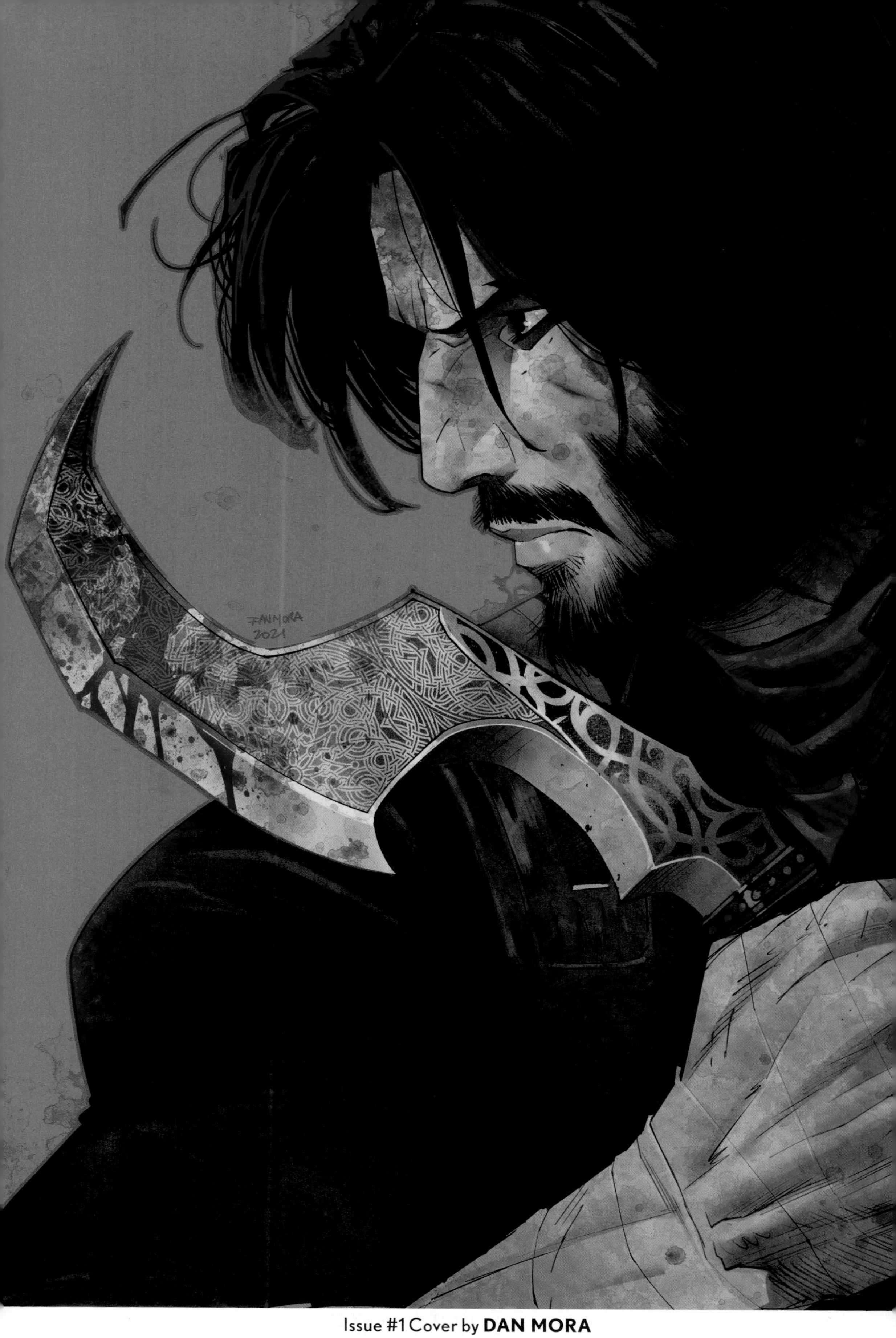
DANMORA
2021

Issue #1 Cover by **DAN MORA**

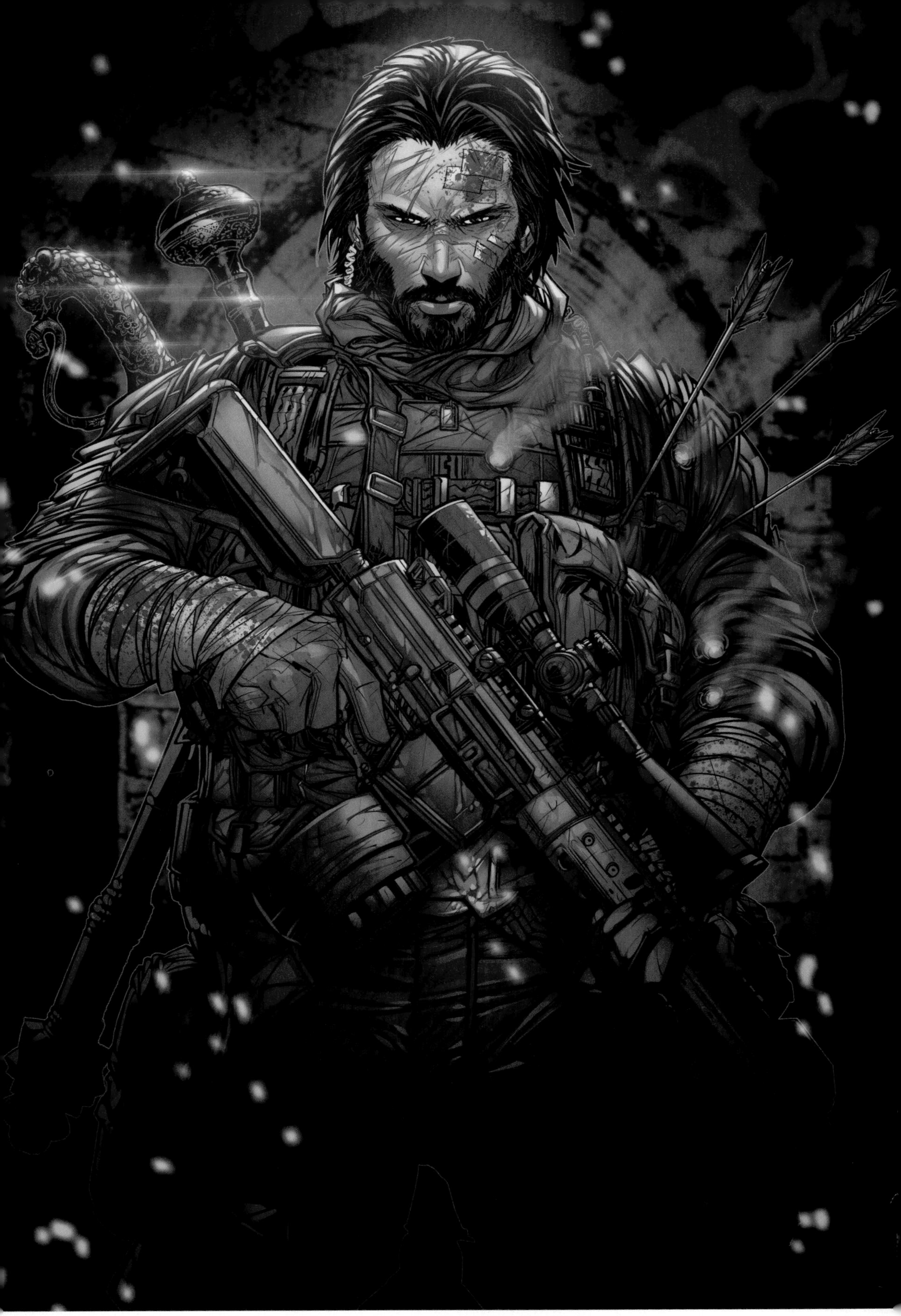

Issue #1 Cover by **JONBOY MEYERS**

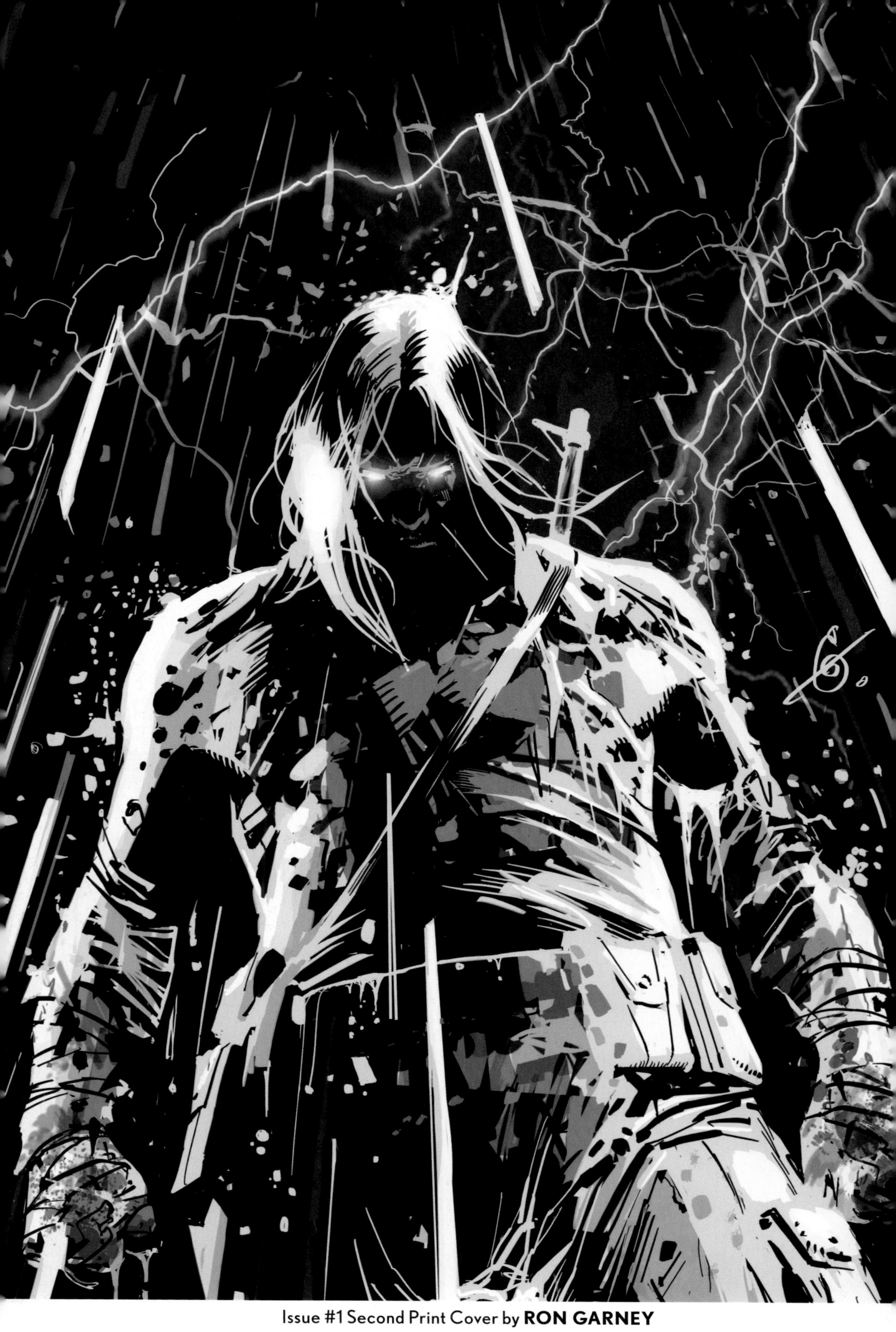

Issue #1 Second Print Cover by **RON GARNEY**

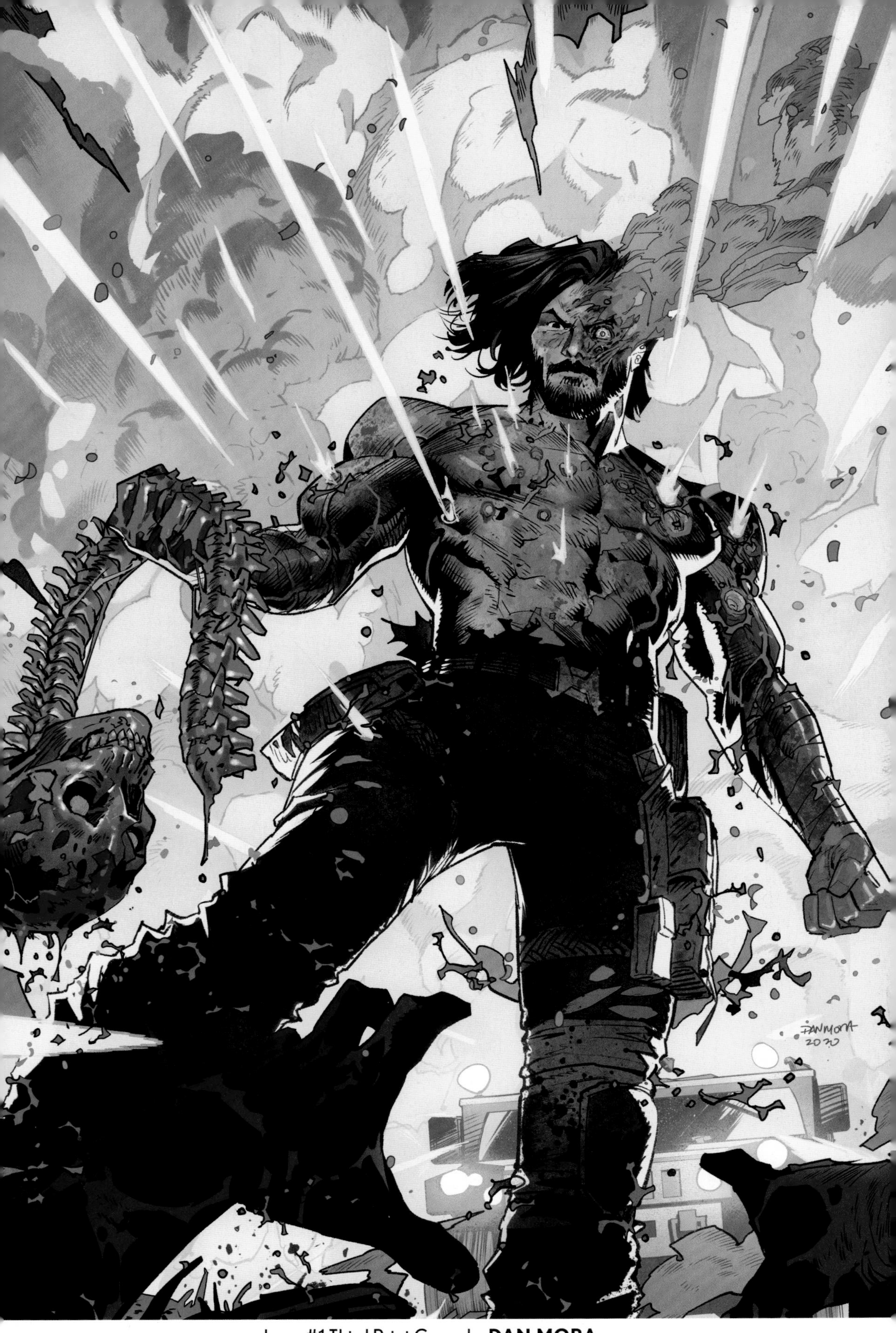
DAN MORA
2020

Issue #1 Third Print Cover by **DAN MORA**

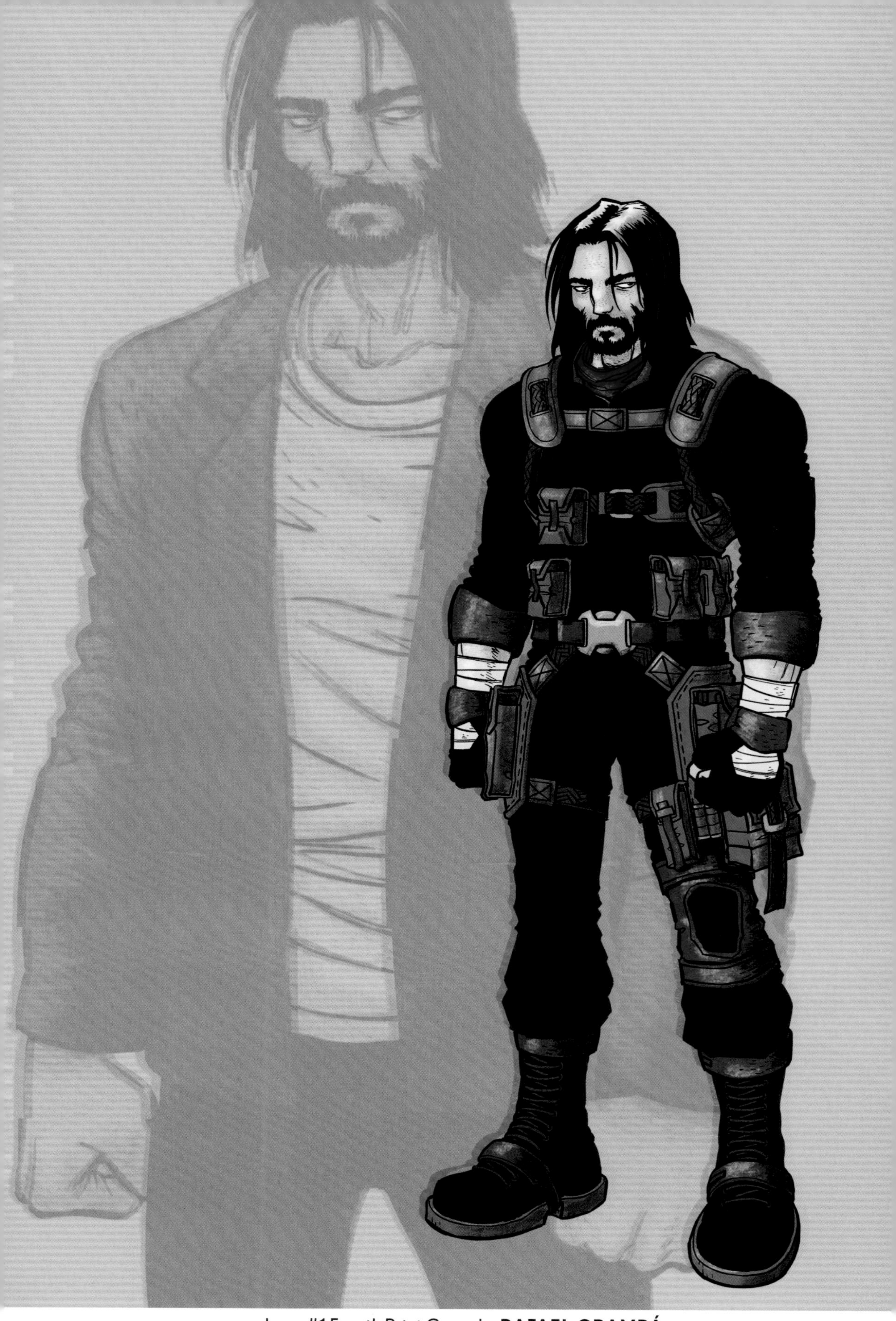

Issue #1 Fourth Print Cover by **RAFAEL GRAMPÁ**

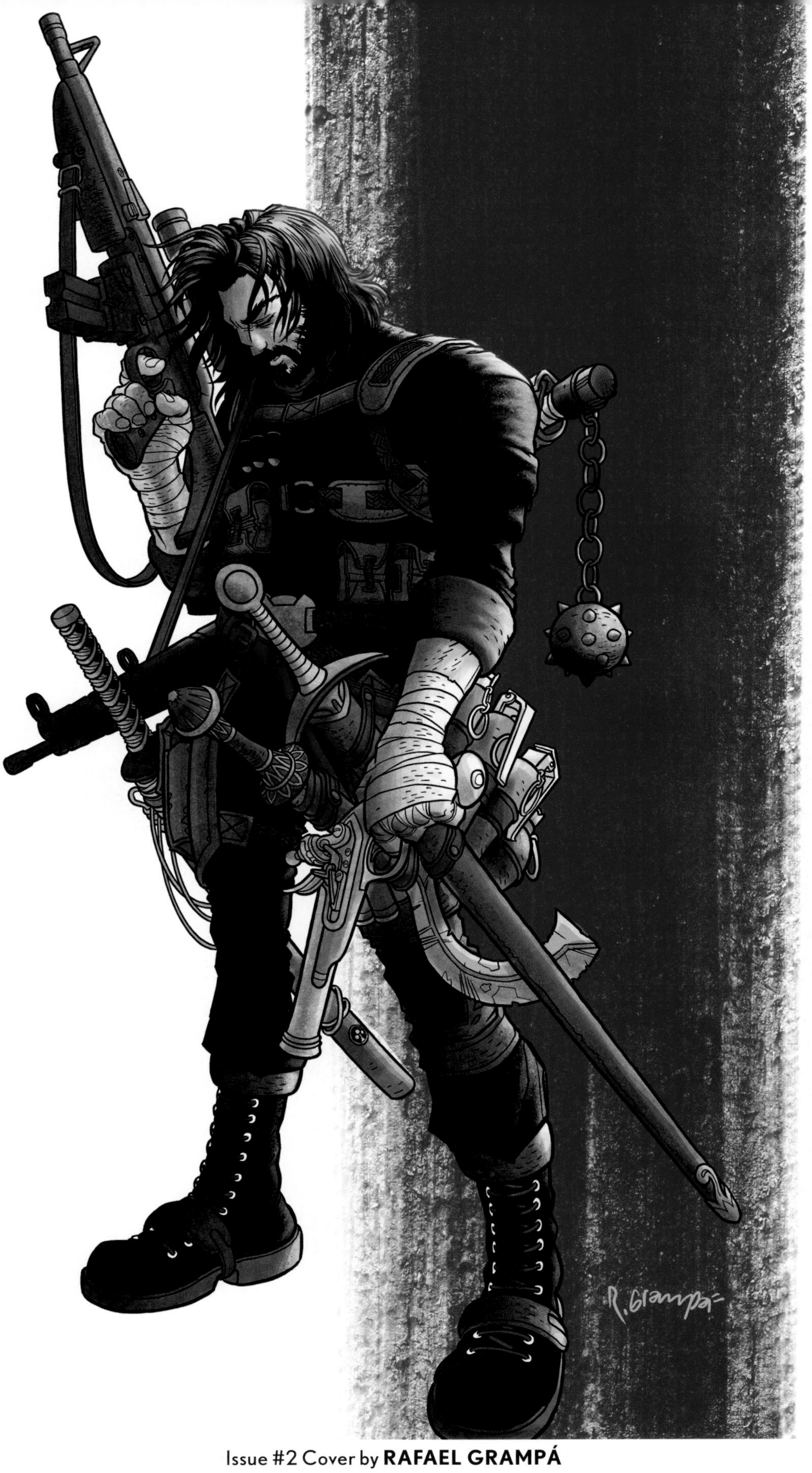
R. Grampá

Issue #2 Cover by **RAFAEL GRAMPÁ**

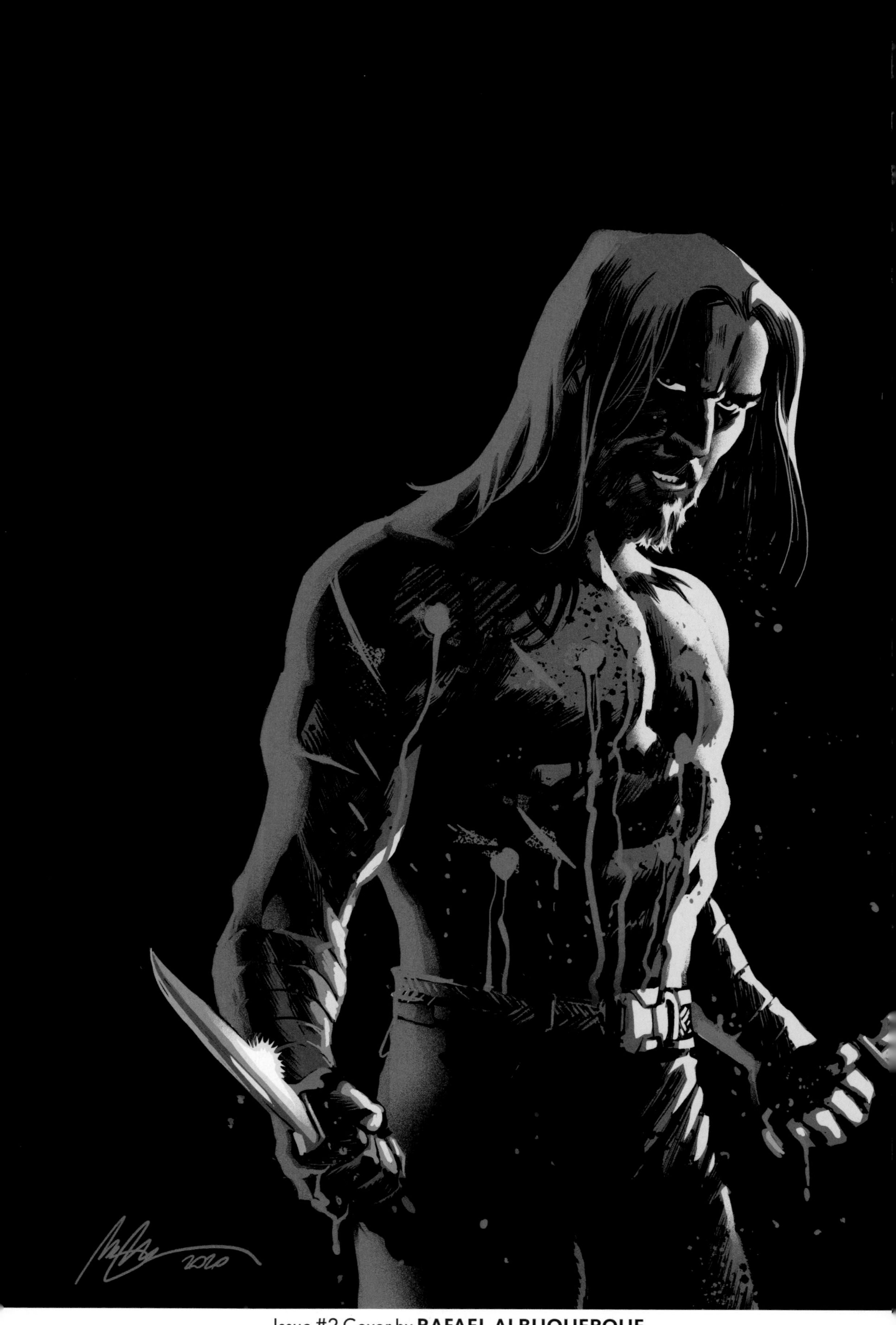

Issue #2 Cover by **RAFAEL ALBUQUERQUE**

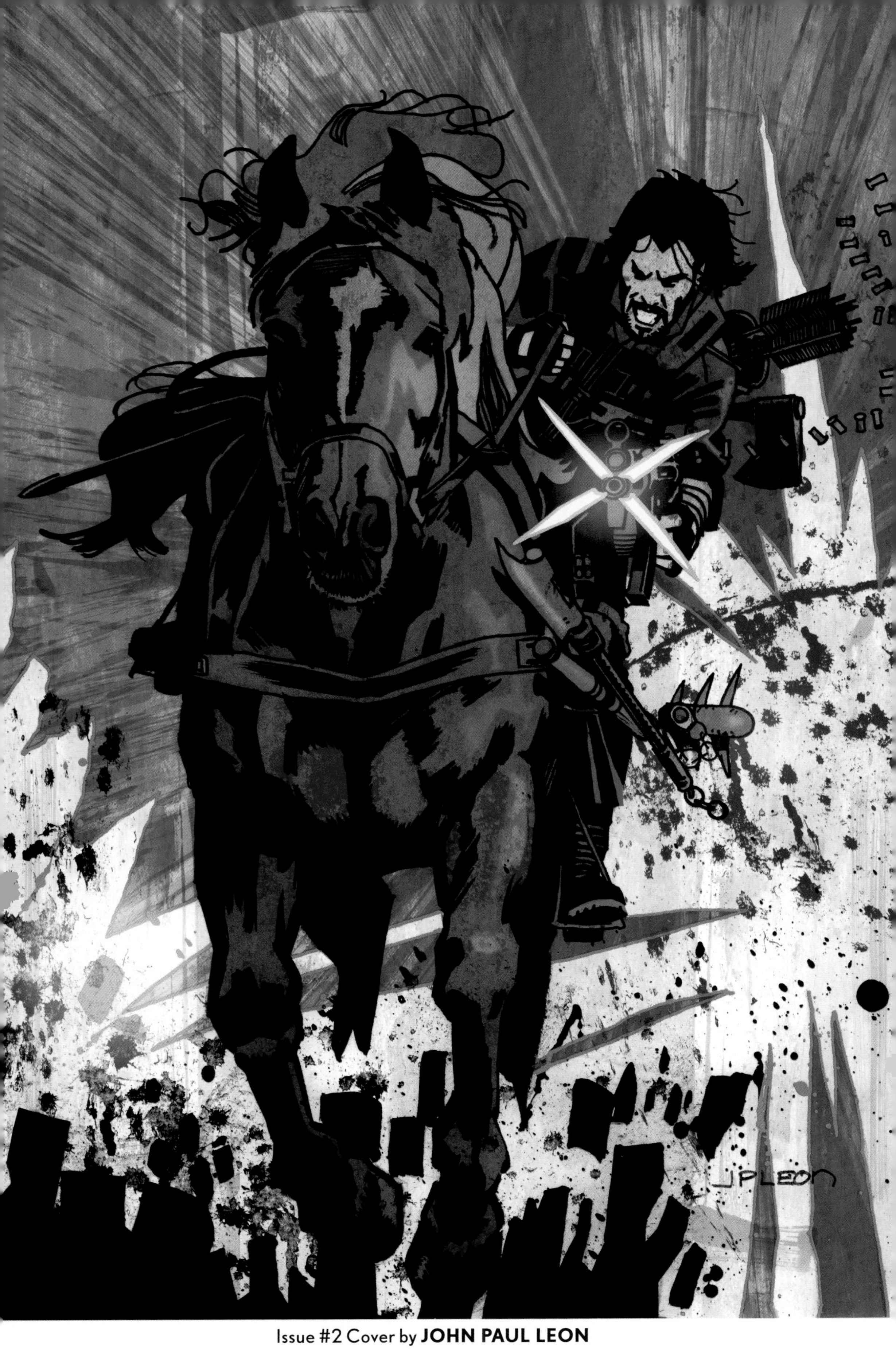
JPLEON
Issue #2 Cover by **JOHN PAUL LEON**

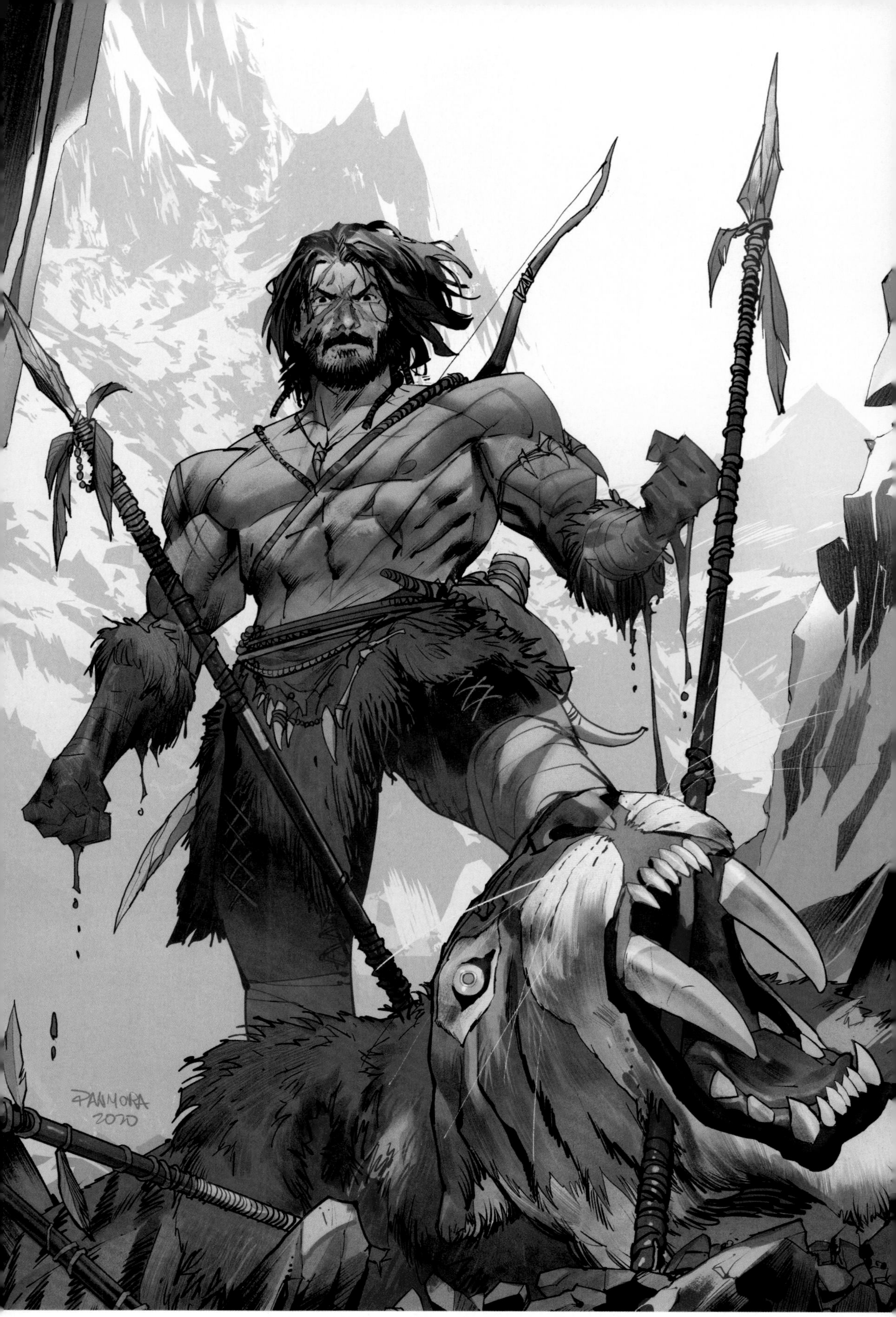
DAN MORA
2020

Issue #2 Second Print Cover by **DAN MORA**

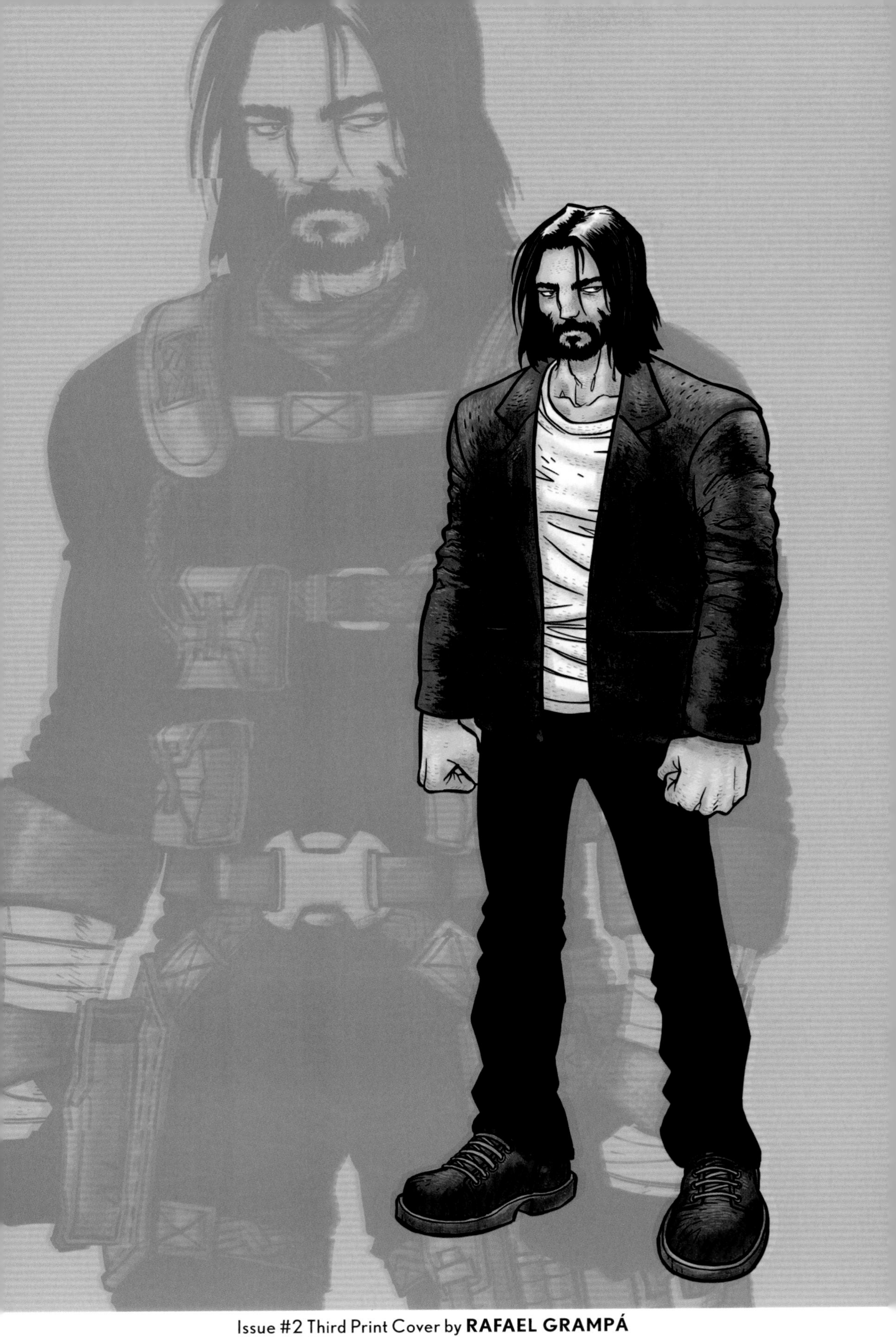
Issue #2 Third Print Cover by **RAFAEL GRAMPÁ**

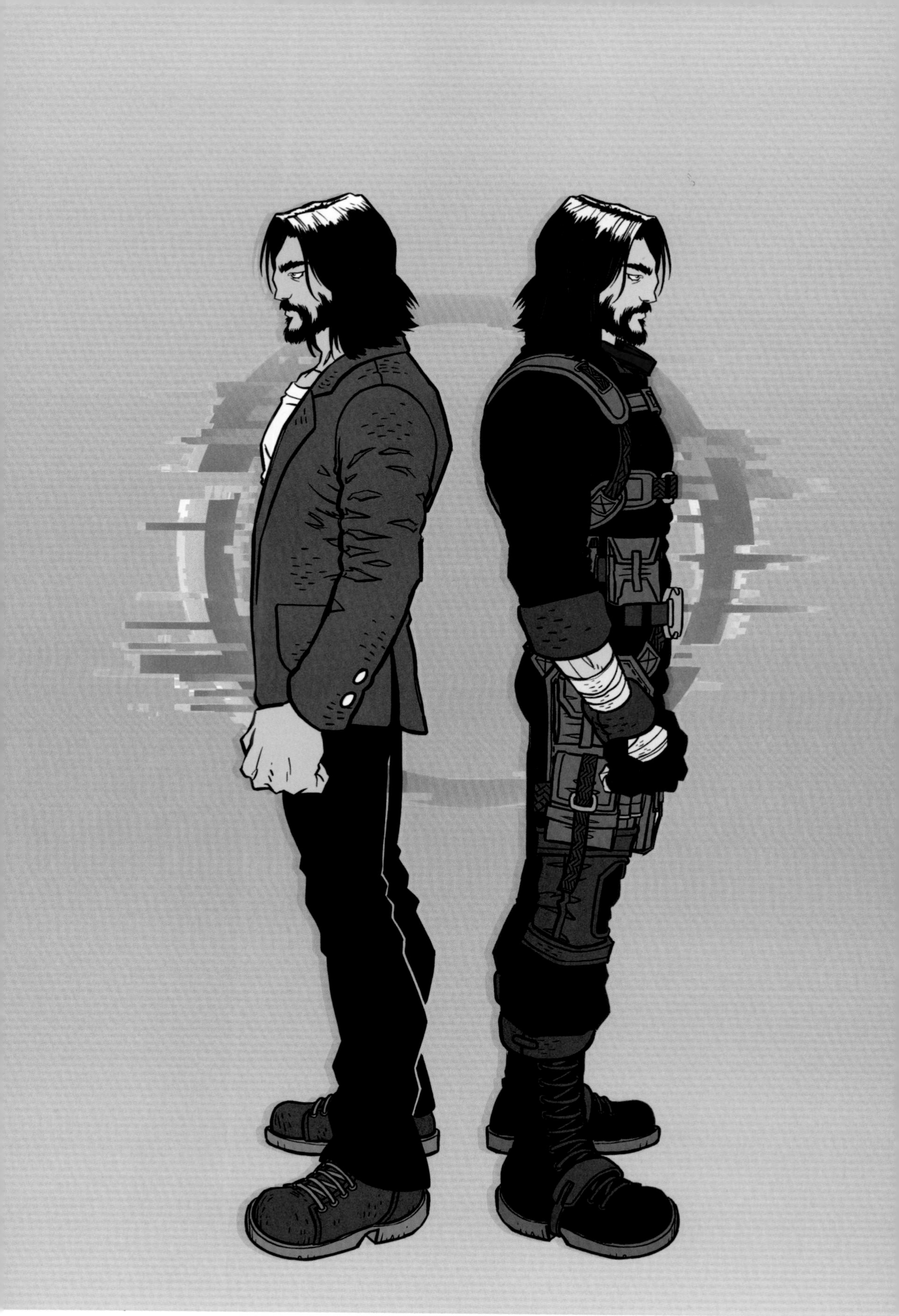

Issue #3 Cover by **RAFAEL GRAMPÁ**

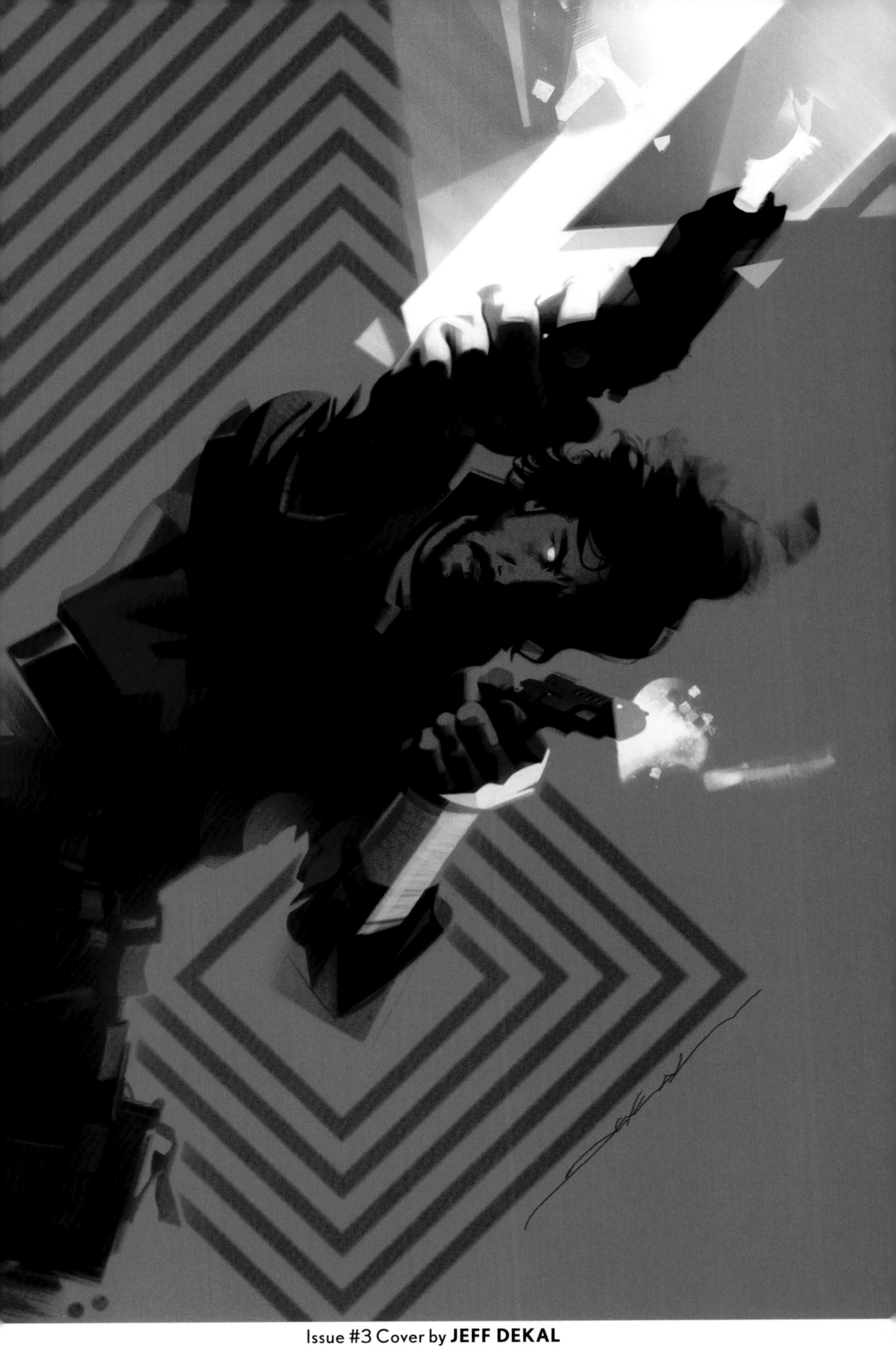

Issue #3 Cover by **JEFF DEKAL**

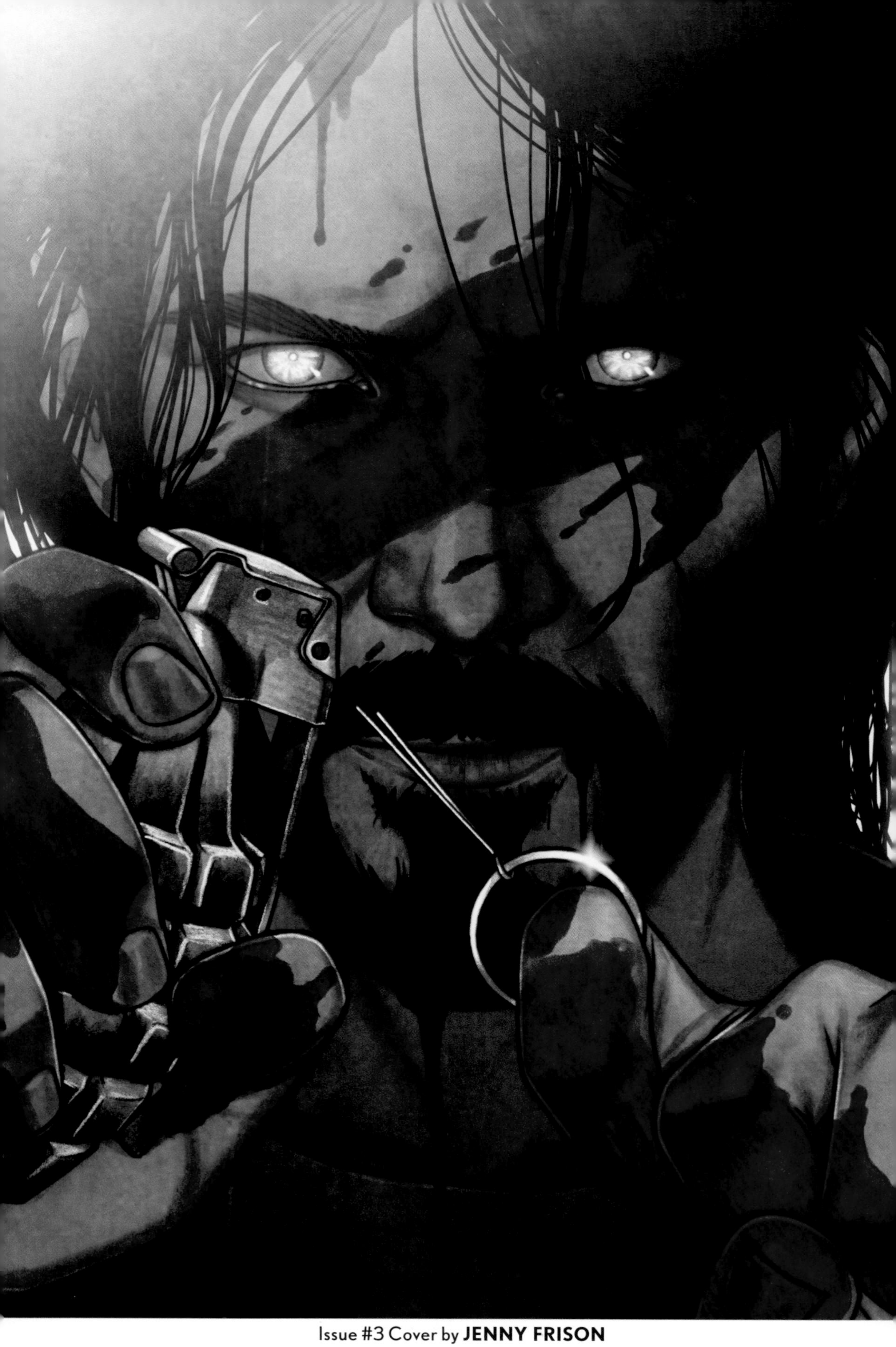

Issue #3 Cover by **JENNY FRISON**

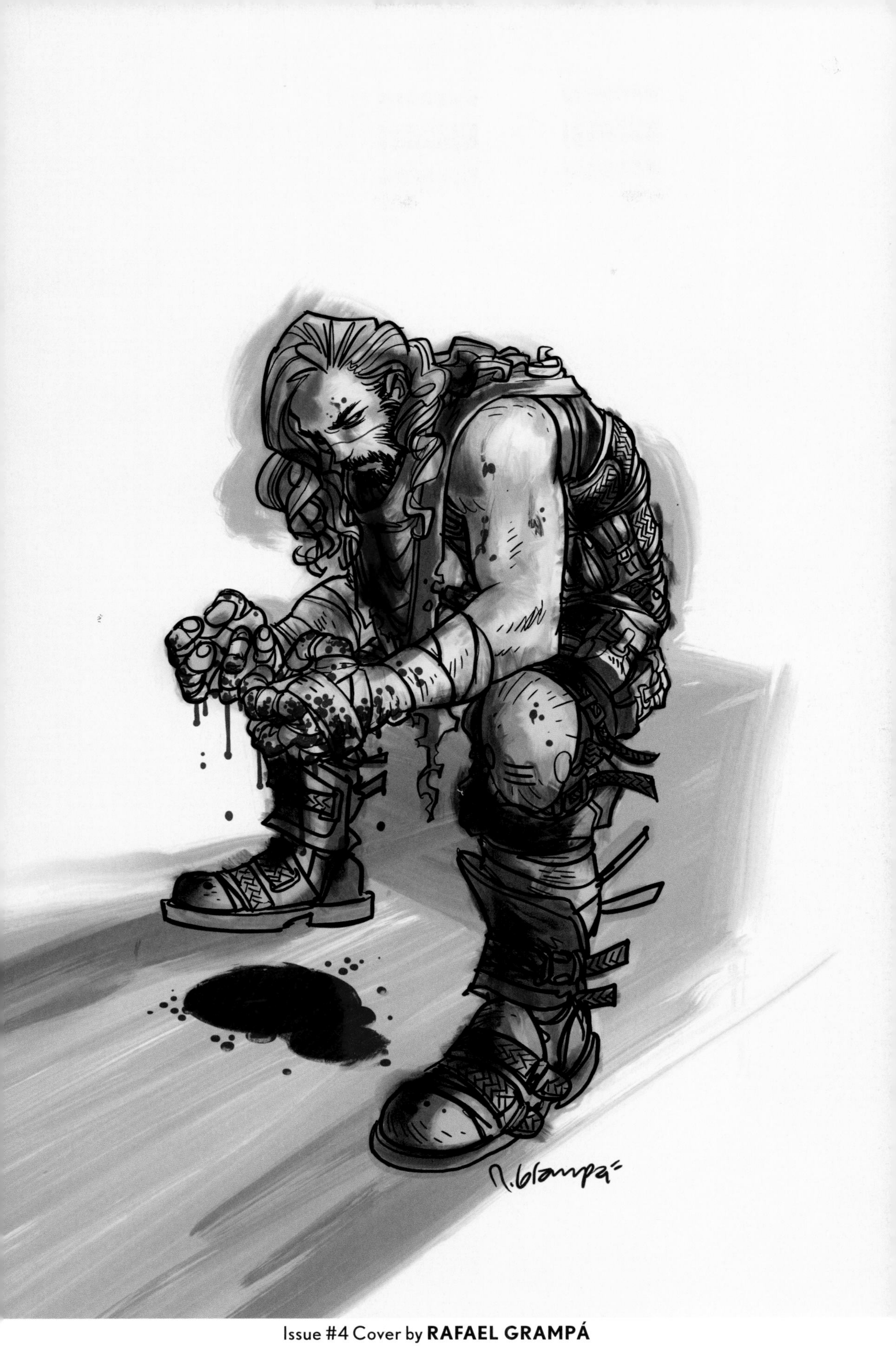

Issue #4 Cover by **RAFAEL GRAMPÁ**

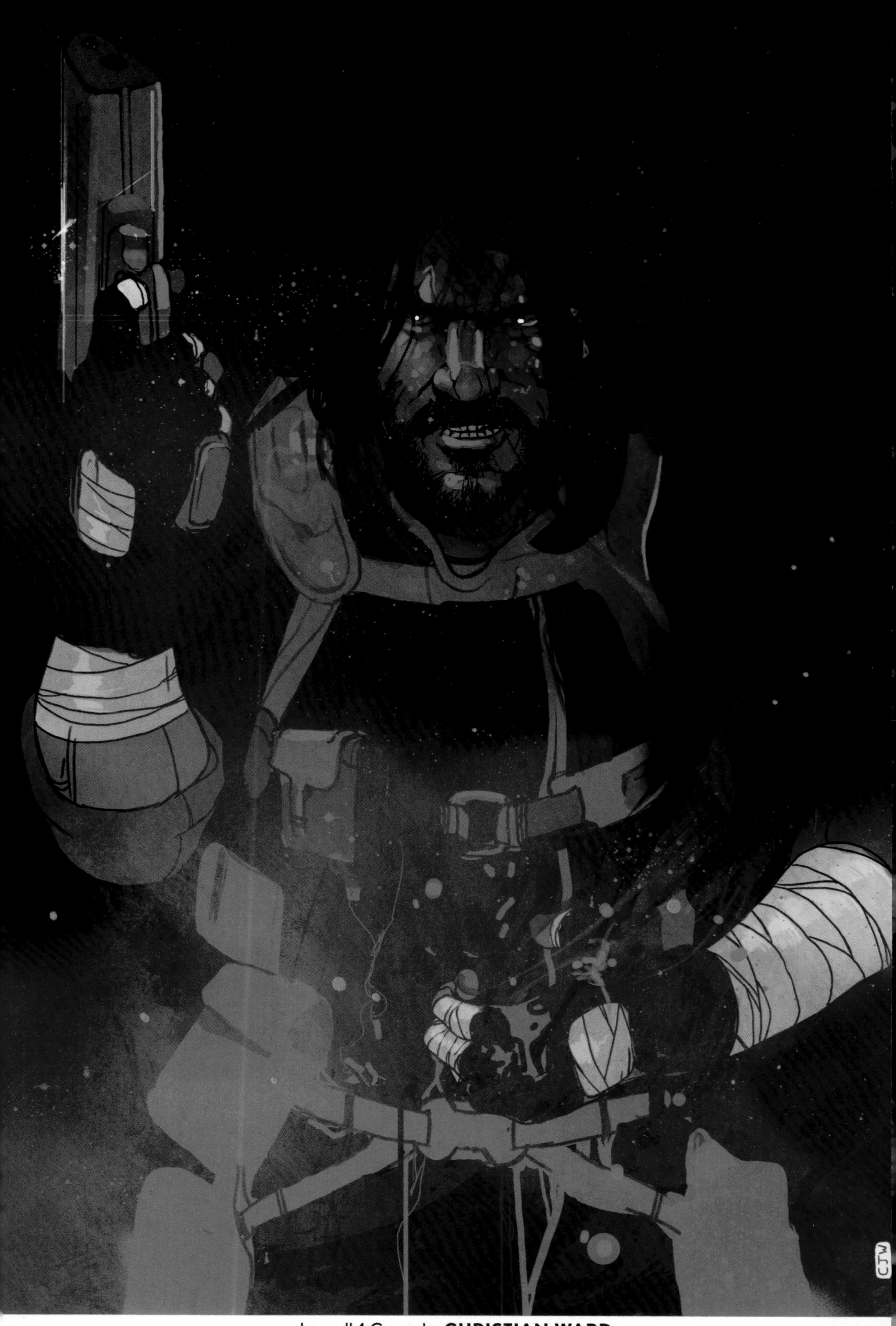
CTW

Issue #4 Cover by **CHRISTIAN WARD**

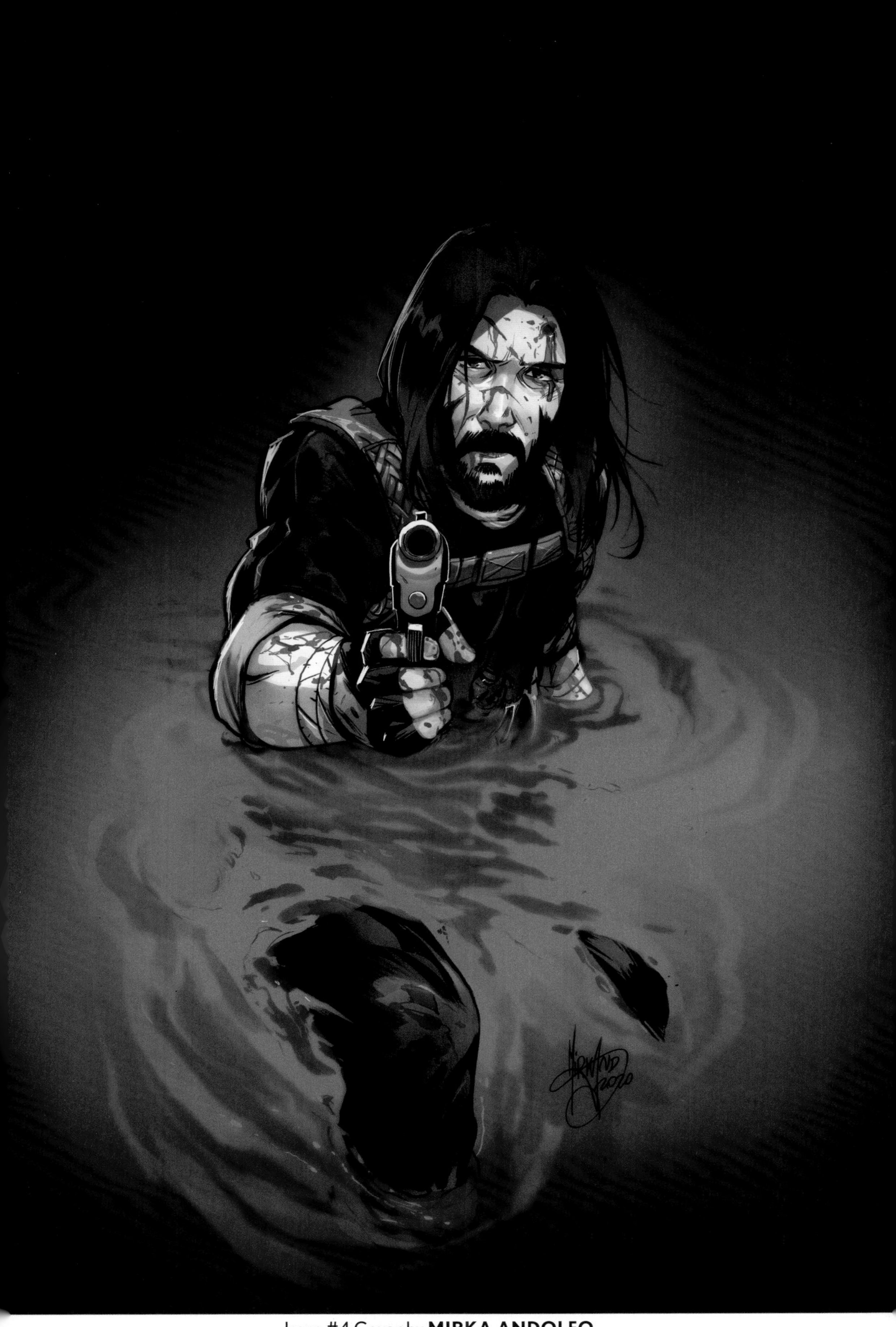

Issue #4 Cover by **MIRKA ANDOLFO**

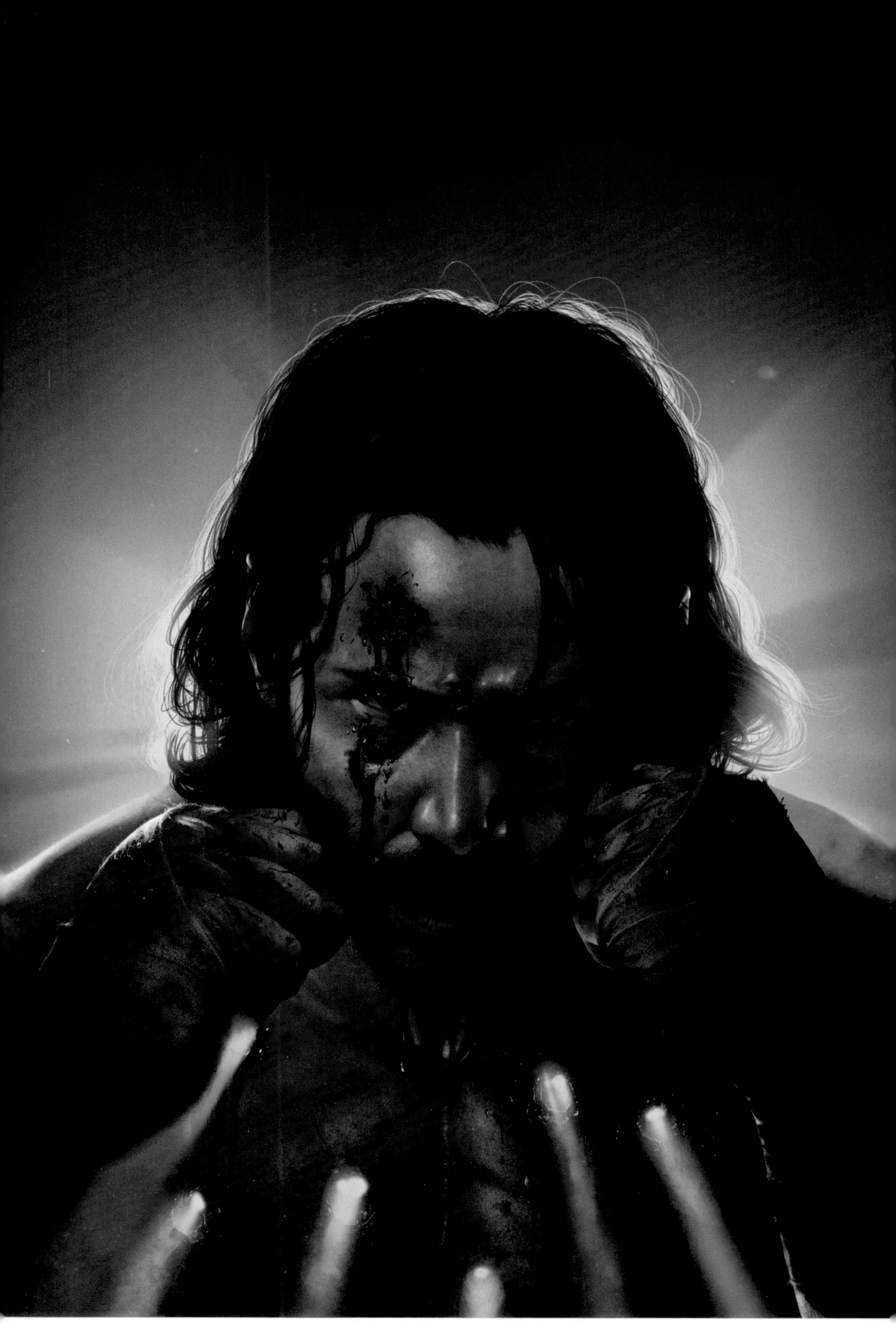

Additional Artwork by **RAHZZAH**

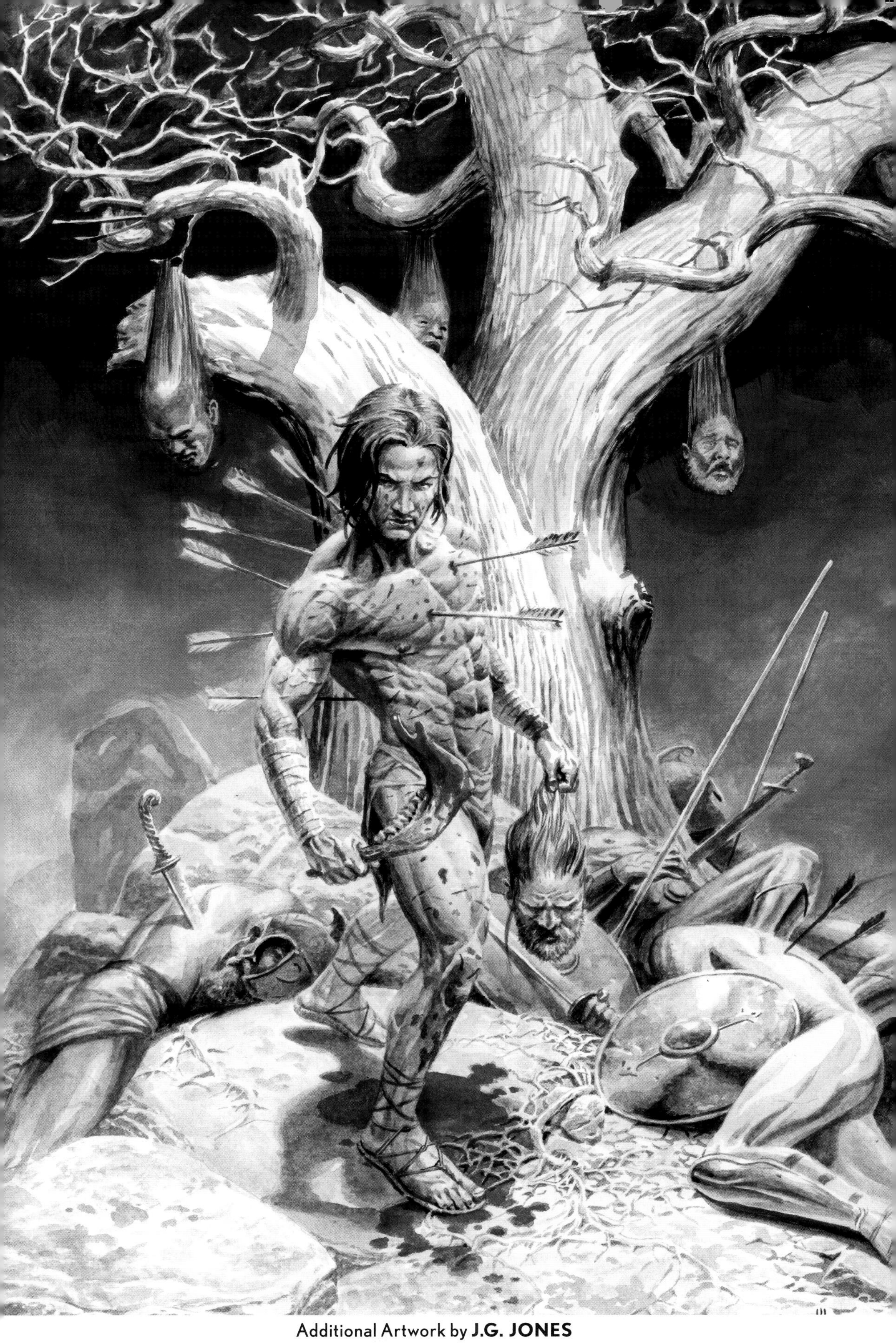

Additional Artwork by **J.G. JONES**

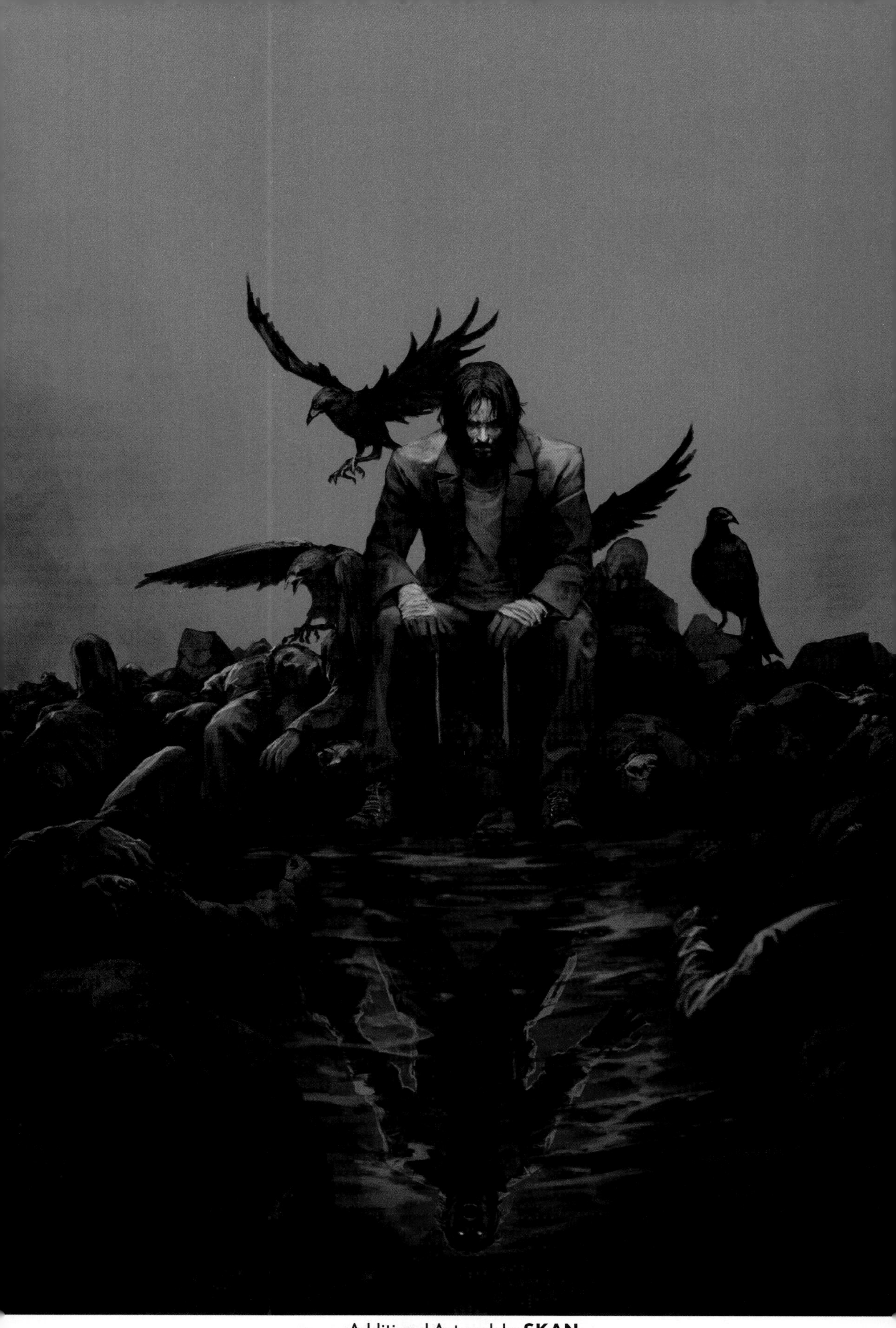

Additional Artwork by **SKAN**

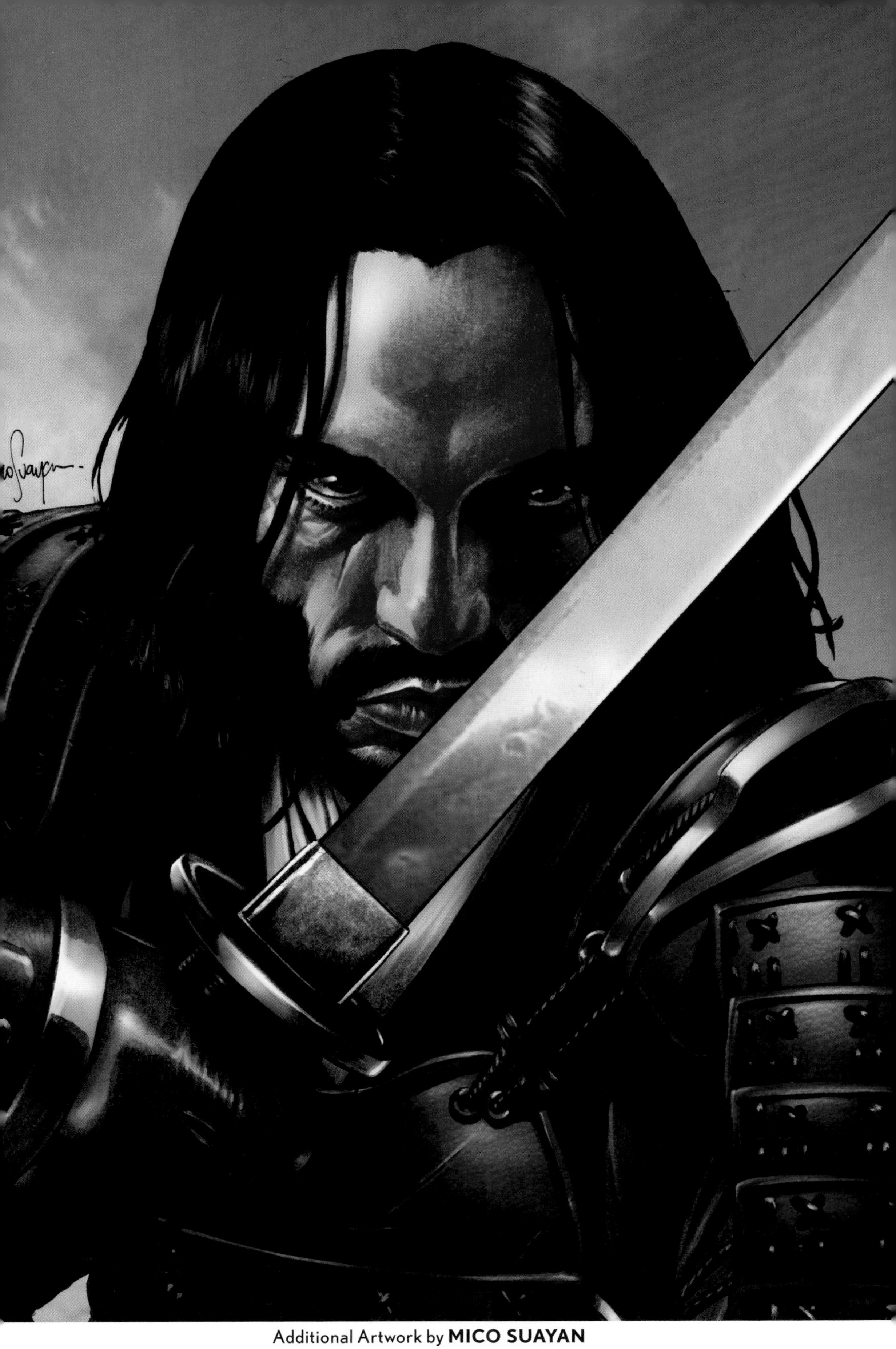

Additional Artwork by **MICO SUAYAN**

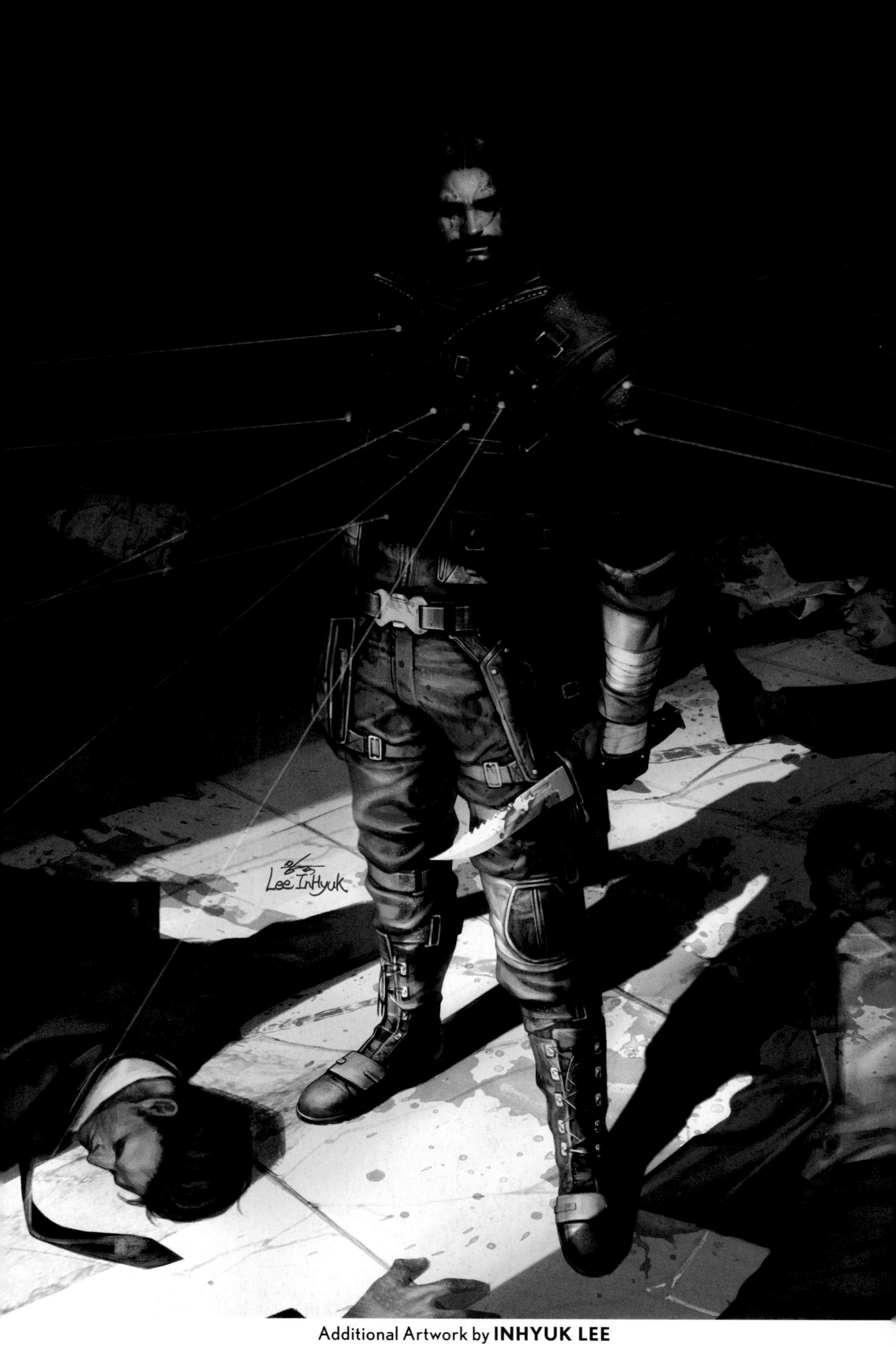
Lee InHyuk

Additional Artwork by **INHYUK LEE**

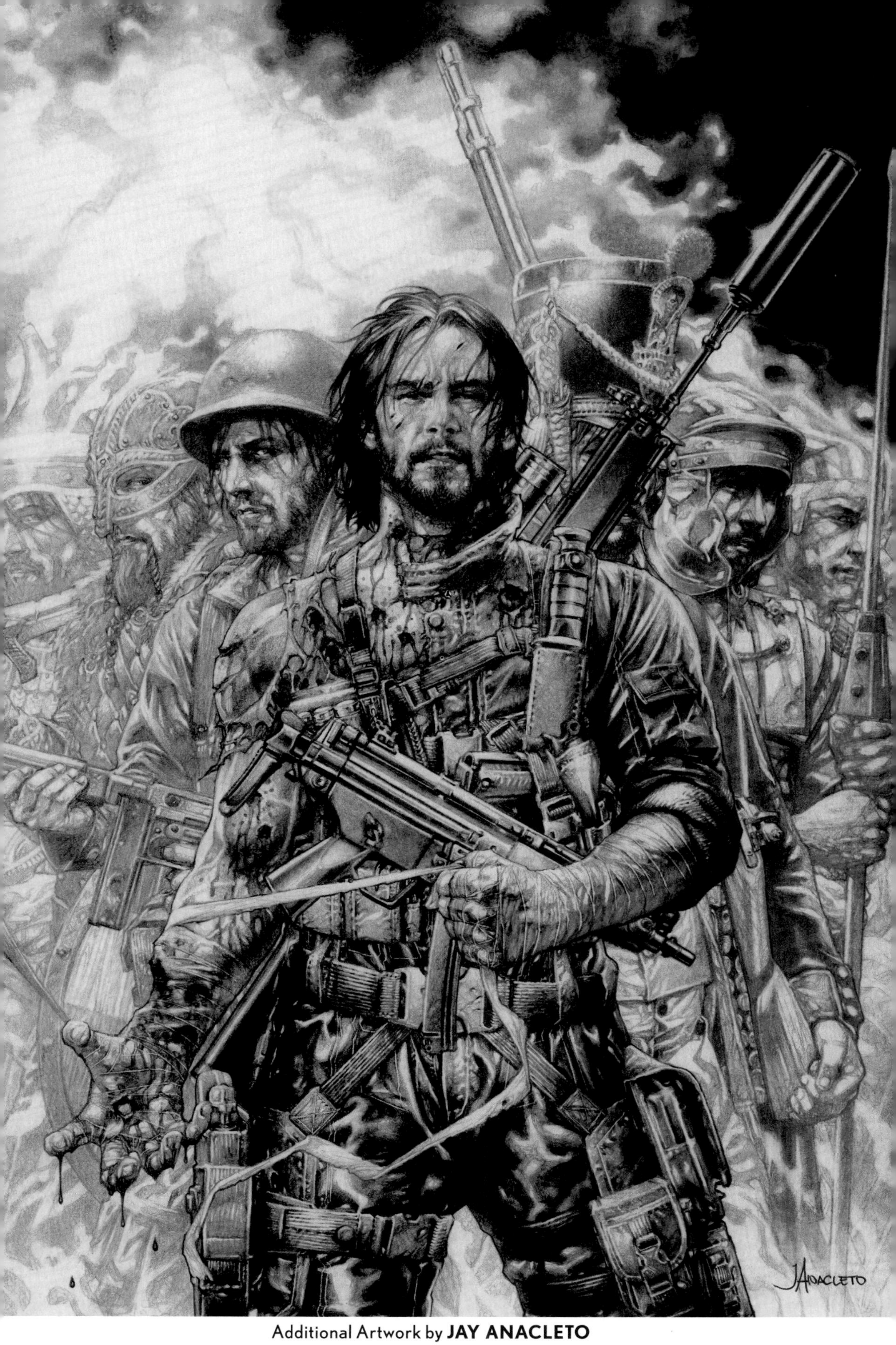

Additional Artwork by **JAY ANACLETO**

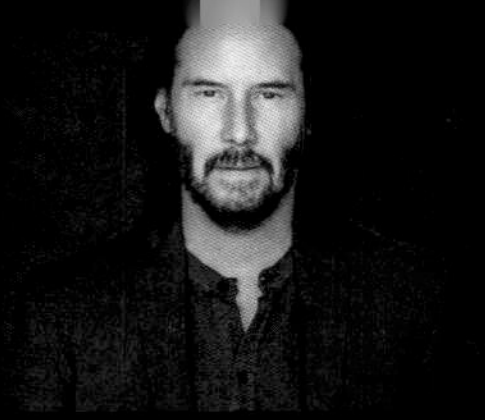

© Jack Guy Photography

KEANU REEVES, the iconic star of feature films such as *John Wick* and *The Matrix*, is the creator and co-writer of *BRZRKR*. Reeves is a celebrated actor whose 35-year film career has garnered enormous success at the box office and received widespread acclaim. *BRZRKR*, his first comic book and graphic novel series, is the highest funded comic book Kickstarter of all time and the highest selling original comic book series debut in over 25 years.

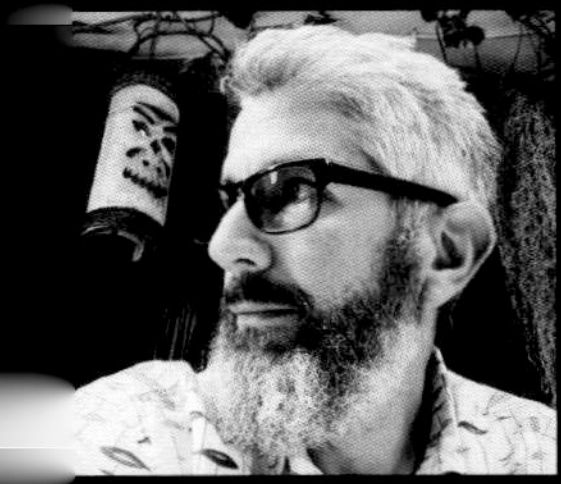

MATT KINDT is the *New York Times* bestselling writer and artist of the comics and graphic novels *Dept. H*, *Mind MGMT*, *Revolver*, *3 Story*, *Super Spy*, *2 Sisters*, and *Pistolwhip*, as well as the writer of *Folklords*, *Black Badge*, and the Eisner Award-nominated *Grass Kings* with BOOM! Studios, *Bang!*, *Ether*, *Fear Case*, and *Crimson Flower* with Dark Horse Comics, *Justice League of America* with DC Comics, *Spider-Man* with Marvel Comics, and *Unity*, *Ninjak*, *Rai*, and *Divinity* with Valiant Comics. He has won the PubWest book design award, been nominated for six Eisner Awards and six Harvey Awards (and won once). His work has been published in French, Spanish, Italian, German, and Korean.

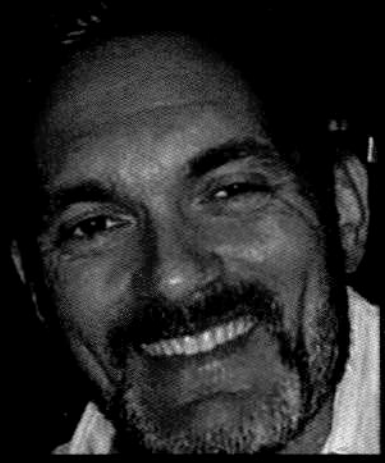

Over the course of his 30-year career, **RON GARNEY** has built a large fan following, illustrating some of the industry's greatest characters including Spider-Man, Hulk, Wolverine, Thor, X-Force, Captain America, Ghost Rider, Moon Knight, Silver Surfer, G.I. Joe, and the Justice League of America, along with original series like *Men of Wrath* with Jason Aaron. He recently completed acclaimed runs on *Daredevil* and *Savage Sword of Conan* at Marvel Entertainment. A perennial "Top Ten" artist during his career, Garney has been nominated twice for the industry's coveted Eisner Awards, for Best Artist and Best Serialized Story (*Captain America* with Mark Waid), and has worked in Hollywood on major projects, notably as a costume illustrator for *I Am Legend* (starring Will Smith) and providing illustrations for Marvel's *Daredevil* on Netflix.

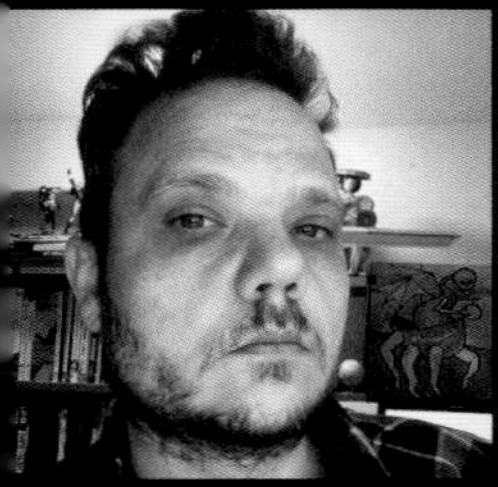

BILL CRABTREE has been coloring comics since 2003. His work has been nominated for Harvey and Eisner Awards. Career credits include colors on *Invincible*, *The Sixth Gun*, *The Damned*, *Bang!*, *Crimson Flower* and *BRZRKR*. He lives in Portland, Oregon with his partner, their daughter, two cats, and a dog.

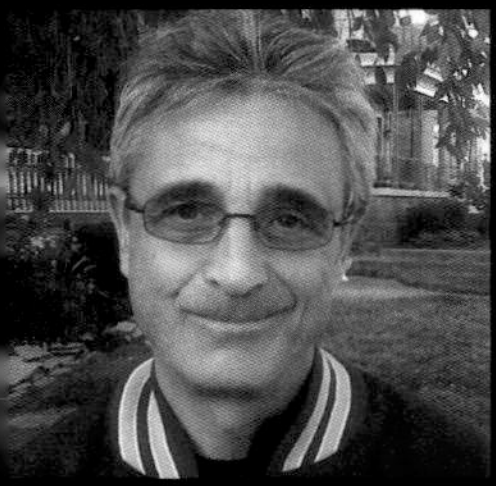

CLEM ROBINS has worked in comics since 1977, and has been all over the place. Projects include *Hellboy*, *X-Men*, *Spider-Man*, *Superman*, *Batman*, *Green Lantern*, *The Fantastic Four*, *Wolverine*, *Teen Titans*, *Preacher*, *Y: The Last Man*, *Deadman*, and many others. His work on *100 Bullets* was nominated for a Harvey Award. He is currently lettering Tom Taylor and Andy Kubert's series *Batman: The Detective*. His 2002 book *The Art of Figure Drawing* was published by North Light Books, and was translated into Spanish, French, Italian, German, and Chinese. His paintings and drawings are in the Eisele Gallery of Fine Art in Cincinnati, and in the permanent collection of the Cincinnati Art Museum. You can see them on his website: www.clemrobins.com.